✠ THREE planes roared away from a dogfight, headed west along the Somme River. In the lead was a Sopwith Camel flown by a green pilot named Wilfred May. He was maneuvering wildly to evade the twin streams of death from the Spandau machine guns of the red triplane on his tail.

The German so intent on destroying the young Canadian was the apparently invincible Richthofen, the Red Baron.

Pursuing Richthofen was Captain Roy Brown, May's superior, desperately trying to save his fledgling. Brown got the triplane in his sights, got in a sustained burst of fire before overtaking his target and losing sight of it behind some trees. He was sure he had scored.

But Richthofen continued his chase through a hail of ground fire after Brown was gone. Then suddenly his guns were silenced and he banked hard to the east, banked sharply again, sideslipped, then glided to earth. He had been killed by a single bullet through heart and lungs.

The Red Baron was downed. His age was twenty-five, his air victories were eighty—two numbers to be associated with his name for all time.

Had Richthofen flown on after receiving his death wound from Brown? Had some unknown Australian gunner killed the Prussian aristocrat? Could the questions about his death ever be convincingly answered?

The great Richthofen controversy had begun.

✠ ✠ ✠

✠ ✠ ✠ ✠ ✠ ✠ ✠ ✠ ✠ ✠

Who Killed the Red Baron?

THE FINAL ANSWER

by P. J. Carisella and James W. Ryan

A FAWCETT GOLD MEDAL BOOK

Fawcett Publications, Inc., Greenwich, Conn.

Member of American Book Publishers Council, Inc.

DEDICATION

To the Australian "Diggers" of the First World War, ever peerless fighters, and more specifically to those of the 3rd, 4th, and 5th Divisions, Australian Imperial Forces.

A special word of gratitude is due to Congressman Torbert H. Macdonald of the Massachusetts 7th Congressional District for the generous services he' provided so graciously in obtaining material for this work, especially in Australia.

CONTENTS

ACKNOWLEDGMENTS

Quite obviously, as will be noted from the preface to this work, P. J. Carisella is indebted to innumerable persons, here at home in the states, and in Canada, Europe, and Australia for their very kind assistance and to many organizations, historical and otherwise, for their invaluable sources in the preparation of this manuscript. Space limitations make it impossible for him to name all of them personally, but he does gratefully acknowledge their contributions and wishes to thank the following individuals and groups.

Cedric Bassett Popkin, Rupert Weston, Robert Buie, Donald L. Fraser, H. Henry, O. Hyder, E. E. Hardaker, John Homewood, Eric Harding, George Ridgway, J. Hocking, J. Inch, J. W. McGreger, R. Radecki, Col. J. M. Prentice, F. A. Pickup, J. Saunders, J. L. Scales, Maj. Gen. L. E. Beavis, R. Burton, John Cusack, E. M. Barker, H. S. Browne, Maj. Gen. J. H. Cannan, John Brake, C. C. Hillary, R. A. Wood, W. A. Aydsley, G. L. Adams, R. Anderson, F. H. Treasure, J. A. Wiltshire, E. T. Wannop, W. M. Williams, W. G. Simmons, C. C. Collins, and Lord Casey.

Also, A. A. Boxall Chapman, P. L. Bulluss, T. L. Baillieu, Air Vice Marshal H. N. Wrigley, Frank A. Sewell, Roderick Ross, Norman Mulroney, Malcolm Sheehan, N. R. Burnell, Dr. David Ellis, E. C. Banks, O. G. Witcomb, J. J. Knapp, L. O. Gyngell, E. J. McCarty, S. C. Morrison, F. Rawlinson, Dr. A. D. Craven, Dr. R. E. Douglas, K. McLeod, J. J. Kitts, Frank Gilfedder, H. Edwards, E. H. Graham, Dr. Paul Hopkins, Frank McGuire, Walter Musiano, Robert W. Carlin, David Workman, and Doug Smith.

Additionally, Baron Karl Bolko von Richthofen, General Karl Bodenschatz, Air Vice Marshal Raymond Collishaw, D. G. Lewis, A. Franklyn, Neville Hewitt, and the following ladies: Mrs. S. M. Garrett, Lady Knox, Mrs. M. E. Simpson, Mrs. E. A. Mart, Mrs. J. Alexander, Mrs. M. Rowntree, Mrs. J. Crawford, Mrs. N. Travers, and Mrs. Ida Bridge.

Special thanks are due these: Australian Flying Corps, Royal Air Forces, Royal Canadian Air Forces, United States Air Forces, Cross & Cockade Society of World War I Aero Historians, Australian Imperial War Memorial, Australian Records Office, Australian R.S.S.L. organizations, *Mufti, Reveille, The Listening Post,* city and town clerks throughout Australia, newspapers throughout Australia, and the surviving members of the Richthofen Jagdgeschwader (J.G. 1).

Last, he extends his sincerest thanks to James W. Ryan of Cohasset, Massachusetts, for his writing talent in the preparation of this manuscript.

PREFACE

Author P. J. Carisella has long been considered one of the most outstanding authorities on the extraordinary life and mysterious death of Baron Manfred von Richthofen, Imperial Germany's Ace of Aces in World War I. Carisella's reputation in this fascinating field is richly deserved and based on the more than thirty years he has devoted to studying the facts of the Red Baron's life and to investigating the pros and cons of the half century controversy stemming from the Flying Uhlan's death. No detail which comes to his attention about the Baron, be it miniscule or vague, is left unprobed. If Carisella believes any such information about the Rittmeister can in some way help to lend new insight into the facts of the German ace's life and death, he is relentless in his quest to prove it to be either factual or worthless.

No individual alive today, including the Baron's surviving brother, Baron Karl Bolko von Richthofen, is more interested and more determined in unearthing the true facts about the twenty-five years the Baron strode the earth, rode to the hunt, stalked his aerial prey, and crashed to his death atop Corbie Hill than P. J. Carisella.

A life-long resident of Wakefield, Massachusetts, and a Navy flying veteran of World War II, Carisella today is acknowledged to be a foremost expert in this area. He is the only American to receive honorary membership in the Society of the Old Grey Eagles, which is composed of the surviving members of the original Richthofen Jagdgeschwader No. 1. In 1968, he again was the only American to be personally invited by Baron Karl Bolko von Richthofen and the Old Grey Eagles to witness the stirring fiftieth anniversary ceremonies marking the death of the Red Baron. The observances were held by the contemporary Richthofen Geschwader (Squadron) at its air base in Wittmund, West Germany.

Carisella's basement den contains priceless relics and memorabilia of Richthofen and his famed red Fokker Dr.-1 triplane 425/17. His collection has drawn World War I aviation buffs, historians, researchers, editors, and writers from around the world to his Wakefield home. Australian authorities have publicly stated that his Richthofen collection is the finest in existence outside of their own Imperial War Memorial.

In addition to this collection, Carisella has files bulging with more than fourteen hundred letters he has received from World War I fliers of both the Cross and Cockade and from other witnesses, now dead or scattered around the globe. Many of these letter writers actually viewed Richthofen's last takeoff, dogfight, crash, and funeral on April 21 and 22, 1918.

When he isn't rereading or cataloguing his daily correspondence, Carisella keeps busy viewing new photographs and films of the Rittmeister. Many of these photographs never before published are included in this book along with pictorial records of his 1968 visit to Bertangles, Poulainville, Corbie, and Cappy. In spare time from his work as a federal government employee, Carisella either delves deeper into his library of more than two hundred volumes devoted to Richthofen and World War I aviation, or adds new material to scores of scrapbooks in his continuing search for the truth.

He once spent three years just tracking down the whereabouts of the goggles flung off by Richthofen seconds before his fatal crash on April 21, 1918. His persistence paid off in November 1963 when he made contact with E. E. Hardaker of Woodburn, Australia. Hardaker, a World War I Aussie with the 11th Brigade, had witnessed the Baron's last fall and recovered the goggles. Today these goggles are in Carisella's collection.

Carisella believes that all the facts regarding the life and death of the Baron are now available after his research of more than thirty years. He intends to present these facts as objectively as possible in this book. His conclusions are those of himself and his coauthor, James W. Ryan. Both are members of the Cross & Cockade Society of World War I Aero Historians. It is Carisella's hope that the facts as recorded within this work will settle for all time the controversy about who killed the Red Baron.

Who Killed
the Red Baron?

✝ ✝ ✝

Chapter 1

BIRTH OF DEATH IN THE AIR

✠ THOSE magnificent men first fought for the sky more than half a century ago at the controls of pint-size birds of prey. The aerial conflicts of those intrepid youths in the dim, dog-eared days of 1914–1918 trumpeted the elevation of man's age-old hatreds and prejudices into the sphere of the clouds.

War for those daring birdmen meant meadow aerodromes in the soft morning mist, dawn patrols, the sweet, nose-tingling odor of castor oil in the prop blast of a Fokker or Spad, the ear-shattering tat-tat-tat of Spandaus and Vickers guns, ambuscades in the clouds, waiting fate from the direction of the sun, and the constant threat of incineration.

The Great War, as it also was known, recorded the first combat deaths in the sky and created the aerial dogfight, in which scores of gaily colored planes thundered at each other, stunting, diving, climbing, closing, clearing and coming together again. With the rattle of death enveloping them, the pilots of the cross and cockade shot their foes to pieces,

16

littering the blue with flaming wreckage and broken, burnt bodies in moments of insanity and pandemonium that marked the ballet of death in the air.

Out of this carnage sprang the myth that those early fighter pilots were a special breed of romantic and chivalric knight-errants, justly paid war's highest wages in the form of fame, decorations, orders, honors, and glory. The myth was perpetuated by, among others, English Prime Minister Lloyd George who rose in Parliament in 1917 to state that the airmen "are the knighthood of this war, without fear, without reproach; and they recall the legendary days of chivalry, not merely by the daring of their exploits, but by the nobility of their spirts."

In our own time, a popular writer, who should have known better, wrote of those early war birds as knights of the air and added: "But the unique development . . . was the fact that the first war in the air unexpectedly returned the ancient concept of the duel to modern warfare, and along with it, a code of conduct which had been considered obsolete for centuries."

Lovely sentiments, but it just was not so. On the contrary, aerial warfare was just as ruthless and unchivalrous as the horrible fighting in the mud-wracked trenches. The truth of this statement is substantiated by the fliers' own records, combat reports, diaries, biographies, and reminiscences. While those members of "the knighthood of the blue" undoubtedly were the finest of their nations' youth, a special breed, if not innately so, at least by virture of their temporary profession, their memorabilia starkly reveals that they expected no mercy and seldom gave it in combat.

As a matter of fact, the lack of chivalry was an indelible part of their makeup. It flawed such great aces as Maj. Edward "Mick" Mannock, the one-eyed enigmatic Irishman who was the Royal Flying Corps' top scorer with seventy-three confirmed kills, and Baron Manfred von Richthofen, Imperial Germany's Red Knight, who tallied eighty official victories before his own death in the air. Maj. James McCudden, victor in fifty-seven sky fights and RFC's fourth-ranking ace of the conflict, wrote in his posthumous autobiography, *Five Years in the Royal Flying Corps,* that he and his flying mates were nothing but "hired assassins."

With few exceptions, any knightly deeds among the airmen

Pfalz DIII Scout. This little plane might have replaced the Albatros after its introduction in 1917 if the Fokker triplane had not grabbed the limelight. Span: 30 ft. 11 in.; length: 23 ft. 2 in.; top speed: 103 mph at 10,000 ft.; climb: 10,000 ft. in 17 min.

were confined mostly on opposing sides to their noncombat activities. For it was on the ground, where the birdmen could try to forget their daily confrontations in the sky, that they felt their deepest kinship for the enemy who shared the same dangers.

Captured fliers traditionally were treated to a night of revelry by their victor and his comrades before being shipped off to internment. The German ace, Oswald Boelcke, graciously loaded up his downed foes with wine, cigarettes, and other creature comforts before their departure for prisoner-of-war camps.

When a flier was shot down across the opposing line, notice of his death or capture usually would be dropped on his home aerodrome or close by, if possible. When Boelcke, the father of pursuit aviation and the creator of the Flying Circus, died in a midair collision with one of his novice pilot's Albatros on October 28, 1916, Allied fliers dropped an inscribed wreath over the German lines on the day of his funeral. The attached note read: "To the memory of Captain Boelcke, our brave and chivalrous foe."

From such noncombat incidents, the myth of chivalry in the air was propagandized by reporters and popular writers in their endless quest for colorful and bizarre material. Mannock, the fey, brooding Irish ace, had little use for their ilk, and usually sent them packing by relating the details of an especially grisly kill in which both the enemy pilot and his observer plunged flaming to the ground. In his diary, he wrote, "Sizzle, sizzle, sizzle . . . I sent one to hell today." To his men, he always gave this admonition: "And when you shoot, don't aim for the plane—aim for the pilot."

Mannock thought nothing of pouring a stream of bullets into a German spiraling to earth in a mass of flames. After the enemy planes crashed, he would fly over, and if he detected any signs of life, he would riddle the charred wreckage with lethal bursts of unerring fire. This was also a practice of many fliers on both sides, including the Red Baron and his cold-blooded brother, Lothar von Richthofen. When his messmates of No. 74 "Tiger" Squadron rose to toast the memory of the Red Baron, Mannock stalked out, growling, "I hope he roasted all the way down."

In consequence of his brutal directness and pragmatic approach to aerial warfare, the writers thought Mannock inhuman. As a result, little was written about him during his lifetime, and his death in July 1918 passed unnoticed by the British public. It was only after his friends had interceded with the minister of air, Winston Churchill, that Mannock's exploits became known, and the Victoria Cross was awarded posthumously.

Before the First World War, none of the great powers had formulated any definite role for the airplane. A few farsighted men, notably Italy's Giulio Douhet and France's Ferdinand Ferber, visualized the possibilities of aircraft in war. But the voice of the prophet is seldom heard in his own land—and the writings of Douhet and Ferber received little attention.

The hardbound traditionalists, especially those still carrying the odor of horseflesh, believed the flying machines would perform a limited role in the way of scouting the enemy's maneuvers and whereabouts. And then, of course, not nearly so well as their beloved cavalry, although the latter's epitaph had been written by the deadly machine-gun years before 1914. The lessons of Omdurman in 1898 and the Boer War had faded from narrow minds.

Gen. Ferdinand Foch, who later was to command the combined Allied armies, including the Americans, stated contemptuously at the French War College in 1910 that the airplane would be "useless" for war. Even the German High Command, after the fighting had been raging for two months in 1914, declared intransigently: "As experience has shown, a true combat in the air as described by journalists and romantics must be considered as sheer mythology. The duty of the aviator is to observe, not to fight. . . ."

So it is not too surprising that military aircraft, as such, did not exist when the war erupted in the summer of 1914. Each nation's fragile flying machines came in every possible shape and design. It was not until the fliers made known the need for aircraft of superior speed, performance, and armament that military planes per se were finally designed and constructed.

In the beginning, England counted 180 flying machines, half of which could not fly the English Channel. The English navy listed another 93 aircraft. France, whose public long had been aviation conscious, possessed about 800 planes, 35 seaplanes, and 37 Zeppelins.

Above—teenage ace Werner Voss.

Right—Oswald Boelcke.

The early birds resembled flying chicken coops, bathtubs, or giant seagulls. A one-hundred-horsepower engine was considered an awesome dynamo. A speed of ninety-five miles per hour was reckless; most aircraft were capable of doing only fifty-five to seventy-five miles per hour. Many of the engines were unreliable, at first. The planes were without armament. Wings snapped off if a pilot got too tricky. The planes lacked self-sealing fuel tanks, and a bullet could quickly turn them into flaming torches. Parachutes were unavailable almost to the end of the war, and then only the Germans used them on a regular basis. The Allied brass kept parachutes from their fliers; they reasoned that their fliers would be too quick to bail out in combat if they were equipped with chutes.

The majority of the pilots were noncommissioned officers when the war began, as they were ranked with the same importance as chauffeurs. The observers, usually aristocrats and considered more intelligent, received the commissions. Later, many of the famed aces, including the famed Red Baron, came forward from the ranks of the useless cavalry units.

Again in the beginning, the fliers had the mission only to observe the enemy and gather information about his whereabouts. When passing, the rival pilots waved good-naturedly at each other; however, the mounting holocaust on the ground soon snapped that outward bond of camaraderie. The casualties in the Battles of the Frontier, at Mons, and on the Marne, and the resulting race to the sea, which climaxed in an ugly line of trenches stretching from Switzerland to the English Channel, demanded that every combatant kill the enemy by any and every means possible.

So the pilots ceased tossing highball salutes to each other as they crossed paths in the sky. Instead, they began taking pot shots at one another with pistols, carbines, and rifles. Then the French produced the idea of dropping bags of bricks or showers of steel arrows on enemy aircraft and their crews. The British, the model of gentlemanly manners, preferred hurling grenades and petrol bombs of canned gasoline at the Hun machines. The Germans unimaginatively countered with shoulder arms and small bombs.

Hostilities were only two weeks old when Germany's Lt. Franz von Hiddeson loosed two tiny bombs from his aircraft onto a Paris suburb. His triumph was short-lived. Shortly afterwards he was downed by primitive antiaircraft fire. About the same time a German sergeant-pilot's Aviatik was felled by ground fire. In that same month of August 1914, a two-placed British aircraft forced down a Rumpler-Taube near Amiens. However, the crew set the machine ablaze and escaped.

On two French aviators, history has bestowed the honor of being the first men to shoot down an airplane in true aerial combat. Sgt. Pilot Joseph Frantz and his observer-mechanic Louis Quenault were aloft in a Voisin pusher biplane on October 5, 1914, when they spotted a two-seater Aviatik and rushed to attack. Hit by repeated bursts of rapid fire from a clip-fed Hotchkiss machine gun, the German bus plummeted downward in swift gyrations to crash into a stand of trees beside a storybook chateau's rose-sprinkled pond at Jonchery, France. The German occupants of the Aviatik were dead when Frantz landed in a field nearby to inspect the wreckage. For their first-in-history triumph, the Frenchmen were handed a freshly picked bunch of flowers by an old woman.

The aircraft as a lethal weapon of war really came into its own when famed prewar stunt pilot, Roland Garros, the son of a lawyer and the first man to fly the Mediterranean, fastened a Hotchkiss machine gun to the cowling of his small Morane-Saulnier monoplane. Previously, machine guns so fixed had shot the propeller to pieces, much to the chagrin, and usually the death, of the plane's pilot. But Garros, a piano virtuoso, with Gallic ingenuity and the assistance of aircraft designer, Raymond Saulnier, bolted triangular steel plates to the propeller to deflect any bullets which might strike it.

Garros was eagerly airborne on April Fool's Day, 1915, to test his new weapon. Sighting an Aviatik at three thousand feet, he closed swiftly and opened fire at one hundred feet. Bullets from the second clip of his twenty-five-round Hotchkiss ripped the German two-seater and it plunged to earth.

In the ensuing eighteen days of glory, Garros shot down four German planes. He was the terror of the skies and France's first air hero of the war. However, his victory skein was short-lived. In scoring his last victory, slugs from his Hotchkiss damaged the propeller, despite the steel plates. He

Richthofen in a rare moment of jollity. *Left to right*—Stephen Kirmaier, Hans Immelman, Richthofen, W. Wortman.

was forced to land behind the German lines where his aircraft was captured before he could destroy it.

Garros' plane was forwarded immediately to Berlin where it was inspected without delay by Dutch plane designer, Anthony Fokker. Within forty-eight hours, Fokker, who earlier had sought in vain to sell his plane designs to the Allies, had improved on Garros' feat by an arrangement of cam and rods attached to the engine of his own plane, the Fokker Eindecker (one-winger). His invention synchronized the firing of a machine gun to permit the bullets to pass through the spinning prop without striking it. Thus was born the "Fokker Scourge," the fearful nightmare of a winged craft spitting out bullets at the rate of six hundred rounds a minute.

Fokker's synchronized machine gun was first flown in combat by Oswald Boelcke on June 30, 1915. With the weapon mounted on an Eindecker, Boelcke forced a Maurice Farman to withdraw. But it was left to Max Immelmann, the vaunted "Eagle of Lillie"—so-called because of the number of aerial victories he was to score over that French city—to tally the initial victory in an Eindecker equipped with the synchronized gun. Remembered to this day for his aerial maneuver known as the "Immelmann turn," he shot a British B.E. 2A out of the sky on August 11, 1915.

In tandem, Immelmann and Boelcke then began a scoring spree that ultimately earned both the Pour le Merite (the Blue Max), Imperial Germany's highest decoration. Its French name extended back to the days of Frederick the Great and his great love affair with everything that was French. Victor in fifteen aerial combats, Immelmann, like so many of the famed aces of the war, including Guynemer, Mannock, Richthofen, Albert Ball, and Frank Luke, crashed mysteriously to his death in June 1916. German accounts said Immelmann died because of technical failure of his aircraft. The British give credit for his fall to Cpl. J. Waller, the gunner of an F.E. 2b, piloted by Lt. G. R. McCubbin.

Boelcke, then Germany's leading ace on "Kanon," as they were called after ten victories instead of the usual five for the Allies, organized an elite unit of fighter pilots called Jagdstaffel 2. A jagdstaffel was a hunting squadron, which usually consisted of some fourteen planes. Boelcke's unit was equipped with the new Albatros DI's and DII's.

The great German ace recruited his own pilots and traveled extensively to get the best possible men. One of his earlier choices was Baron von Richthofen. Only in his early twenties, Richthofen was just beginning to rack up his first kills when Boelcke crashed to his death. Victor in forty sky battles, Boelcke's end came when his craft collided in midair with that of a fledgling pilot, Lt. Erwin Boehme, an officer from German East Africa. The collision tore his wing fabric and Boelcke's bus spiraled down. The date was October 28, 1916; Boelcke was twenty-five.

The ace's name was not permitted to die with him for the Kaiser issued a decree renaming Jasta 2 as Jasta Boelcke.

With the invention of the synchronized machine gun, the first aerial successes of Garros (who escaped years later from his German prison only to die fighting seven Fokkers five weeks before the end of the war), Immelmann, Boelcke, and the English flier, Lanoe Hawker, and the increasing production of sturdier and faster planes to fit the combat pilots' needs, the air war, by 1916, evolved into a conflict of lone aerial duelists, the aces, before giving way to formation flying and tactics.

With their much improved birds of prey, the fliers learned to take advantage of the clouds, to use solitary observation and scout planes as decoys to tempt rash opponents into lethal ambushes, and to attack with the sun behind them and their quarry blinded to the onrushing peril. Replacements learned fast in the finest tradition of such movie films as *Dawn Patrol* and *Hell's Angels*. Greenhorns seldom lived to regret a mistake. The life expectancy of fliers usually was figured at about three weeks. It was much less for RFC pilots during the headlong German successes of "Bloody April" in 1917.

In most instances, the more famous aces rose to fame by blasting enemy planes without warning. Surprise was the key to victory; it was not very sporting or chivalric, but it was the quickest way to rack up victories and to win the medals and glory that followed. The favorite tactic was to sneak up on an enemy plane without being seen, or while its pilot was busy tailing another bus, and riddle it with fire.

British ace, Jimmy McCudden, summed it up succinctly in his autobiography when he wrote: "The best way to get a Hun is to find him before he sees you. Of course, I hate to

Albatros DIII's of Richthofen's Flying Circus. The "vee-strutter," as Allied forces call this Albatros, appeared on the Western Front in the spring of 1917 and, during "Bloody April" of that year, they were largely responsible for destroying 368 British aircraft. For six weeks they maintained supremacy—until the new Sopwith Camel, the S.E. 5, and the improved Bristol Fighters took over. The Albatros DIII had a 29-ft., 7-in. span, 24-ft., 2-in. length, could do 120 mph at sea level. The DIII was powered by the 175-hp Mercedes motor or the 200-hp Austro Daimler.

shoot a Hun down without his seeing me. It's against what little sporting instinct I have. But it's in accordance with my doctrine and theory of fighting, and it seems to work well."

Youthful—many of them were only in their teens—competitive fliers, eager for the decorations and recognition accorded the aces, fattened their scores by gunning down aircraft whose propellers had failed and were attempting desperately to disengage. Indeed, these pilots, without hesitation, riddled aircraft whose crews had surrendered and were seeking a place to land. Downed pilots were usually shot at from the air.

Baron von Richthofen, like McCudden and many other Allied fliers, constantly sought to impress one fundamental rule of aerial combat on his men. Again and again he was heard to say, "Never shoot holes in a machine. Aim for the man and don't miss him. If you're fighting a two-seater, get the observer first. Until you have silenced the gun, don't bother about the pilot."

In all fairness, it must be remembered that the fliers, like their brethren locked in muddy combat in the trenches, were also motivated by the emotions of anger, hatred, and revenge, the fever of battle, and the fear of death in its most awful forms. Nations cannot stumble as blindly into war as they did in August 1914 and then damn the men who must do the fighting and commit the slaughter.

As the war in the air progressed, the heyday of the lone sky duels gave way slowly to formation fighting. In numbers there was strength, and when the opposing groups clashed, the dogfight evolved. Simultaneously, the numerous combatants, including the United States, which never designed an aircraft used in combat, began to give serious study to aerial tactics. Those studies in time led to the great national air forces that we know today.

Still, when one recalls those first aerial fights of more than half a century ago, the images conjured up mostly are those of the aces and planes they flew and the dogfights in which they engaged. The top Allied fliers included Britain's Mannock, Billy Bishop, McCudden, Ball, Beauchamp-Proctor, George McElroy, and Raymond Collishaw. America's top scorer was Eddie Rickenbacker with twenty-six victories. Other U.S. aces were Frank Luke, the headstrong "Balloon Buster" from Arizona; his flying pal, Joe Wehner from Everett, Massachusetts; Elliot W. Springs; and the mysterious Gervais Raoul Lufbery, the brilliant star of the Lafayette Escadrille.

France contributed more than her share to the roster of the shooting stars who streaked across the heavens in those years of 1914-1918. There was glory-seeking Rene Paul Fonck; fragile George Guynemer who scored fifty-four victories in six hundred aerial fights before his enigmatic end at age twenty-two; Charles Nungesser, who survived the war with forty-five kills only to perish in an abortive transatlantic flight in May 1927; Georges Madon who died in a plane crash on Armistice Day, 1924; Maurice Boyau; and Alfred Heurtaux, who was the highest scoring French ace still alive at this writing.

The Allies also boasted such famed aces as Belgium's Willie Coppens, victor in thirty-seven sky battles; Russia's Capt. A. A. Kazakoff; and Italy's Major Francisco Garacca, thirty-four confirmed victories; Lt. Silvio Scaronl, with twenty-six; and Lt. Col. Pier Ruggiero Piccio, twenty-four.

The top aces of the black cross were Germany's von Richthofen, eighty official victories; Ernest Udet, runner-up as Germany's leading ace, with sixty-two victories; Boelcke; Max Ritter von Mulzer, the "Second Eagle of Lillie"; Teenage ace Werner Voss; Edward Ritter von Schleich, the "Black Knight," so-called because he painted his aircraft all black; Rudolph Berthold, the "Iron Knight" who scored forty-four kills and survived the war only to be throttled by German Communists; Heinrich Gontermann, the "Balloon Strafer," with thirty-nine kills, including eighteen observation balloons; and Hermann Goering, who racked up twenty-two victories and later commanded Adolph Hitler's Luftwaffe in World War II.

Sharing almost equal fame with the aces were the cheeky little planes they flew; planes which were never built to bear the dust of museums. They were designed to fly and fight; to conquer or to be killed, and if vanquished, to bear their birdmen to the grave. The names of those birds of prey live on in the annals of aviation history. They are treasured relics in museums scattered around the globe. They are sold today at fantastic prices to collectors. Models of them are prominent items in any first-class hobby shop.

The list of those famed aircraft included Britain's Sopwith

Schoolchildren visiting Richthofen at his home in Schweidnitz, 1917.

Camel, called the "big pup" by the RFC fliers. A compact craft, it appeared at the Front in June of 1917. The Camel was the first Allied aircraft equipped with two Vickers machine guns synchronized to fire through the propeller. It was baptised "Camel" because the weapons were mounted on top of the fuselage, their breeches enclosed in a humplike metal cowling. With a top-notch pilot at its controls, this "tricky beast" could easily out maneuver any enemy aircraft except the Fokker triplane. In six minutes, it could climb to 6,500 feet, level off and shoot along at 100 knots (115 mph), and reach an altitude of 19,000 feet.

During the war the Camel was used increasingly on offensive patrols, escort work, and ground strafing. It held the single honor of destroying more enemy aircraft than any other type of aircraft during the course of World War I. A product of the Sopwith Aviation Company, this "fierce little rasper" was credited with downing 1,294 enemy machines.

All together, some 4,188 Camels saw service before the end of the war.

This was the plane Capt. A. Roy Brown was flying when he allegedly shot down the Red Baron on April 21, 1918, atop Corbie Hill.

Other notable British aircraft were the Sopwith Pup, Tripe and Snipe; the famed S.E. 5A flown by Mannock, McCudden, and McElroy at the time of their deaths within a three-week period during July 1918; the Bristol Fighter; D.H. 2 and the R.E. 8; and Vickers Gun Bus. The French planes best remembered are the Breguets, Caudrons, Nieuports 17 and 28, Salmsons, and the Spads S. 7 and XIII.

The most famous German aircraft developed during the war were the Albatros DI, DIII, D.V, and CIII; the various Fokkers, including Baron von Richthofen's tripe and, of course, the D.VII; the Halberstadts; Pfalz Scouts, a pretty aircraft which made up for its slow rate of climb and speed by its maneuverability, as well as the dependability of its 160 horsepower Mercedes engine; Rolands and Rumplers; and the Hannoveraner C.L. II.

Fokker's Dr.-1 triplane undoubtedly was the deadliest mount of the war when flown by such men as von Richthofen and Werner Voss. It had a wing span of 23.5 feet and a length of 19 feet. Its top speed at 8,000 feet was 121.5 mph when equipped with the 110 horsepower Oberursel-Le Rhone engine. A heavier model with a 145 horsepower Oberursel-Le Rhone engine could reach an altitude of 3,280 feet in two minutes at a gross weight of 1,375 pounds.

The tripe's fuselage was formed of welded steel tubing, braced by diagonal wires. It was fabric covered except for triangular plywood fillets from the cowling to the area behind the cockpit. The top decking also was made of plywood. The tail section was fashioned of the same steel tubing, as was the undercarriage. Its axle was also fitted with a large fairing, which provided additional lift.

For armament, the tripe carried twin Spandau machine guns which were synchronized to fire through the airscrew arc. With its excellent rate of climb, the Fokker Dreidecker (three-winger) could outmaneuver the Camel. Some 320 of the Dr. 1's were built before production ended.

Although Richthofen was still flying the Dr. 1 when he was killed, he already had switched his allegiance to Fokker's D.VII. After testing the D.VII, his enthusiasm for that machine was immeasurable and he had ordered them for his own Jasta. They appeared over the Front the same month he died. From April 1918 until the end of the war, the D.VII reigned as Germany's greatest fighter plane. Eighty percent of Germany's front-line squadrons were flying the craft by July. Some three thousand of them saw service in the last months of the conflict.

The famed bus was a biplane of cantilever wing design. It was powered by a 200 horsepower BMW or Mercedes engine and capable of reaching a top speed of 130 mph. The plane could climb to 6,600 feet in a flat four minutes and then continue on to a ceiling of nearly 20,000 feet. Pilots loved it because it had no vicious habits which could kill them in a moment of carelessness. An easy plane to fly, the Fokker D.VII's were the only German aircraft specifically mentioned as reparations in the Armistice treaty. The United States alone received 142 of them after the war.

As the war progressed, the role of the bombers became more prominent. The Italians were pioneers in their construction and their best-known product was the various Capronis. The main British contribution in this area was the Handley Page 0|400, capable of hauling eight 250-pound bombs and eight 112-pound bombs. The Germans developed a number of big bombers. The most famous were the so-called

Left to right—Lothar von Richthofen (40 victories) and his older brother Manfred (80 victories) pose by a Fokker triplane.

"Giants," which were used to strike against England. Britain experienced its hell from the air long before the attacks of Hitler's Luftwaffe. The Giants included Gothas and Zeppelin-Staakens which carried out 52 bombing missions against England in 1918. These raids killed 857 persons and injured 2,058, but they did little in the way of damaging strategic targets.

The much-feared Zeppelins also achieved little material success. The prediction that the German lighter-than-air machines would destroy English and French cities never proved so. The first Zeppelin attack was launched against English coastal towns in January 1915, and London was raided in May of that same year. The raids caused more terror than destruction. By 1916, the British had aircraft capable of dealing with the Zeppelin threat.

No history of World War I aviation would be complete without a mention of French Escadrille N-124 or, as it was more familiarly known, the Lafayette Escadrille. Surprisingly the French first opposed the idea of a flying unit composed strictly of American volunteers. The United States was neutral, and France did not want to tip that vast reservoir of manpower and equipment into the hands of the Boche. However, Gallic common sense, brought around by the insistent pressure of American expatriates, soon perceived the propaganda value of such a Yankee flying corps. The squadron originally was organized as L'Escadrille Americaine, but protests by the German ambassador in Washington forced the French to change the name to that of the legendary Lafayette Escadrille.

The first American volunteers to join the unit came from the ranks of the French Foreign Legion, French Flying Service, and the Ambulance Service. Dated March 14, 1916, the initial roster included these names: Norman Prince, William Thaw, Bert Hall, Kiffin Rockwell, Elliot Cowdin, Victor Chapman, and James McConnell. Four of them, Prince, Rockwell, Chapman, and McConnell, died in action.

It was during the prolonged battle of Verdun that the squadron first saw action. That was in May 1916. The squadron remained operational until February 18, 1918, when it was removed from the French order of battle. At that time, most of its pilots transferred to American flying units. While operational, the Lafayette Escadrille's pilots racked up thirty-nine confirmed aerial victories. It suffered the loss of six fliers in combat, two dead in operational accidents, and one downed by antiaircraft fire. Five other members of the squadron were hospitalized with wounds.

The name of the famed unit did not die in the postwar period. The French had a squadron with that name through the 1920's and 1930's, and until the end of World War II. About an hour's drive from Paris, at Villeneuve l'Etang, just outside of St. Cloud, there is a handsome monument to the World War I dead of the unit. Many of them rest there today.

With the signing of the Armistice, France maintained it had destroyed 2,049 German planes. The French admitted that 8,255 of its airmen were killed, wounded, or missing as the result of air action. The British claimed 7,900 confirmed and unconfirmed enemy machines against a loss of 2,810 craft. The United States reported that it destroyed 781 enemy planes and 73 balloons. The Americans acknowledge the loss of 289 planes and 48 balloons. The Central Powers, including Germany, never issued any reliable figures and many of their records have since been lost.

It is doubtful whether any of these figures can be substantiated with any great accuracy, especially those of the British and the Americans. The British fliers were notorious for their victory claims. It was once said that if all the victory claims put in by the British pilots had been confirmed, they would have totaled far more than the number of machines the Germans built during the entire war.

But for the fliers of that long ago time, the only concern was their war in the air. For the victor, there was the adulation of the nation; for the loser, there was a shallow grave, a shovel in the face, and a wooden cross. Chivalry was wonderful, but there was no place for it in aerial conflict. Survival, by any means possible, was much preferred.

✠ ✠ ✠

Chapter 2

LIFE OF THE RED BARON

"Richthofen's end is as legendary as the death of Siegfried."

—GERMAN CHRONICLER

✝BARON Manfred von Richthofen was born a hunter and he died a hunter in pursuit of an elusive quarry. The instinct for the hunt dominated his character throughout his brief life. For him the hunt was the very breath of life itself. Stalking prey, whether of the four-footed variety in the Silesian uplands and the Black Forest, or of the winged class in the French skies, was his ultimate joy. Be the target deer, boar, pheasant, or man, he exulted when the hunted was fixed forever in his sights and his eager finger squeezed the trigger to still the quivering heart.

The hunt was his passion; its trophies were his dearest relics. In peacetime, he killed game at every opportunity; in war, he killed men indiscriminately and with the same deadly imperturbability and finesse. In peacetime, his trophies were the horns, antlers, skins, and the stuffed animals and birds with which he filled the rooms of his parents' home. In war, his trophies were every possible decoration the grateful Fatherland and its allies could bestow upon him, remnants of downed Allied aircraft, and grisly photographs of foes he had slain.

He was born to glory, born a knight, and born a Prussian aristocrat. No writer could create a more romantic and incredible figure. He was proud and haughty, aloof and unemotional, a finely molded product of his environment and his day in history. A legend in his own lifetime, the boyishly handsome nobleman of the unsmiling demeanor became an even greater legend following his mysterious death during an aerial dogfight over the Somme Valley on April 21, 1918.

He grew to only medium height but was exceptionally robust and imbued with unflagging vitality. He was blond and small of waist. His eyes were steely blue and difficult to fathom except when he exploded into righteous anger at the laggard and the pusillanimous in his flying units. The nose was strong and slightly jutting. It curved like that of the falcon which he most resembled when aloft in his heavenly element. His lips were full and carefully drawn; they seldom smiled. The jaw was firm.

In the short twenty-five years of his life, he knew the frenzied adulation experienced by few men. He was the idol of his nation, lionized by millions. In his daring aerial exploits, the German people forgot for a few moments the horrors of the trenches.

Women worshiped him and offered him a host of proposals, legal and illicit. Yet his heart supposedly belonged to only one of them—a woman who has never been named. Some say he even married her about six weeks before his death. Then others, more unkindly, said he did not know women intimately, preferring instead the company of only a few close male friends of similar background and tastes. They noted that he remained mostly to himself on the aerodromes of France; he hardly ever took part in the hell-raising parties of wine, women, and song arranged for Germany's birdmen in Berlin's Bristol Hotel by airplane designer, Anthony Fokker; sipped liquor only occasionally; and smoked at the rarest of times. They did not really understand that, for the Baron, nothing really mattered except the hunt.

Newsmen, visiting wartime quarters, noticed that he often slipped away from his pilots' parties. But one of his fliers explained: "He likes to be alone at night. He reads a lot and he plans tomorrow's operations and he thinks. The rest of us

The Richthofen home in Schweidnitz, where Manfred grew up following the aristocratic pursuits of riding and hunting.

eel that we're better off if we don't think." Richthofen, by nature, was dour and aloof, and his personal shyness prevented him from participating in many of the celebrations at his headquarters. However, he always saw to it that, whenever possible, his men dined on the best food and wine that the black market could provide. One writer, after visiting his headquarters during the war, described him as "the pampered aristocrat of the war, the golden youth of adventure."

His Emperor and Empress deferred to him. He was the Teutonic knight incarnate. He was the Wagnerian image of flesh and blood. The chief of the German General Staff, Field Marshal Eric Ludendorff, himself had said: "He was worth as much as three divisions." His name was a household word among the dwellers of castles, landed estates, farmhouses, and urban apartments and hovels. Photographs of him were as readily displayed as those of the late President John F. Kennedy in our own day.

He remains a true German hero, emulated to this very day by the new breed of Luftwaffe pilots. The anniversary of his death is always marked by traditional pomp and circumstance and speeches evoking his fighting spirit and sense of duty to the Fatherland. His memory is bereft of any political stigma; it lives on as a stark symbol of all that is most admirable in those who fell fighting for God and Country. Why, the contemporary fliers of the Richthofen Geschwader ask, should they not honor the man who officially destroyed eighty Allied aircraft in eighteen months and who commanded a group of elite airmen who shot down 644 enemy planes while losing only 56 pilots themselves? Could any hunter be more worthy of remembrance?

Manfred von Richthofen was only a child, hardly shorn of the long blond curls and the dresses in which his mother loved to clothe him, when his love for the hunt initially manifested itself. Visiting his grandmother, he took his first air rifle and slipped away from the grownups to seek some targets for his pellets. They turned out to be four of his grandmother's tame ducks who, unfortunately, caught his attention while swimming in a nearby pond.

The future ace felt neither shame nor remorse for his action. Indeed, in the manner of the typical Junker lad of the late nineteenth century, he rushed to his grandmother to boast of his prowess with the air rifle.

His mother, the Baroness Kunigunde von Richthofen, outwardly did not appreciate the trophies collected by her excited son. She began to scold young Manfred, but the grandmother hushed her: "He has confessed his deed like a man. And like a man, he has killed his prey. So it is like a man, all be it a young one, that we should treat him."

The Baroness, although a bit perturbed, secretly was proud of her oldest boy. For years she treasured a cluster of duck feathers affixed to a section of brown pasteboard by crimson sealing wax. The feathers, she proudly told all those who visited the Richthofen home in Schweidnitz, were relics of Manfred's first kill.

Rittmeister Manfred Freiherr von Richthofen, who was to become the most colorful figure in the history of military aviation and the center of endless controversy, was born at Breslau on May 2, 1892, the eldest son of Albrecht von Richthofen, an officer of the 1st Regiment of Cuirassiers. His mother was a member of the wealthy von Schickfuss and Neudorff family.

In German, the name Richthofen means court of justice. It is a sort of title stemming from ancestors who had been mayors, judges, and councilors in Silesia since the seventeenth century. The province of Silesia now is a section of Communist East Germany. The patent of nobility had been bestowed upon the male line of the Richthofen family by Frederick the Great after he had overrun Silesia, once a part of romantic Bohemia in 1742.

It is also interesting to note that the Motif of the von Richthofen family contains a sentence which, being translated, states: "Clear like a crystal without a shadow, remained the glory of the name." Germany's great fighter pilot sought successfully during his life to conform in all his deeds to those ringing words.

Manfred was the eldest son of the Richthofens. His brother, Lothar, was born in 1894. Lothar, in seventy-seven days at the front, scored forty confirmed kills and tied for the tenth spot among the ranking German aces of World War I. Manfred was always slightly envious of his younger brother's rapid rise and fun-loving personality, and never quite approved of his cold-blooded manner in chalking up kills, a manner which was more detached than even his own.

Lothar also had the good fortune to survive the war,

unlike his oldest brother, but his good luck was short-lived. On July 4, 1922, the small commercial airliner he was piloting was stricken with engine trouble. Lothar tried to reach the safety of the runway at Fuhlsbuttel Airfield near Hamburg, but the aircraft quickly lost altitude and slammed into a tree. Lothar was fatally injured and died en route to a hospital.

There was also a third son, Karl Bolko, who was born in 1903. He was never old enough to serve in the war. He lives today and is a successful businessman in West Germany. There was one daughter, Ilse, who served as a nurse during the war. Death took her in 1962.

Manfred was small as a child but developed a healthy constitution through constant exercise and participation in sports. Like the other boys in his country squire class, he was extremely fond of the outdoor life, particularly riding, shooting, and hunting. Keen eyesight was a great assistance to him in the latter endeavor. His remarkable agility was demonstrated at every opportunity by turning somersaults without using his hands.

In his autobiography, *The Red Battle Flyer*, published as German propaganda during the war, he relates how "as a little boy of eleven, I entered the Cadet Corps. I was not particularly eager to become a cadet, but my father wished it. So my wishes were not consulted."

Albrecht von Richthofen perhaps was motivated in pushing his oldest son into the military profession because of his own premature retirement from the cavalry. He had been placed on the disabled list because of deafness contracted when he plunged into a frigid river to help rescue three men of his Life Cuirassier Regiment during winter maneuvers.

In any case, as the future ace noted, the son's wishes were not consulted. It is unlikely, however, that Manfred would have objected. "Der Vater" had spoken and the Junker son obeyed unquestioningly. Unwavering obedience, a sharp sense of duty, and admirable self-discipline were to be the outstanding traits of young Richthofen.

The father selected the German Military School at Wahlstatt to educate his son. The school formerly was a monastery and, as far as Manfred was concerned, it still was because the cadets lived like monks. Food and furniture were scarce. Discipline was severe and unending.

At Wahlstatt, Manfred quickly began to demonstrate that he was not lacking in courage. He wrote in his autobiography: "I had a tremendous liking for all risky foolery. For instance, one fine day, with my friend, Frankenberg, I climbed the famous steeple of Wahlstatt by means of the lightning conductor and tied my handkerchief to the top. I remember exactly how difficult it was to negotiate the gutters. Ten years later, when I visited my little brother [Bolko] at Wahlstatt, I saw my handkerchief still tied up high in the air."

From Wahlstatt, Manfred went on to the Royal Military Academy at Lichterfelde, which he said he "liked very much better" than the cadet school. At Lichterfelde, he wrote, "I did not feel so isolated from the world and began to live a little more like a human being." After finishing his studies there, he went to the Berlin War Academy, graduating at the age of nineteen in 1911.

In the fall of 1912, he won his second lieutenancy and was posted to the crack 1st Regiment of Uhlans, named after the Russian Emperor Alexander I. Richthofen personally sought service with this unit because it was garrisoned in his "beloved" Silesia. He said at the time, "It is the finest thing for a young soldier to be a cavalryman."

Richthofen's admiration for the "arme blanche" was not reciprocated, much to his chagrin on countless occasions. He dearly loved his mounts, but the romance was the old story of unrequited love. His peacetime days with the cavalry reveal constant references to his being thrown by several mounts, resulting in a number of broken bones. But he repeatedly demonstrated his determination and self-discipline by remounting as quickly as possible.

In 1913 he rode a charger named Blume in a cross-country race for the Kaiser's Prize. Richthofen had only ridden two miles when the horse pitched him on his head. "I suddenly stood on my head," he recalled later. The young officer suffered a broken collarbone. Undaunted, he refused to give in to the agony wracking his shoulder and remounted Blume. With Spartan courage, he galloped another forty miles to win the race.

II

The Great War, which raged for four years and claimed thirty million victims, came as a surprise to the twenty-two year old cavalry officer. For months there had been nothing but talk of such a war and the newspapers had been filled with lurid accounts of the impending conflict. Richthofen and his comrades, however, reached the point of ennui because of the barrage of such reports.

"We had so often packed our service trunks that the whole thing had become tedious. No one believed any longer there would be a war," he wrote afterwards.

But the leaders of Europe, in their stupidity, were hellbent on war in that halcyon summer of 1914. The troublesome Balkans were once more a tinderbox. No one proposed any constructive action to lessen tensions. Let war come. It would be short and glorious, a carbon copy of von Molkte's smashing victory over France in 1870.

The war came swiftly after June 28, 1914. On that date, Archduke Francis Ferdinand, the Hapsburg heir to the crown of the ancient Austro-Hungarian Empire, was assassinated with his duchess in the streets of Sarajevo, the capital of Serbia. The assassin was Gavrilo Princip, a youthful member of a Serbian nationalist group, which had sought to annex Bosnia, a part of Emperor Franz Joseph's empire.

The Austrians issued an ultimatum to Serbia. It was summarily rejected. Austria declared war on little Serbia on July 28, 1914. Russia mobilized to protect her fellow Slavs. France followed. Germany, an ally of Austria, declared war on Russia July 31 and against France August 3. Each nation, its population whipped into a state of patriotic fervor, was convinced the war would be of short duration and the troops would be in the enemy's capital by Christmas.

The day before the hostilities erupted, Richthofen's lancer regiment was stationed at Ostrowo in Silesia, some six miles from the Russian frontier. The 1st Uhlans consisted of a depot and four squadrons of horse. Its main duties, in the event of war, were to scout ahead and act as a screen for the army. No duties were considered more dashing at the time.

On that day, Richthofen and his fellow officers, still uncon-

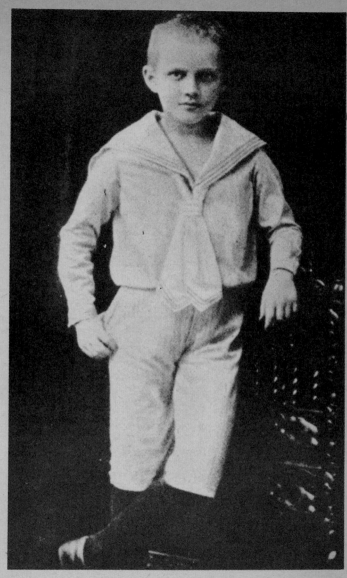

Manfred at the age of seven.

vinced that hostilities were inevitable, sat in the officers' club eating oysters, drinking champagne, and gambling. "We were very merry. No one thought of war," the Baron said later. Even the stern admonitions of a headquarters officer that war was only hours away failed to convince the gay group of the seriousness of the situation.

The next day the Uhlan regiment received its dispatches to take the field. Richthofen's orders, which he had memorized thoroughly, were to lead a troop of lancers across the frontier and take up a position near the Polish village of Kielce. From there he was to report back any enemy troop movements.

Richthofen prepared to move his horsemen at midnight. A few minutes prior to that hour he made a final inspection of the men and their mounts. Then, alone for a moment and using his saddlebag for a desk, he wrote a brief note to his family: "These are to be my last lines, written in a hurry. My most hearty greetings to you. If we never see each other again take these, my most sincere thanks, for everything you have done for me. I leave no debts behind me. I have, on the contrary, saved a few hundred marks which I am taking along with me. Embracing every one of you, I am, your grateful and obedient son and brother, Manfred." This done, he signaled his men to mount, and, amidst the creaking of leather harness and equipment and the clatter of ironshod hooves on the cobbles, he rode off to his greatest hunting adventure. He was twenty-two years old.

Young Manfred's war did not prove to be nearly as exciting as he had expected. In the first week of the great adventure, there was a narrow brush with a body of Cossacks and his return to camp to learn that he had been reported killed in action at Kalisz. Condolences already had been received by his family. Manfred hastened to reassure them of his existence. A few days later his regiment was ordered to entrain for the Western Front. Debarking at Busendorf, the cavalryman rode across Luxembourg into Belgium and joined the Crown Prince's German 5th Army in the Ardennes Forest.

Richthofen, at the head of fifteen lancers, experienced his first real taste of warfare, and an unforgettable mouthful it was, on the lovely, bright, sunlit day of August 21 in the woods near Virton. As his men entered the dense forest,

Manfred excitedly drove them in hot pursuit of a large body of French cavalry. He was thirsting for a fight. His brother Lothar's dragoons had already reached the front, and the thought that his younger brother might distinguish himself first was particularly galling. He was determined that he would always be first, especially in the hunt.

His eagerness overcame his usually cautious nature, and the Uhlans ran head on into a deadly ambush. Enemy fire swept their ranks from behind a concealed barricade to the front and from both sides. Several Uhlans and horses went down. Manfred's own orderly fell at his side, unwounded, but pinned beneath his mount. Richthofen gave the signal for his men to close up and follow him. To stand and fight would be useless. Their survival lay in flight. The Uhlans withdrew in haste and disorder; Manfred, smarting from shame, galloping along with them.

"The enemy had certainly surprised us," he modestly commented later. "They had probably observed us from the beginning and had intended to trap us and catch us unaware as is the character of the French," he added, in a face-saving explanation. But the lesson of the ambush was not lost on the youthful officer. Later, he would use the same tactics repeatedly to win fame in the hostile skies of France.

More patrols and scouting missions followed in the weeks ahead. Still embarrassed from the drubbing he had taken, Manfred sought constantly, but unsuccessfully, to distinguish himself in action. "I am trying hard to win the Iron Cross," he wrote his mother. Decorations, the outward trappings and baubles of valor, were important to him. He was proud and anxious to win the visible trophies of war to match the numerous trophies he had gained in peace. And all the time, there was the growing fear that Lothar would be the first of the Richthofens to distinguish himself in battle.

The days of the cavalryman in World War I passed quickly on the Western Front. Trench warfare had come of age. The Crown Prince's forces were brought to a halt before Verdun and both sides began to dig in along the heights of the Meuse River. With the end of the war-of-movement phase, Richthofen and his fellow Uhlans were dismounted and attached to infantry units. Manfred himself became a supply officer and knew the constant sting of being referred to as a "rear-echelon warrior." It rubbed his hunting instinct to realize that in the great time of killing, he was not part of the killing.

Stuck in the mud of the trenches, young Manfred turned his eyes skyward when an occasional aircraft droned overhead. How lovely they were, he thought, wheeling and soaring above the clouds. As a cavalryman, he realized bitterly that the airplane had taken over the horsemen's role as the "eyes of the army." He wondered what it would be like to fly, a free spirit adrift in the blue, so far above the mud-filled trenches and their human wreckage. At times he thought of applying for flying duty, but always hesitated because he thought the war would be over before he finished his training. Glory would escape him. Lothar might realize it first.

In the fall of 1914, he was awarded his first decoration, the Iron Cross (Second Class). He received it for the cavalry patrols he had carried out in the early weeks of the war. It was not actually much of a decoration; some five and a half million men won it between 1813 and 1918, but Manfred treasured it as his very first trophy of the killing time. To his mother he wasted no time writing: "I come with glad tidings. Yesterday, I was decorated with the Iron Cross . . ." He continued, however, to speak enviously of Lothar and of how he "would like so much to earn the First Class Order of the Iron Cross."

Christmas came and passed and with it the hopes of a quick victory by any of the warring nations. Winter passed and spring's touch softly caressed the scarred earth, and still Manfred found no release from his tedious duties as a supply officer and then an ordnance officer of an infantry unit before Verdun. His boredom was compounded by the neverending inspections and paper work. He found a slight outlet for his boundless energies by escaping occasionally from the trenches to go hunting, especially the wild boar that abounded in the woods well behind the German lines.

It was April, and nine months had passed and he saw no end to the fighting. Yet, where was the glory he had counted on so eagerly when he rode so valiantly off to the war in the summer of 1914? Many of his cousins and schoolboy friends had seen much more combat than he. Many of them had been wounded and quite a few killed. But all he had really known was the war of waiting. It was not his kind of war.

The impasse was broken at the end of April when he

received orders to return to duty in the supply service. The orders stated that he would carry out his duties as a supply officer even further back from the front lines. The Uhlan officer, despite his strong sense of duty, exploded and wrote the following scathing letter to the general commanding his division: "My Dear Excellency: I have not gone to war in order to collect cheese and eggs, but for another purpose." The remainder of the unmilitary letter contained a request for a transfer to the flying service. Surprisingly, Manfred was not disciplined, probably because of his family's aristocratic connections and also because his zeal for battle was admired by his general. At the end of May 1915, his "greatest wish was fulfilled" when orders came down approving his request for transfer to the flying service.

III

The delighted Richthofen hurriedly departed for Cologne where he and thirty other officers went through the standard four-week observer's course as members of Fliegerersatzabteilung No. 7. At this time, the observers in the German Flying Service were always officers, while the pilots usually were noncommissioned officers, the reason being that the observers' duties were considered far more important than those of the pilots. The course consisted of numerous classroom lectures on navigation, map reading, observation, and photography, the workings of the internal combustion engine, and, of course, several hours of actual flight.

Richthofen was exhilarated by his first flight. In preparation for it, he went to bed earlier than usual, not that he was much of a "night owl" anyway, and rose thoroughly refreshed and ready to go the next morning. Before he knew what was happening, the pilot was roaring down the air strip. The craft shook all over while Manfred hung on for dear life. Suddenly, the shaking ended. The plane was airborne.

Aloft, the cavalry officer cautiously began "to look over the side at the country." How small everything seemed to him, even the great cathedral of Cologne. He thought it resembled a toy. "It was a glorious feeling to be so high above the earth, to be master of the air," he wrote afterwards. "I didn't care a bit where I was and I felt extremely sad when my pilot thought it was time to go down again."

Richthofen took to the air like a born falcon. He quickly recognized it as a new element to conquer, one which held the promise of novel hunting thrills. He was determined to master it, to stake it out as his domain. To be high in the blue was a thousand times better than the existence he had known in the trenches. Once again he could serve as a cavalryman. Truly he was, at last, a flying Uhlan. The vast blue acres beckoned, expansive in their glorious immensity, an open invitation for daring young birdmen to fly and fight.

Manfred was ranked at about the midlevel of his class when it passed out of the course and he was sent on to FEA No. 6 at Grossenhain to finish his training. With that out of the way, he was delighted when orders assigned him, in June, to action with Feldfliegerabteilung No. 69 on the Eastern Front, only about one hundred miles distant from his beloved Silesia. The unit's chief responsibility was to report enemy troop movements to the 6th Austrian Corps in the army of General von Mackensen.

Richthofen was assigned as an observer to First Lieutenant Zeumer, one of Germany's earliest pilots and one of the 69th Squadron's crack fliers. It was quite an experience for the youthful Junker. Zeumer was dying of tuberculosis. He knew it and was inordinately reckless when aloft, determined to die in action rather than in bed. He was to get his wish eventually but not until June 1917, and then on the Western Front. In the meantime, he flew like a maniac, constantly courting death. For Manfred, who was not so anxious to die, at least not before he knew real fame, it was an unforgettable experience to fly with Zeumer.

Still, Manfred described those days aloft in an Albatros CI or BII with the fearless Zeumer at the controls as "my most beautiful time." The Baron considered life in the Flying Corps very much like life in the cavalry. He and Zeumer were airborne every day over the scorched Russian countryside, reconnoitering the Russian army, and on numerous occasions, bringing back valuable information.

But the team split up within a month with the arrival at 69th Squadron of Count von Holck, a sportsman and a prewar automobile enthusiast. In the former Uhlan officer, Manfred sensed a kindred spirit, especially when he arrived at the air field, not in a tender, but on foot with his hunting dogs after a thirteen-mile hike from Jaroslav where his train

Richthofen joined the First Regiment of Uhlans in 1911 and entered many prewar riding competitions. At a Breslau meet he is third over the obstacle.

had been held up. The Count was most agreeable to being Richthofen's pilot. It actually made little difference to him who his observer was as long as he could fly and raise havoc with the enemy. His daring equaled that of Zeumer and almost cost him and Manfred their lives on several occasions. Once Holck flew so close to the ground that smoke from a burning town choked off the Mercedes engine of their Albatros, forcing them to land in what they thought was enemy territory. The craft was wrecked on impact. Holck and Manfred escaped injury and ran into nearby woods to hide from the Russian infantry which seldom deigned to take prisoners alive. Fortunately, the area that very day had been seized by the Prussian Guards and the intrepid pair was rescued unharmed.

With victory realized for a time in the East, Richthofen and Holck, along with thousands of other Germans, were transferred to the West about the middle of August 1915. While both men were to die in aerial combat, Holck's end came first and was witnessed unknowingly on May 1, 1916, by Richthofen. Aloft at the time, Manfred saw a Fokker Eindecker engaged with three French two-seaters above Fort Douaumont on the Verdun front. Before he could join the fight, the Eindecker suddenly dove straight down through the clouds. Later, the Baron learned that the pilot, shot through the head, was his old comrade, Count von Holck.

On his arrival at Ostend, Belgium, on August 22, 1915, Richthofen was assigned to a super-secret outfit called the Ostend Carrier Pigeons—Brieftauben Abteilung Ostend (BAO). A mystery squadron, the BAO, with that cover name to mask its real function, was established to begin the long-distance bombing of England. Manfred teamed up with another old flying mate from the Russian front, Zeumer, to begin training on the A.E.G. GII, one of Germany's earliest two-engine bombers. Manfred was not a great admirer of the Grosskampfflugzeug (large battle plane). The two-seater crafts lacked speed and maneuverability, and Richthofen deridingly referred to them as "big apple barges." The plans to use the large aircraft to bomb Britain never materialized, and Richthofen and Zeumer were put to work bombing, instead, Belgium cities occupied by the British Expeditionary Force. The Baron enjoyed dropping the bombs but was prevented from seeing their impact by the construction of the aircraft.

Once, when attempting to view the explosions, he extended his left hand to signal Zeumer to come about. Overeager, he forgot the whirring propeller and suffered the loss of the tip of his little finger. The Flying Uhlan had given his first drop of blood for the Fatherland.

It was on September 1, 1915, that Manfred experienced his first aerial combat. With Zeumer once again at the controls of the "big apple barge," Richthofen spotted a Royal Flying Corps Farman and ordered his pilot to close in. As the two ships passed within about one hundred yards of each other, the Baron fired four shots from his automatic rifle. He missed, but the observer in the Farman scored several hits on the A.E.G.

Later the same month, while flying in an Albatros with Lieutenant Osteroth as his pilot, Manfred sighted a lone Farman some three miles behind the French lines in the Champagne sector. He immediately ordered Oseroth to attack. The Albatros wheeled into good position and Richthofen loosed his entire supply of one hundred machine-gun rounds at the two-seater Allied bus. Fatally hit, the Farman spiraled down to crash nosefirst into a large shell crater. Manfred was elated, but his victory remained uncredited as it occurred too far behind the enemy lines to be confirmed. However, he was quite philosophical about the loss of confirmation, noting that the "chief thing is to bring a fellow down. It does not matter at all whether one is credited for it or not."

The team of Richthofen and Zeumer broke up on October 1, 1915. At the time, both were assigned to Brieftauben Abteilung Metz (BAM)—the Metz Carrier Pigeons, another cover name for a German bomber unit. Richthofen carried on with his observer's duties, but Zeumer was assigned to fly one of the few Fokker monoplanes attached to the unit for protection duty.

On the train to Metz, France, Richthofen met the man who was to have the most marked influence on him and to bring him eventually to the fore as the ace of aces of World War I. The meeting occurred when Manfred was seated at a dining-car table next to one occupied by a "young and insignificant-looking lieutenant." Richthofen's heart leaped excitedly when he recognized the officer as one of his great heroes, Oswald Boelcke, then Germany's ranking fighter pilot. A Prussian officer did not betray any outward emotions, but Boelcke was an air god to the youthful Richthofen. He could not let the moment pass without engaging Boelcke in conversation. There was much Manfred wanted to hear firsthand about aerial combat, and who was more knowledgeable about the subject than the man seated opposite him.

Excusing himself, Richthofen made his introductions and then inquired how Boelcke "managed" to shoot down the enemy birdmen. A modest man, Boelcke, at first, was embarrassed by the obvious adulation contained in Manfred's voice. However, he quickly recognized how important the question was to Richthofen and he replied, "Well, it is quite simple. I fly close to my man, aim well, and then, of course, he falls down." Manfred shook his head. He explained how he did the same things but his opponents failed to go down. Boelcke explained that the difference was that he flew a Fokker fighter while Manfred fired from a large battle plane.

After his meeting with Boelcke, Richthofen resolved to emulate his hero. He, too, would become a pilot. He, too, would learn to fly a Fokker. Then, perhaps, his chances for great success in the air would brighten. He no longer was happy to be an observer; he must learn to fly his own aircraft. At the controls of his own plane, he, too, could join ranks with those German heroes of the air to whom the German nation was beginning to pay so much respect and award honors beyond imagination. On his arrival at Metz, he immediately urged Zeumer to teach him to fly. In every spare moment, the pair was aloft in an old B-type craft. Ten days after his chance meeting with Boelcke, Zeumer said, "Now go fly yourself" to the Baron.

Afraid, but not willing to admit it, Manfred, his head full of Zeumer's final instructions, climbed into the familiar cockpit and prepared for takeoff. With the engine full on, the chocks were removed from the wheels, and the ungainly craft rolled down the field into the wind. As the fragile bus left the ground, Richthofen felt his fears dissipate. Once again he knew an unheralded exhiliration that he had not felt since his first flight. This feeling, though, was even more intense. He was alone at last at the controls and alone at last in the blue.

"I did not care for anything," he wrote afterwards. "I should not have been frightened no matter what happened."

What happened next piqued his pride and gave him a few bruises. He brought the machine in for the landing, but his actions were too mechanical. He was never to be a great flier at any time, and he especially was not during that solo flight. The machine did not respond as he had expected. Suddenly, it lurched. Confused, he tried to put it back on an even keel by the book. He overcorrected and the bus slammed into the ground at a high rate of speed. It nosed over and fell apart. A much wiser Uhlan officer extricated himself from the wreckage, unhurt but shaken, as Zeumer and his comrades came running.

Undaunted, and determined more than ever to follow in the footsteps of his idol, Boelcke, Manfred followed Zeumer's instructions to the letter for the next two days. Satisfied that he would not make the same mistake twice, he soared aloft again on another old B-type plane. His passionate practice paid off. He made several good landings. Two weeks later he presented himself for the pilot's examination, confident that he would pass without difficulty. But to his great surprise, since he flew without mishap, he failed to pass.

Another month passed, with Richthofen fulfilling his observer responsibilities and practicing flying solo in his spare time, before the examining officer was satisfied. His ambition had seen him through. But the examination he had passed was only of a preliminary nature. The German Flying Corps required the most demanding examinations before a flier could go to the front, especially at the controls of a fighter plane. Manfred was shipped to Doberitz near Berlin on November 15 for additional training. During this phase of his training, Richthofen combined business with pleasure. On a training flight, he would put his bus down at the Buchow Estate where he was well known by the family. Then he would spend several hours hunting boars before returning to base.

IV

On Christmas Day, 1915, Manfred received the one present he wanted above all others—word that he had passed his final examination and was rated as a full-fledged pilot. Now he could honestly visualize himself at the control of a single-seater fighter in deadly pursuit of Germany's enemies.

Elusive glory was at last within his grasp. Up there in the sky he would show Boelcke and Immelmann and the other early flying heroes his worth and mettle. Now he had the jump on brother Lothar.

A pilot he truly was, but he had to wait until March 1916 before going to the Front and an active-service flying unit. He was assigned to the 2nd Battle Squadron in the Champagne sector. His excitement was somewhat dampened by the announcement that he would fly a two-seater Albatros rather than single-seater fighters. The Baron kept his disappointment to himself, for he knew his time would come. In the meantime, he must get in all the flying possible to be ready for that day. At the same time, there was nothing in the rule books that said he could not make his reconnaissance ship more battleworthy. So, unmoved by the laughs and jeers of his fellow pilots, he fixed a machine gun onto the upper wing of his Albatros. The idea came to him after inspecting a downed Nieuport biplane. It was not enough for him that his observer had a machine gun. He, too, was a hunter and wanted his own weapon.

On April 26, 1916, he had his first opportunity to use his personal weapon. On a scouting mission, he spotted a French Nieuport below him. The enemy flier turned and dashed back over his own lines, but Richthofen was after him in a flash. Diving from above, he overtook the French bus and swooped below it so he could bring his machine gun into play. He fired a few well-directed bursts. The Nieuport staggered from the impact of the gunfire, slowly dropped over backward, and began falling end over end.

The Baron, figuring the pilot was attempting a ruse, watched for the French plane to straighten out and run for home. But the enemy plane continued its downward plunge; the pilot either was dying or dead. The Nieuport splashed into the woods near Fort Douaumont. Manfred's observer leaned forward to pat him on his head and offer heartiest congratulations. The Baron was elated but knew he undoubtedly would not receive confirmation for this second success as it too fell behind the opposing lines.

On his return to base, he simply reported, "I had an aerial fight and have shot down a Nieuport." He was correct in surmising that the higher-ups would not credit him with the victory. Yet, paradoxically, the Germans included the kill in

Teutonic Knight and squires; dressing for takeoff.

their war communique for that day: "Two hostile aircraft have been shot down in aerial fighting above Fleury, south and west of Douaumont." A jubilant Manfred dashed off a brief note the next morning to his mother, the Baroness: "In haste—some gladsome news. Look at the communique of yesterday, April 26th. One of these planes was shot down by my machine gun and is to my credit." The hunter had flushed and killed his quarry in the sky. The unacknowledged victory was sweet. He longed for an acknowledged victory. That would be sweeter.

Richthofen did experience several flights at the controls of a Fokker monoplane, two of which he wrecked in mishaps, before his posting once again to the Russian Front. The move to Kovel was made because the relentless German assaults against Verdun had failed. The elan of the poilus had smashed the Kaiser's elite regiments on the bloody highlands bordering the Meuse. Assigned to fly a C-plane, the Baron participated in a series of light bombing attacks against the Tsar's forces. He enjoyed the flying but burned impatiently within to return to the Western Front, where the Battle of the Somme was raging, at the controls of his own little fighter. The glory and idolization that cast a godlike aura around Boelcke beckoned him.

The opportunity to grasp for his own chunk of fame made itself known to him on a hot, humid day in August. Richthofen and several flying mates, dripping with perspiration, were holding a bull session when one of the fliers happened to remark that Boelcke was scheduled to visit the Kovel airfield that very day. The Baron immediately became excited. At last he was going to have a second meeting with his great hero. He inquired about the reason for the visit. His excitement increased when informed that Boelcke, returning from an inspection of Turkish Forces, was recruiting pilots for a crack Jagdstaffel he had been given a free hand to form.

Manfred, however, was too proud to present himself to Boelcke who was interviewing applicants for his new flying circus in one of the unit's railroad cars. He hung back as the pilots filed in one at a time to talk to Boelcke. An inner voice told him to go up and reintroduce himself. But his stubbornness held him back. The interviews ended, and the dejected

Richthofen went off to his quarters and sleep. Tossing and turning, he cursed himself for his foolish pride.

Early the next morning, he was awakened by a peremptory rapping at the door. He staggered sleepy-eyed to open it and found Boelcke himself standing there, with the coveted Pour le Merite fixed below his choker collar. The Baron was overwhelmed. There was his idol presenting himself in person. The Baron also was lucky. Boelcke had remembered their initial meeting on the train to Metz. Hearing that young Richthofen was attached to the K.G. 2, he had sought him out, his curiosity aroused at the Baron's failure to present himself during the interviewing of the previous day.

"Are you no longer interested, my young friend, in being a fighter pilot?" Boelcke asked the incredulous Baron.

"Yes, of course, sir." Manfred blurted out. Quickly recovering his usual poise, he waved the Saxon flier to a chair. "Please be seated, Herr Lieutenant."

In a few staccato sentences, Boelcke explained the reason for his visit. The Baron was well aware of the reason but listened politely and with the greatest interest.

"Affairs are going badly for our airmen on the Somme Front. The enemy has seized control of the air. You know what that means. Their aircraft are directing artillery fire without interference. Their fighters are incessantly strafing our infantry. The effect on the morale of our men is abysmal. Our flying service is being derided. The front-line troops are saying: 'May God punish England, our artillery, and our air force.' And the infantry is asking, 'Has anybody seen a German airman?' I have been ordered to recruit a group of select fliers and form a crack squadron and drive the enemy from the air. How about you, Baron, would you like to join me on the Somme and see some real fighting?"

The Baron was beside himself with excitement. His greatest wish was coming true, but he could hardly believe it possible. The great Boelcke himself was asking him to be a member of his squadron. What better opportunity for a hunter? And what prey could be more challenging than the daring British airmen prowling the skies above the Somme. His answer was immediate and in the affirmative.

Three days later, Manfred was in a train speeding across Germany. Watching the countryside flash by, he remembered how one of his flying mates, left back at the Kovel airfield, had called out to him at his departure, "See that you do not come back without the Pour le Merite [Blue Max]!" Manfred had smiled; he seldom laughed; nodded his head confidently and waved his last farewell to Russia. "From now onward," he said afterwards, "began the finest time of my life." The hunter, at last, was to have his just share of the killing time. Now he would show them—and especially his younger brother. Fame no longer would be denied him. He knew it instinctively.

Boelcke, as commander of the newly formed Jagdstaffel No. 2, did not fling his new cubs into the air at once. He knew the need for additional German airmen was desperate. But to send his cubs aloft without first inculcating in them the principles and techniques of air fighting would only result in heavy losses. Impatient as they were to flaunt their wings in combat, the cubs first must be properly prepared. They would have their fill of combat soon enough.

With the arrival of additional new Albatros DII's on September 16, 1916, Boelcke decided that his cubs had had enough practice in formation flying, team tactics, and aerial gunnery. He would lead them into combat against the enemy.

September 17 dawned bright and clear and developed into a glorious late summer day. Roaring down the runway at Lagnicourt, Boelcke, still the leading German ace and a hero of the Fatherland, led seven of his cubs in the direction of the lines. ". . . for the first time we flew as a squadron commanded by the great man whom we followed blindly," Manfred recalled later. Boelcke spotted eight B.E. 2c's of No. 12 Squadron, RFC, and an escort of six F.E. 2b's of No. 11 Squadron, RFC, and true to his own teachings, signaled his men to climb so they would have the advantage of altitude. At the same time, he maneuvered his formation around between the sun and the Englishmen.

While the Britishers excitedly watched the results of their bombs erupting on the Marcoing railway station, Boelcke chose to attack. The eight German aircraft swooped down on the fourteen RFC planes. Manfred quickly picked out one of the RFC's F.E. 2b's as his own victim and headed straight for it. When the distance between his Albatros and the target narrowed rapidly to fifty yards, he opened fire. His bullets had no effect. The "lord," obviously no stranger to aerial combat, banked his bus from side to side to permit his observer to fire back over the top wing at Richthofen. Startled by the unexpected bursts from the Lewis gun, the Baron dove quickly out of range. He ducked his Albatros into a cloud and then arced out below and behind the F.E. 2b. He closed to a killing distance, unseen by his opponents, and sprayed the RFC craft's engine and nacelle. The lethal spray mortally wounded both the pilot, 2d Lt. L. B. F. Morris, and his observer, Lt. T. Rees.

The badly stricken aircraft nosed over to begin its final plunge. The Baron had to fling his Albatros about to miss a collison. In his eagerness to score, he had almost rammed the F. E. 2b. As he followed the crippled bird down, the dying Morris summoned sufficient strength to right his bus and bring it to a rocky landing near a German airfield. The jubilant Baron—"I nearly yelled with joy," he said afterwards—made a hasty landing nearby and rushed to the English machine. Rees was dead and Morris died en route to a field hospital. The hunter was overjoyed. This kill could not be kept from him.

Boelcke also was delighted with the performance of his cubs. They had lived up to all his expectations. In addition to Manfred, Erwin Boehme and Reimann had tallied confirmed kills. And Boelcke himself had chewed up another victim. As a memento to his esteem, Boelcke presented each of the successful fighters with ornamental beer mugs, a traditional presentation piece in the officers' mess of numerous nations.

Richthofen, ever the relic collector, decided to do Boelcke one better. The hunter would present himself, from then on, with a silver cup for each of his victories. He wrote immediately to a Berlin jeweler and ordered a plain sterling silver cup to be inscribed "1 Vickers 2. 17.9.16." The cup was to measure five centimeters in height and three centimeters in diameter at the mouth. Although Richthofen had incorrectly identified his victim as a Vickers aircraft rather than a F.E. 2b, the cup, and all the others which were to follow, would serve to commemorate his aerial conquests.

To his mother, the proud Baron wrote in part: ". . . Making for them (an English Squadron), I shot one down. Its occupants were an English officer and a petty officer. I was rather proud over my tryout. Naturally, I have been credited with the downed plane." After posting the letter in

Cambrai, the Baron visited the fresh graves of Morris and Rees. For a few moments, he quietly studied the two mounds of earth and the crosses at their head. They were his first two Englishmen. He vowed that many more would suffer a similar fate. The Fatherland demanded it.

Later, the Baron, rehashing his thoughts about that initial confirmed victory, wrote: "At that time, I did not have the conviction, as I later had in similar cases: the conviction best described by the sentence—He must fall. In this, my first encounter, I was curious to see if he would fall. There is a great difference between the two feelings. When one has shot down one's first, second, or third opponent, then one begins to find out how the trick is done."

V

Manfred apparently determined quickly how the trick was done. His second victory came the very next Saturday. Jasta 2 tangled with a unit of Martinsyde Elephants of No. 27 Squadron, RFC. The Elephants, built as single-seater fighters, were appallingly unsuitable for that role as they responded much too slowly to their control. The Baron's Albatros, with its two deadly Spandau machine guns, easily shot one of them out of the air. Thrilled by his second victory, he landed and motored to the crash site. From the wreckage, he deftly removed a piece of fabric bearing the number "G.W.174." From that time on, the hunter began to send home, when they became available, relics of his aerial kills. Carefully packed for shipment, they were lovingly uncrated and placed in a display at the home in Schweidnitz. In time, the trophies of his successes grew to museum proportions. His mother was not always overjoyed, however, to receive such relics. She knew only too well that each represented human lives and a fate that could also take her own dear son, Manfred.

Another letter was dispatched to the jeweler in Berlin. The Baron asked for a second cup, exactly of the same design as the first. It was to be engraved as follows: "2 Martinsyde 1. 23.9.16." The jeweler was to fill orders for sixty of these grisly trophies before the war depleted Germany's supply of silver. As a result, Richthofen was unable to commemorate his last twenty victories in the sky by dead men's cups. The cups remained with the Richthofen family in the Schweidnitz

The Red Baron in the cockpit.

home until the Russian army overran Silesia in the closing days of World War II. Their ultimate disposition has never been determined. One report says they were recognized as historical items and packed for shipment to Moscow where they remain still crated to this day in some unidentified warehouse.

A week passed and Manfred scored his third victory. His victim was another F.E. 2b. It fell in flames from a height of twelve thousand feet, burning its two occupants beyond recognition. The wreckage only yielded a battered number plate for the trophy-hunting Richthofen. The usual order went off to the Berlin jeweler. "Liebe Mamma" heard about the kill in a letter written a week later. In the first paragraph, Manfred wrote "On September 30th, I brought down my third British-er. His plane was burned when he crashed to the ground. One's heart is beating a bit more quickly when the adversary, whose face one has just seen, goes down enveloped in flames from an altitude of twelve thousand feet. Naturally, nothing was left, either of the pilot or the plane when they crashed. I picked up a small plate as a souvenir . . ."

The Baron now had come into his own element. The traits of the born hunter manifested themselves in his fast climbing record of confirmed victories. He kept his body in the finest possible condition. He constantly studied the tactics of the top aces, especially those of Boelcke. He scrutinized his prey before closing in for the kill. He skipped the nights of revelry so his hunter's instincts would always be at their peak when he roared aloft. Never a great flier, he disdained aerobatics and chose, instead, to garner his victories by maneuvering into the most favorable position before loosing his unerring fire.

He always listened intently as Boelcke, ever his mentor, analyzed the results of each of his men's fights and constantly hammered home his dicta: "Always keep your eye on your opponent and don't let him deceive you by ruses—try to get behind your foe to attack. If you are yourself dived upon, do not try to evade the onslaught, but turn to meet your enemy."

Manfred's willingness to learn and his determination to succeed paid the inevitable results. By October 17, the Baron had scored six confirmed kills. Boelcke, at the same time, had raised his tally to thirty-five victories. A week later, Boelcke had shot down his fortieth enemy plane. He stood alone as the idol of the German nation. No other flier of any nation could boast such a victory record in the air. Enemy pilots began to believe he was invincible. They were wrong. No man is immortal, as we were so well reminded by the fall of the giants among us in the period from November 1963 to June 5, 1968.

On October 28, 1916, Boelcke, the fourth of six children of a school teacher, used up all his time on earth. He already had led three patrols that day and was airborne on his fourth when his number came up. It was late in the day, and the sky was dark and forbidding when Boelcke led his men aloft to provide air cover for the infantry. Above Pozieres, the German war birds tangled with a group of D.H. 2's from No. 24 Squadron, RFC. Boelcke and Erwin Boehme, who had come east from the Kovel airfield with Richthofen to join Jasta 2, dove in tandem on one of the single-seaters. Boelcke got under the craft for a shot at the defenseless underbelly. At that moment, another Britisher, being pursued closely by the Baron, shot across the flight path of Boehme. The maneuver forced both Boelcke and Boehme to bank their planes. In the split second the damage was done. The wheels of Boehme's Albatros DII ripped the upper wing of Boelcke's bus on the port side. It was the lightest of collisions, but the wind quickly grasped the rent fabric and peeled it loose. The leader's plane swerved to the left and nosed downward in a spin. Boehme, Richthofen, and the other members of Jasta 2 followed anxiously in his wake, praying for a miracle. Their prayers went unanswered. Boelcke's Albatros slammed into the ground. Thus died Germany's "father of fighter aviation" at the age of twenty-five.

Richthofen learned officially of Boelcke's death on his return to base. He and his mates could hardly believe it. He was pained by Boelcke's loss but philosophical, too. "Nothing happens without God's will," he said. "That is the only consolation which any of us can put to our souls during this war." Boehme was inconsolable, convinced that Boelcke's death was his fault. A court of inquiry, however, was to clear him of any guilt in the tragic accident. He would return to the air and score twenty-four official victories before going down in flames on November 29, 1917, near Ypres.

On the morning of November 3, Richthofen scored his

seventh victory—once again an F.E. 2b. In the afternoon he attended Boelcke's funeral in the Cathedral of Cambrai. Describing the affair in a letter to his mother, the Baron wrote: "During the funeral services and in the procession, I carried a pillow displaying his [Boelcke's] decorations. The funeral was like that of a prince. During six weeks we have, out of twelve pilots, six dead and one wounded while two have suffered complete nervous collapse. Yesterday I brought down my seventh, shortly after my sixth. The ill luck of others has not yet affected my nerves." His iron will and nerves were to remain unassailable until he was wounded and shot down in the next year.

With Boelcke dead and buried, the German airmen swept aloft to avenge his death. The Jasta was renamed in Boelcke's honor and command was given to Oberleutenant Stephen Kirmaier, who was to die in action some three weeks later. The surviving cubs now were full-grown lions, rampaging through the skies over the Somme, seeking out the British whom they blamed for the death of their great teacher. No quarter was given; none was sought. The ruthlessness of aerial combat following Boelcke's death brought the British charge that the Germans were "like mad dogs." Any thoughts that the war in the air was one of gentleman against gentleman quickly dissipated as losses soared on both sides.

Six days after Boelcke's fall, the Baron chalked up his eighth kill. Ordinarily, Richthofen would have received the coveted Pour le Merite on achieving that score. But he was to be greatly disappointed. The German General Staff had decided, because of mounting intensity of aerial warfare, to establish sweeping reforms in the award of the Fatherland's top decoration. Immelmann and Boelcke had received the medal after garnering eight kills, but the High Command ruled that henceforth a pilot had to score sixteen victories to qualify for the Blue Max. The Baron would have to wait, but he vowed to make the waiting period as brief as possible.

On November 20, Manfred scored his first "double kill" of the war. In the morning, he fastened onto the tail of an F.E. 2b and shot it down after expending three hundred rounds of Spandau ammunition. Airborne again in the afternoon, he encountered a B.E. and quickly dispatched it. Since the B.E. was his tenth victim, he decided that from then on a cup of double the size of the others would be ordered to signify each successive tenth victory.

Three days later, during that month of revenge for Boelcke's death, the Baron fought his famous aerial duel with Major Lanoe Hawker, the RFC's top ace with nine kills and a holder of the Victoria Cross for routing three enemy aircraft in one engagement. The victory served to complete the Baron's metamorphosis into a very confident man-killer. Here is the manner in which Manfred described the action with Hawker in his own diary:

"I must confess that it was a matter of great pride to me to learn that the Englishman I shot down on November 23, 1916, was the English equivalent of our great Max Immelmann. Of course, I did not know who he was during the fight, but I did know from the masterly manner in which he handled his plane and the pluck with which he flew that he was a wonderful fellow.

"It was fine weather when I flew away from our aerodrome that day. I was in the best of spirits and keen for the hunt. Flying at an altitude of about ten thousand feet I observed three British planes. I saw that they saw me, and from their maneuvers, I gathered that our hopes for the day's fun were mutual. They were hunting bent, and the same as I.

"I was spoiling for a fight, and they impressed me much the same. They were above me, but I accepted the challenge. Being beneath and in no position to attack, I had to wait till the fellow dived on me. It was not long to wait. Soon he started down in a steep gliding dive, trying to catch me from behind.

"Both of his motors are speeding [Hawker was flying a D.H. 2 of No. 24 Squadron, which he commanded] to the utmost; still neither of us seems to gain on the other. We are exactly opposite each other on the circumference of the circle, and in this position neither of us can train our single forward shooting machine guns on the other.

"First we would go twenty times around to the right and then swing into another circle going around twenty times to the left. We continue the mad race, neither gaining an advantage. I knew at once that I was dealing with no beginner, because he didn't appear to dream of trying to break off the fight and get out of the circling. His plane was excellent for maneuvering and speed, but my machine gave me an advantage of being able to climb better and faster. This enabled me at last to break the circle and maneuver into a position behind and above him.

"But in the circling fight, both of us had lost height. We must have come down at least six thousand feet because we were a little more than three thousand feet above the ground. The wind was in my favor. Throughout the fight, at the same time we kept getting lower, the wind was gradually drifting us back to the German lines. I saw that now we were even behind the German lines in front of Bapaume, and my opponent should have noticed it was time for him to back out of the fight because he was getting further into my territory.

"But he was a plucky devil. With me behind and above him, he even turned around and waved his arm at me, as though to say: 'Wie gehts?' We went into circles again, fast and furious and as small as we could drive them. Sometimes I estimated the diameters of the circle at between eighty and a hundred yards. But I always kept above him and at times I could even look down almost vertically into his cockpit and watch each movement of his head. If it had not been for his goggles, I could have seen what sort of face he had.

"He was a fine sportsman, but I knew that in time my close presence behind and above him would be too much for him, particularly as all the time we were getting lower and lower and farther behind my lines. We were getting so close to the ground that he would soon have to decide whether he would have to land behind our lines or break the circle and try to get back to his own side.

"Apparently the idea of landing and surrender never occurred to this sportsman, because suddenly he revealed his plans to escape by going into several loops and other maneuvers of equal folly. As he came out of them, heading back for his own lines, my first bullets began whistling around his ears because up to now, with the exception of his opening shots, neither one of us had been able to range on the other.

"The battle is now close to the ground. He is not a hundred yards above the earth. Our speed is terrific. He starts back for his front. He knows my gun barrel is trained on him. He starts to zigzag, making sudden darts right and left, right and left, confusing my aim and making it difficult to train my guns on him. But the moment is coming. I am

Manfred and Lothar von Richthofen.

fifty yards behind him. My machine gun is firing incessantly, we are hardly fifty yards above the ground and just skimming it.

"Now I am within thirty yards of him. He must fall. The gun pours out its stream of lead. Then it jams. Then it reopens fire. That jam almost saved his life. One bullet goes home. He is struck through the back of the head. His plane jumps and crashes down. It strikes the ground just as I swoop over. His machine gun rammed itself into the earth and now it decorates the entrance over my door. He was a brave man, a sportsman and a flier."

When he was informed of Major Hawker's prominence, Manfred flew over the English lines and dropped a note to inform Hawker's men of his fate. The Baron's comrades arranged the burial services for the English ace, but as was the custom, Richthofen did not attend. It was considered in bad taste for the hunter to attend the funeral for his victim. The order, of course, was posted off to the Berlin jeweler. Hawker was recalled, until the Russians came, by the simple inscription on one of the Baron's cups: "11 Vickers 1. 23.11.16." Once again, Manfred had incorrectly identified an enemy plane as a Vickers.

VI

Promoted to a flight commander with Jasta Boelcke, he was aloft as often as possible, depending, of course, on the restricted flying weather caused by the poor late autumn weather and the fact that the Germans usually only flew one patrol a day. However, these factors notwithstanding, he destroyed a D.H. 2 on December 11 and added a second "double" to his hunter's bag on December 20. With Immelmann and Boelcke dead, the Fatherland was eagerly searching for new air heroes to glorify. The Baron was determined to fill that demand. He visualized, too, what a dashing figure he would cut with the handsome Blue Max suspended from its black and silver ribbon around his neck. It had slipped from his grasp before when he had scored his eighth victory; he would not let it get away again. Of all of Germany's colorful medals and decorations, none seemed more desirable to him than the Pour le Merite.

In the meantime, the hunter's ego would be satisfied in

another way. His self-esteem demanded it. He had his speedy Albatros DII painted bright red, similar to the color of the Nieuport flown by French ace, Jean Navarre, at Verdun. Such a bright color, the Baron thought, would let the enemy know of his presence. From then on, they would know the adversary they faced. To accept his challenge was to engage in a duel to the death with Germany's ace fighter pilot. From then on, too, he was to become known along the Western Front as the "Red Baron," or sometimes as the "Red Devil" or "Red Falcon" by the British and as "le rouge teufel" by the French. During the war, he was never known as the "Red Knight."

Two days after passing Christmas with his father, then recalled to the colors as a reserve major, and his brother, Lothar, who had left the dragoons to enter the Flying Service, the Red Baron felled another F.E. 2b. His sixteenth victory was a Sopwith Pup, piloted by Flight Lt. A. S. Todd of No. 8 (Naval) Squadron. Todd rashly had attacked three Albatros biplanes, one which was piloted by Richthofen. His derring-do was his undoing. While he was hotly engaged with two of the German buses, the Baron winged in behind the Pup and shot it out of the air.

The jubilant Baron was awarded the long-sought Blue Max on January 16, 1917. The medal, accompanied by a special citation from the Kaiser, brought him instant national fame and attention. Letters and wires of congratulations flooded the quarters of the Fatherland's new hero. The German people claimed a new personal champion. Headlines blazoned his name throughout the empire. His prowess in the air was unchallenged. He was twenty-four years old.

The Pour le Merite was not his only reward. As one of the nation's most successful surviving aces, he was promoted to the rank of captain or Rittmeister (riding master) since he was an Uhlan. That was not all. The Baron was informed that he was to leave Jasta Boelcke and take up command of his own Squadron, Jasta 11, then at Douai. His Jagdstaffel No. 11 had been in existence several months but had yet to score a victory. Richthofen vowed to change that situation immediately, and he wrote in his diary: "I had never imagined that it would be so delightful to command a chasing squadron. Even in my dreams I had not imagined that there would be a Richthofen's squadron of aeroplanes."

The Baron wasted no time in showing his men how he had earned the Blue Max. Leading a flight of seven Albatros biplanes on his very first patrol with the new units, he spotted a group of single-seater F.E.'s above the trenches near Lens and attacked. Singling out one of the pusher craft, the Baron closed to fifty yards, loosed one hundred and fifty rounds, and set the RFC bus afire. It was his seventeenth victory. The very next day, Manfred swept into the blue at the controls of a new Albatros DIII and shot down a two-seater F.E. 2b. As he dove down in pursuit of the Britisher, the wing of his new plane cracked and he swiftly put the bus down near the RFC craft. The observer of the F.E. fed the Baron's esteem by telling him his all-red craft was known to the RFC. His enemies, the Baron learned with obvious satisfaction, referred to his machine as "le petit rouge," the little red one. He was disturbed, however, at the structural failure of the Albatros DIII. It was one thing to be shot down by a skillful opponent, but to fall to one's death because of the limitations of a designer was unnerving. His confidence shaken in the Albatros products, he switched, for a time, to the Halberstadt DII.

The winter weather of January and February restricted flying and cut down on his scoring. Still, he was in the air every possible moment and had raised his record of confirmed kills to twenty-one by the end of February. "I was trying to compete with Boelcke's squadron," he admitted quite frankly in his diary. "Every evening we compared our bag. However, Boelcke's pupils are smart rascals. I cannot get ahead of them. The Boelcke section has an advantage over my squadron of one hundred machines downed. I must allow them to retain it," he admitted ruefully.

At that time he also put down some of his thoughts on aerial warfare: "The great thing in air fighting is that the decisive factor does not lie in trick flying [he wasn't any good at it] but solely in the personal ability and energy of the aviator [he had plenty of both]. A flying man may be able to loop and do all the stunts imaginable and yet he may not succeed in shooting down a single enemy. In my opinion, the aggressive spirit is everything and that spirit is very strong in us Germans. Hence, we shall always retain the domination of the air."

His personal opinion of his French opponents was unflat-

tering. He thought they were too tricky; that they "like t
put traps and to attack their opponents unawares." (The ver
tactics he used so often.) The French attacking spirit he sai
"is like bottled lemonade. It lacks tenacity." For the Englis
he had much greater admiration. They were, after all, o
"Germanic" blood. "Sportsmen take easily to flying, an
Englishmen see in flying nothing but sport." The Baron wa
less an admirer of the Englishman's flying skill. "They take
perfect delight in looping the loop, flying on their back, an
indulging in other stunts for the benefit of our soldiers in th
trenches. All these tricks may impress people who attend
sporting event, but the troops at the front are not as appreci
ative of these things. It demands higher qualifications tha
trick flying. Therefore the blood of English pilots will have t
flow in streams."

While there are those writers who disparage the Baron'
fighting tactics because so many of his victims were two
seaters and his combats were usually fought on the Germa
side of the lines, it is interesting to note that Group Capt. J
E. Johnson, who finished World War II as the top-scorin
RAF fighter pilot with thirty-eight confirmed victories, con
siders Richthofen the outstanding fighter pilot of the Firs
World War.

In Johnson's opinion, as put forth in his book *Full Circle,*
study of air fighting tactics, Irish ace, Mick Mannock, re
vered by his men, has to take a slightly rear seat to the Re
Baron. He notes, as have the authors, that air fighting wa
not a sport but a "killing time." For the Baron, aeria
warfare was a deadly business, "where a calculating leade
tried to destroy the enemy's reconnaissance aeroplanes, which
did far more damage than the scouts. There can be no
doubt," Johnson believes, "that the tactics fashioned by the
wily and highly elusive Richthofen were perfectly suited to
the conditions under which he fought." Johnson also points
out that many of Richthofen's kills were scored behind his
own lines because the German Army, during much of the
war, was on the defensive "and those units of the German Air
Service deployed behind that army were employed in an
ancillary and similar defensive role."

With the advent of improved weather in March, the Re
Baron was constantly seeking new victims for his bag. The
grisly toll zoomed to twenty-four by March 9 when he nearly

uffered the fate to which he had sent so many enemy irmen. The frightening experience occurred when he led our men of his staffel down upon nine F.E. 8 pusher fighters o kick off a dogfight that was to rage for half an hour. As he opposing aircraft dived and climbed, closed and fired, everal D.H. 2 fighters joined the melee. Richthofen, whirling round in the midst of the midair carnage, shot down one of he D.H. fighters and smiled in satisfaction as his mates lowned four of the F.E. 8's and forced four others to break away with various degrees of damage.

The Baron was beginning to round up his victorious bird-men of Jasta 11 when he realized his machine had been hit. He knew it instinctively. His suspicions were confirmed immediately when he smelled gasoline and felt the resulting oss of engine power. Then he spotted the telltale white pume of gasoline. It was the tip-off that his craft would ourst into flames momentarily. Richthofen quickly shut off his engine and glided down for a safe landing. An inspection of his Halberstadt revealed bullet punctures in his engine and dual fuel tanks. About this episode, he wrote: "Today I got nto trouble but I escaped with a whole skin."

When April came around, the Rittmeister's score stood at hirty-one confirmed victories. The Baron, of course, was ecstatic. He was Germany's indisputable top hunter. He was n the forefront of the quick and the strong. Anything he wanted, he got as fast as it was humanly possible. He asked hat his charming and witty brother, Lothar, be transferred to Jasta 11. Shortly Lothar, who had passed his flying exami-nation in December 1916, was posted to his famous brother's squadron. He wanted to display his aerial technique to his brother; so the very first time Lothar flew in combat with his brother, the Baron shot down an adversary. How sweet it was to have the kill witnessed by his younger brother. As the Baron noted: "It is a splendid thing to fly together with one's brother and do so well."

The Baron had done more than well during March. The figures for the month showed that he had scored ten official victories. But April was much better. In April, twenty-one enemy machines fell before his guns. The toll and carnage during April was awesome. The RFC lost five planes for every one it shot down during April. Its aircraft just could not match the Albatros DIII flown by the Germans. The

Major Albrecht von Richthofen visits his famous son at St. Nicholas Hospital in Courtrai.

onth would forever be remembered by the RFC as "Bloody pril."

Manfred equaled Boelcke's score of forty on April 11 hen he shot down a B.E. 2 near Willerval. The Baron, owever, was generous. He agreed that Boelcke's mark undoubtedly would be nearing the "century mark, if he had not een killed in the collision with Boehme's machine. The emark was a tip-off to another one of the Baron's wishes: to ore one hundred confirmed kills in the air. Such a figure, urely, could never be challenged by any flier on either side.

Visited by his father on April 29, the Baron decided to ntertain the "old man" by shooting down an enemy plane rithin his vision. He always enjoyed showing his father how ell he could hunt. Richthofen quickly was airborne in the ompany of his brother and Kurt Wolff. Ranging the skies, ney encountered three Spad S. 7's of No. 19 Squadron, FC, shot two down, and drove off the third. On the return o the aerodrome at Douai, Lothar was the first out of his lbatros. In the correct manner of the Prussian military amily, he saluted Maj. Albrecht Freiherr von Richthofen nd reported that he had shot down an Englishman. The Red aron landed his craft and made a similar report. Describing nis exhilarating incident later, Richthofen wrote: "The old nan felt very happy, and he was delighted with our reports. "hat was obvious. He is not one of those fathers who have ears for their sons. I think he would have liked very much to et into a machine and help us with our shooting. We all had meal together."

The downing of the Spad was only the start of an exceptional day for the Baron. Before the sun set, he scored three nore confirmed victories on April 29. The other victims onsisted of an F.E. 2b of No. 18 Squadron, RFC; a B.E. 2d f No. 12 Squadron, RFC; and a Nieuport, piloted by Capt. Frederick Laycester Barwell. His feat of four victories called or a celebration.

A sumptuous dinner was arranged, and among the gay elebrants was the Baron's proud father. The climax of the vening was reached when Richthofen received the following vire from Kaiser Wilhelm: "I have just received the message oday you have been for the fiftieth time victor in an air attle. I heartily congratulate you upon this marvelous success with my full acknowledgment. The Fatherland looks with thankfulness upon its brave fliers. May God further preserve you."

The very next day, April 30, Richthofen had his famous fight with Billy Bishop, the Canadian ace who ended the war with seventy-two confirmed kills. Bishop's score placed him second behind Major "Mick" Mannock on the list of the RAF's top fighter pilots. The Red Baron was flying with four other Albatroses out of Douai when he spotted two Nieuports, one flown by Bishop and the other by his pal, Jack Scott. They rendezvoused above Drocourt, east of Lens about two o'clock in the afternoon.

The Albatroses and Nieuports darted straight at each other. Richthofen opened fire first; sharp bursts from his Spandaus raked Scott's engine. Scott zipped away in a desperate attempt to escape. Bishop was left alone in the midst of the Albatros pack. Above and to his right, he spotted Richthofen diving at him. Bishop's Nieuport banked away but he was not fast enough. Bursts of fire from the Red Baron's guns ripped into the fuselage just behind the cockpit. Later, Bishop would recall: "The best shooting I have ever seen."

Bishop dived, twisted, and rolled in an effort to elude the German's fire. But the all-red Albatros was always one step ahead of him. The fire from the Spandaus was incessant and telling. A burst thudded into his machine. One slug pierced his flying coat. Another burst slammed into his instrument panel. Oil spewed over Bishop's face.

Enraged by his inability to shake off Richthofen, Bishop pulled back on his control stick and shot upwards. As he reached for more sky, he kicked the rudder bar. The Nieuport flashed over and roared down at the Albatros. The angry Bishop opened fire at sixty yards. Bullets from the Nieuport hit home. Richthofen's bus turned over on its back. Bishop dove after it. A big smile creased Bishop's face when he spotted black smoke streaming from the Albatros.

For a moment he was convinced he had triumphed over the mighty German ace. His happiness turned to gloom soon enough. The fall was a ruse. Richthofen's plane flattened out after diving four thousand feet and rushed eastward. A much-chagrined Bishop winged homeward. His gloom was lightened somewhat when he came across Scott, limping home in his badly shot-up Nieuport.

Richthofen took leave the following day, and on May 2

as presented to the Kaiser. The Emperor, obviously briefed since forwarding his message, congratulated the Red Baron on scoring fifty-two kills and again upon marking his twenty-fifth birthday. It was the last birthday the Baron ever would celebrate.

Following his meeting with the Kaiser, Richthofen flew to the German retreat of Bad Homburg where he gave a demonstration of his flying skill to the Empress. Afterwards, he lunched with the Empress and she also gave him a birthday present. He then spent the rest of the month of May hunting in the Black Forest and other choice locations, including the Pless Estates where the hunter had the thrill of shooting bison, and visiting his mother in Schweidnitz. Everywhere the popular hero went he was toasted by dignitaries, embarrassed by admiring throngs of frauleins, and trailed by hero-adoring children. It was all heady business for Germany's top ace. Although extremely reserved and self-conscious over outward demonstrations, he still enjoyed every minute of the adulation and outright worship paid him by the German nation.

Manfred had only been on leave a week when he received a telegram that Lothar had been wounded. He immediately telephoned Jasta 11 to hear all the details. He was quickly assured that Lothar's wound was not fatal. His younger brother, he was informed, had suffered a serious leg injury during a fight with an English fighter. Lothar, at the time, had scored an amazing twenty-two victories in four weeks and had been left in command of Jasta 11 during his brother's absence. He actually had neither the rank nor the experience to assume the command, but the German High Command wanted to keep the name of Richthofen before the eyes of the people.

VII

The Red Baron returned from leave on June 14. Three days later his old friend, Zeumer, the "lunger," from the Russian front, finally kept his own rendezvous with death. The following day, Richthofen, flying his all-red Albatros DIII, zipped down on a R.E. 8, which was busy spotting for the Allied artillery. Zooming in so close that he almost collided with the British bus, the Rittmeister raked the enemy plane with machine-gun fire. Both occupants slumped dead, and the R.E. 8 circled down to crash in a farmyard and burst into flames.

The Baron had not lost any of his old skills. Three more victories followed so that he had an official score of fifty-six on June 26. On that day, the German High Command formed its first Jagdgeschwader. The word literally translated means a "group of hunting echelons." In other words, four Jasta were to be grouped together into a composite unit known as Jagdgeschwader No. 1. The Jastas assigned to J.G. 1 were 4, 6, 10, and 11. Richthofen, who best personified the admirable qualities of leadership, organizing acumen, and fighting ability, was given command of the elite unit.

Thus was born the famed German "Flying Circus" of World War I, and its most famous "Circus Master," of course, was the Red Baron. Orders from headquarters directed that J.G. 1 was to be moved to any section of the front that required its services. This mobility, plus the brightly colored aircraft flown by the Germans, accounted for the nickname Flying Circus.

For the next week, Manfred was busy around the clock organizing his new fighting unit. Anxious to spend as much time as possible aloft, he selected his administrative and personnel officers with the greatest of care. Ever a shrewd judge of character, he was especially careful in the selection of his Jasta leaders.

Ernst Udet, who took command of Jasta 11 in March 1918, noted: "If von Richthofen liked a man it was for purely material reasons. His estimate of a man was formed by what that man achieved for the cause, and whether he happened to be a good fellow or not was of a secondary consideration."

Udet, who survived the war as Germany's second, top fighter-pilot with sixty-two victories, also observed that once a man "had proved his worth, he [the Red Baron] supported you by every means in his power and with his whole personality. If you were a failure he dropped you without a second's hesitation, without a flicker of an eyelid."

He was a demanding leader but never asked his men to do anything that he himself would not do. All newcomers to his Jastas were minutely interviewed and given a flying test before their final acceptance. Even in the midst of a dogfight, Richthofen somehow found time to observe his men in action and afterwards would compliment or criticize them, depending on their performance in action.

Carl August von Schoenebeck, who flew with the Baron, and survives today, recalls in his correspondence with Carisella: "Each time we came back von Richthofen told us what we had done right and where we had made mistakes. Thus I noticed, to my great astonishment, that he never lost sight of us even when fighting for his life. ... We knew we could depend on him like a rock. If things were going badly, if we were ever in a hole, he'd notice it and pull us out. It gave the Jasta a great feeling of safety."

Von Schoenebeck, who was personally instructed on how to fly the Fokker tripe by Richthofen on his arrival at Jasta 11, described the Baron in this manner: "He was about average height, stocky, dark blond with blue eyes. A voice of middle range, his manner of speech clipped, clear and concise. He had a noble way of speech and never swore or used foul language of any kind. There was always a discussion after a flight and during these discussions he was calm and self-controlled and spoke with much humor, no matter how dangerous the action might have been. One could not help but feel and be touched daily by his extraordinary energy and will power. He shone with calm in the most ciritical moments, which quite naturally exercised the most salutary influence on all of us."

When von Schoenebeck left Jasta 11 in March 1918 to assume command of his own Jasta 33, he was given this advice by the Rittmeister: "The leader is the deciding factor for the success of every squadron. Even the best fighter pilots can prove their full worth only if their leader makes proper use of them."

He stressed the importance of meeting the enemy with a bold and united front. But once the initial attack had dissipated itself, he was not adverse to his elite pilots fighting individually. As his Jasta 11 was practically his entire existence, so J.G. 1 became his only great obsession. "Duty above all" was his motto. Pilots who obeyed and fought well had the honor of remaining with his Jastas. Those who could not follow the "Dicta Boelcke," as adapted by Richthofen and who demonstrated a pusillanimous character in combat were quickly sent packing to another flying unit or even stripped of their wings and returned to the misery of the trenches. Flying and fighting, stalking and hunting, shooting and killing were the only things that really mattered to the Rittmeister. His shyness and reserve prevented him from mingling with his fellow officers. He usually dined alone. No hobbies interested him; neither did the theater nor music. He remained mostly to himself on the ground; occasionally he would be found playing billiards or strolling with his huge Danish hound, Moritz, whom he had bought as a puppy while stationed in Ostend. Mostly, though, his thoughts were in the sky and the next chance to tangle with the enemy buses.

With the organization of J.G. 1 underway, Manfred roared aloft in his telltale, all-red Albatros on July 2 in search for his fifty-seventh conquest. He soon spotted a group of R.E. 8's out on reconnaissance and swept down to attack the foremost one. "After my first shots," he wrote requesting acknowledgment of the kill, "the observer collapsed. Shortly thereafter, the pilot was wounded mortally, I believe by my shots. The R.E. fell, and I fired into it at a distance of fifty yards. The plane caught fire and dashed to the ground."

The Red Baron had a taste of the fate to which he had consigned so many men four days later on July 6. Flying an Albatros D.V., he led his Jasta 11 toward the front and soon sighted six F.E. 2d's of No. 20 Squadron, RFC. Jasta 11 swept into the attack. The F.E.'s closed ranks and formed a defensive circle in a desperate attempt to protect themselves from the easily recognized members of Richthofen's dreaded Flying Circus. More German planes joined the fight. Four Sopwith triplanes of No. 10 Squadron hustled to participate in the aerial fray. The observer in one of the F.E.'s fired a long-range burst at an Albatros D.V. although the range was some three hundred yards, one slug whammed off the left side of the Red Baron's skull. Here is the way the Circus Master described the incident while recuperating in the hospital at Courtrai:

"Suddenly something strikes me in the head. For a moment my whole body is paralyzed. My arms hang down limply beside me. My legs flop loosely beyond my control. The worst was that a nerve leading to my eyes had been paralyzed and I was completely blind.

"I feel my machine tumbling down—falling. At that moment, the idea struck me: 'This is how it feels when one is shot down to his death.' Any moment, I wait for the wings to break off. I am alone in my bus. I don't lose my senses for a moment.

"Soon I regain power over my arms and legs, so that I grip the wheel. Mechanically, I cut off the engine, but what good does that do? One can't fly without sight. I forced my eyes open, tore off my goggles, but even then I couldn't see the sun. I was completely blind. The seconds seemed like eternities. I noticed I was still falling.

"From time to time my machine caught itself, but only to slip off again. At the beginning I had been at a height of twelve thousand feet, and now I must have fallen at least six to nine thousand feet. I concentrated all my energy and said to myself: 'I must see. I must see. I must see.' "

By sheer willpower, the Red Baron fought to stay conscious and stave off the swooning sensation that constantly threatened to black him out again. Suddenly, he could see black and white spots—his eyesight had returned. Grabbing the controls, he brought the Albatros down to a landing near Wervicq. With his remaining strength, he tumbled out of the aircraft and collapsed. With the blood flowing from the helmet over his ashen face, he was first taken for dead. But first-aid soon brought him around, and he was sent by ambulance to St. Nicholas Hospital in Courtrai. Physicians shaved his scalp to examine the wound. It was "quite a good-sized hole . . . a wound of about ten centimeters in length," the Baron wrote. At one spot, as big as a dollar coin, the bare white skull-bone lay exposed. "My thick Richthofen skull had proved itself bulletproof." The doctors treated the wound and prescribed a regimen of careful nursing.

The Baron returned to J.G. 1 toward the end of July, taking official command on the 26th. But he was still a sick man. He was constantly bothered with headaches and dizziness. Several times he had to return to the hospital to have bone splinters removed from his skull. Mentally, he was changed, too. Germany's idol inevitably realized that he had no rightful claim on immortality. He, too, was vulnerable to death. He worried about his brother, Lothar, who was still convalescing from his own wound. He thought him much too rash and criticized the headlong manner in which Lothar

The Albatros D.V flown by Richthofen on July 6, 1917, when he received a severe head wound and crashed near Wervicq, Belgium.

flung himself into battle, depending more on luck to see him through than a carefully thought-out plan of attack. He no longer was certain, either, of final victory. The war for the hunter was no longer so attractive. Others were also hunting his familiar all-red plane, which he had for too long tossed like a gauntlet in their faces.

It was three weeks after returning to J.G. 1 before the Rittmeister ventured to the front in hunt of prey. He still experienced faintness and dizziness as he took off shortly after dawn in his Albatros D.V. Sighting a Nieuport, he raced in for the kill and shot it down over the shattered remnants of Houthulst Forest. Then he quickly flew home, tired and weak and fighting nausea. The evening of the very next day he joined his men in a celebration at a local casino in Marcke. Jasta 11 had recorded its two hundredth victory that day.

Richthofen received a wire from headquarters congratulating him on his first victory since returning to action. However, the Baron was urged to take the best possible care of himself and not to fly until he was in tip-top physical condition. The hunter realized that he still was not in peak form, yet he had to be upstairs. To rest on his laurels was to be overtaken by other young and ambitious German warriors. Lt. Werner Voss, the teen-age ace and a born flier who seemed to have no sense of fear, was chalking up kills at an incredible rate.

On August 26, ignoring the advice of his superiors, the Baron led four members of Jasta 11 on an early morning sweep. A Spad was spotted several thousand feet below. Maneuvering until he had the sun at his back, the Rittmeister swooped down. Too late, the Spad sought to escape into nearby clouds. Richthofen's machine guns blazed a stream of fire at the enemy bus. Mortally hit, the Spad exploded in the air. Sick at the sight, the German ace returned to Marcke to ask confirmation of his fifty-ninth victory.

Two days later, the Circus Master received one of Anthony Fokker's new triplanes. Airborne in the new bus, which his ground crew quickly had painted all-red, he and four of his men spotted a lone R.E. 8 on September 1 over Zonnebecke. While the others held back, the Baron roared in for an easy kill. The two occupants of the "Harry Tate," apparently believing the oncoming plane was one of their own

Sopwith tripes—since the German triplanes were unknown on that section of the Front—made no preparations to defend themselves. The German ace closed within one hundred yards and ripped the RFC plane with a burst of twenty rounds. The R.E. 8 fell to its doom. Two days later, the Baron and his men tangled with a group of Sopwith Pups and he tallied his sixty-first victory.

On September 6, the Circus Master left J.G. 1 on convalescent leave. It was a leave he looked forward to with great expectations as the government had invited him to hunt rare elk on an East Prussian Reservation. His bag during the two weeks on the reservation, as he wrote his mother, "has been far from bad; a large elk, three excellent stags, and a buck. I am rather proud of my record because Papa has only shot three stags in all his life. I am leaving for Berlin today and will be with you in less than a week." His mother was never to see him alive again after his visit to Schweidnitz that September.

The Baron was still on leave on September 23 when Werner Voss, who had racked up forty-eight kills, died in a spectacular dogfight with seven S.E. 5A's led by English ace, James McCudden. The Britisher, who was to die in a tragic flying accident the following July, wrote: "As long as I shall live I shall never forget my admiration of that German pilot, who, single-handed, fought seven of us for ten minutes, and also put some bullets through all of our machines. His flying was wonderful, his courage magnificent, and, in my opinion, he was the bravest German airman whom it has been my privilege to fight." During this period, Lothar recovered from his wound, returned to take command of Jasta 11.

The Baron himself finally returned to leadership of J.G. 1 on October 23. At that time he was once more eager to resume combat flying. He was sure that the sight of his all-red machine and its sinister black crosses would serve to rally Germany's birdmen and cast a spell of doom upon the enemy's fliers. When exhorted to leave off flying because of the disheartening effect his death might have upon the Fatherland's populace, he wrote: "I should indeed consider myself a despicable person, if, now that I have achieved fame and wear many decorations, I should consent to exist as a pensioner of my dignity and to preserve my life for the nation, while every poor fellow in the trenches, who is doing his duty equally as much as I, has to stick it out." Coward, certainly he was not.

A month passed before the Baron scored his next kill. At that time, J.G. 1 had been shifted hurriedly to the Cambrai front to help the ground troops defend against a serious attack by the British 3rd Army. Flying an Albatros D.V, rather than a tripe, the Circus Master, that late November day, shot down a D.H. 5 over Bourlon Wood. Two days later, he racked up his sixty-third kill when he and two other German birdmen, including brother Lothar, were attacked by ten S.E. 5A's above the same Bourlon Wood. Again at the controls of an Albatros D.V, the Baron whirled about in the melee, firing at several enemy buses, before his lethal fire connected at one hundred yards and one of the S.E. 5A's exploded in midair. The wreckage fell in a small copse of woods near Moeuvres.

With the advent of December, air activity lessened over the Western Front. On December 11, Manfred wrote the following to his mother. "There is little doing here at present and things are consequently rather dull. I am leaving for Speyer today to look over an airplane plant. Christmas I intend spending with my squadron, together with Papa and Lothar. My orderly has already sent a parcel to Bolko, and I trust I have succeeded in meeting a cadet's tastes."

Bolko, then a cadet at Wahlstatt, undoubtedly was grateful for the package, but again entreated his famous brother to pay him a flying visit. The youngster, quite understandably, longed to show off his brother before his fellow cadets. The Baron, however, begged off, explaining that the adjacent terrain had been turned into a quagmire by the weather and was unsuitable for a safe landing. To soften Bolko's disappointment, he indicated that he would make every effort to fly to Wahlstatt in the late spring or early summer. It is likely, though, that the Baron realized he would never live to make the trip. That Christmas he was the sole survivor of the original group of pilots recruited by Boelcke to form his legendary Jasta 2.

Right after the New Year of 1918, the Rittmeister went to Brest-Litovsk as an observer attached to the German delegation that dictated peace terms to the revolutionary delegates of a defeated Russia. Quickly wearying of the politicians' doubletalk and machinations, the Baron, accompanied by brother Lothar, slipped away to stalk bison and red stags in the Romanoffs' old hunting preserve at Bialowicza. He wrote his mother that the hunting sojourn had done both him and Lothar a "world of good." From there he went to Berlin arriving on January 20, while Lothar went to Schweidnitz to visit their mother. For the next several weeks the Baron was kept busy in Berlin by the authorities' demands upon him to make comparison tests of various prototype aircraft and to give them the benefit of his experience in the examination and testing of new airframe and engine types and individual major components. During his stay in the German capital, he constantly heard the acclaim of the populace and was beseiged by well-wishers and autograph collectors everywhere he went. But the huzzahs of the people no longer thrilled him. Daily reports from J.G. 1 clearly demonstrated that the Allies were seizing air supremacy with their Camels and S.E. 5A's, Spads and Nieuports. Outwardly he remained optimistic about eventual victory, but inwardly he no longer was confident that he would survive the war. In a letter to his mother on February 11 after he had returned to the Front, he said, ". . . Now I think I will not come back to Germany for a long time. Keep Lothar with you as long as possible . . ." He was determined to give Lothar every opportunity to survive.

VIII

The High Command had other ideas. The great German spring offensive of 1918 was to be shortly launched. All leaves were canceled and Lothar reported back to Jasta 11. The pilots of J.G. 1, Richthofen's Jagdgeschwader, flocked into the hostile skies of France. On March 12 the Red Baron, grimly determined to recapture his old fighting form, swept aloft at the controls of an all-red Fokker triplane. Accompanied by Lothar and another German aviator, he attacked a flight of nine two-seater Bristol Fighters 2.

When one of the Brisfits broke away to dive on an unsuspecting German two-seater aircraft, the Circus Master was after it in a flash. Bursts of machine-gun fire from the tripe quickly incapacitated the rear gunner. The pilot of the RFC bus attempted to flee home, but the Baron fastened onto his tail and followed him right down to nearly ground level. The Brisfit pilot, recognizing that he could not escape, touched down in Germany territory, and he and the observer were speedily captured. The victory was Richthofen's sixty-fourth.

March 13 was an unlucky day for Lothar von Richthofen. His tripe was shot up during an aerial melee with the very same Bristol Fighters of No. 62 Squadron. As he tried to sideslip on approaching the earth, his tripe crashed. Lothar was slammed forward and suffered severe facial injuries that were to keep him hospitalized for weeks. The Baron was not so unfortunate. During the same sky fight, he charged a Sopwith Camel of No. 73 Squadron, and fire from his Spandaus struck the enemy plane's fuel tank. The Camel crashed to the ground behind the German lines, killing the pilot J. M. Millett of Windsor, Nova Scotia.

Five days later Richthofen was in the thick of the great battle of Le Cateau. In that unforgettable aerial fight, the Baron chalked up his sixty-sixth kill. This is the way he described the action: "At about 10:30 A.M. on March 18th I took off with thirty of my squadron and led all three staffels in close order against the enemy, flying at a height of 5,300 meters. When we approached the front, I saw several English squadrons that had just flown over our lines and were making for Le Cateau. I met the first squadron, which consisted of two-seaters, in the neighborhood of La Catelet (15 kilometers north of St. Quentin), at a height of about 5,500 meters. With Lieutenant Gussmann (Jagdstaffel No. 11), I shot at the last of these opponents, a Bristol Fighter. The wings broke away. Lieutenant Gussmann brought him down in the vicinity of Joncourt.

"Afterwards I reassembled my thirty machines, rose to 5,300 meters and followed two English squadrons that had broken through and reached Le Catelet. When our opponents endeavored to curve away and return to their lines, I attacked them near Le Cateau. I was the first to come into contact with the enemy, and with Lieutenant Lowenhardt I shot down the machine flying nearest to us, a Bristol Fighter. I saw the English machine go into a dive and break to pieces in the air.

"Meanwhile, my staffels were engaged in a fierce encounter with the squadrons of enemy single-seaters that suddenly came down from a great height to protect the English two-

A popular portrait of the Red Baron.

seaters. At the same time, several staffels of Jagdgruppe No. 2, including Jagdstaffel No. 5, hastened up and joined in the battle. A long circling fight took place. It was impossible for us to retain our squadron formations. Everyone attacked the enemy flying nearest to him. The consequence was a confused melee of single combats. It was often quite impossible to distinguish friend from foe. The air was thick with white streams of phosphorous ammunition. Through it, one saw machines shot down in flames or going down out of control.

"I picked out a Sopwith Camel bearing streamers and forced it to land in the vicinity of Molain-Vaux-Aubigny. The occupant was a Canadian who had led one of the two one-seater squadrons. The enemy's total loss was fifteen machines, nine of which were shot down by my staffels. Our only loss was one machine from Jasta No. 10."

Three days following this memorable ballet of death, the Germans launched their great offensive. It was preceded by a four-hour bombardment that shook the front held by the British 3rd Army. Richthofen and his fellow birdmen rejoiced as infantrymen from fifty-four divisions swept forward. Mist, however, hovered over much of the battlefield and limited the support role of J.G. 1. Richthofen himself did not fly until three days after the onslaught was underway. On March 24, he received orders from the 2nd German Army headquarters mentioning the fact that advancing German troops were being incessantly harassed by enemy aircraft. The Rittmeister was requested to immediately put an end to this aerial activity of the RFC pilots.[1]

That same day, March 24, the Baron, flying a tripe, led twenty-five members of his various Jastas in an attack on ten S.E. 5A's of No. 56 Squadron. Singling out an S.E. 5A piloted by an American, Wilson Porter, Jr., he directed withering blasts of fire at it. The British craft instantly broke up and fell over a wide area, killing young Porter.

The Rittmeister really got back into high gear as March came to a close. It was the killing time once again for the German hunter. His hunting instinct was never better. On

---

[1]Authors' Note: The original copy of this order was among the items found on the Baron's body April 21 and today is in the collection of Neville Hewitt, an Australian, along with other personal papers of Richthofen. Hewitt was gracious enough to forward a copy of this German order and the Baron's ID card to P. J. Carisella.

March 25, he shot down his sixty-eighth victim, Lt. Donald Cameron, who was flying a Sopwith Camel. The next day the Baron scored a "double," consisting of a Sopwith Camel and an old R.E. 2. March 27 was even better. He scored a "triple," downing two Bristol Fighters and another Camel. The two occupants of an Armstrong Whitworth 2 were killed when Richthofen attacked them near Mericourt. The latter craft was headed for home when the Baron cut it off, raked it with one hundred rounds, and sent it down in flames. His last victory in March raised the Red Baron's official record of aerial victories to seventy-four.

April came and the Baron had three weeks left of life. That same day the Royal Flying Corps and the Royal Naval Air Service were amalgamated into the Royal Air Force. The Germans were still advancing, but most of the lightning impact had disappeared from their offensive. As the German infantry moved forward, J.G. 1 accompanied them, transferring from one advanced airfield to another. On April 2, Richthofen was with some of his birdmen at Harbonnieres. Shortly after lunch the Circus Master took off in his tripe on a "lone wolf" patrol. He sighted an R.E. 8 at twenty-five hundred feet and swept down. He was within fifty yards of the RAF machine before the observer spotted his all-red plane and opened fire. Too late. Manfred closed to within ten yards and riddled the R.E. 8 with unerring fire. The old "Harry Tate" exploded in a mass of flames, roasting the two youthful occupants alive.

Back at his field, Richthofen observed: "Queer but the last ten I shot down all burned. The one I got today also burned. I saw it quite well. At the beginning it was only quite a small flame under the pilot's seat, but when the machine dived, the tail stood up in the air and I could see that the seat had been burned through.

"The flames kept showing as the machine dashed down. It crashed on the ground with a terrible explosion, worse than I have ever witnessed before. It was a two-seater but its occupants defended themselves well."

Reproached by one of his men for flying too close to the enemy plane, the Baron responded with a smile and agreed that it had been close. "I had to come up quite close. I believe that observer, whoever he was, was a tough party, a first-class fighting man. He was a devil for courage and energy. I flew within five yards of him until he had enough, and that despite the fact that I believe I had hit him before. Even to the last minute he kept firing at me. The slightest mistake and I should have rammed him in the air."

It was on that very day Richthofen received the last decoration his grateful Fatherland was to confer on him. The Emperor himself forwarded the Order of the Red Eagle with Crowns and Swords (Third Class) and the accompanying citation, the twenty-sixth citation he received for bravery and service. The hunter had no further trophies to collect. He had them all, all but one. The one he did not yet possess was the wooden cross. He would earn that shortly.

Four days afterwards, the Red Baron dove his tripe on a flight of low-flying Camels of No. 46 Squadron. A few slugs from his machine guns ripped into the craft flown by Capt. S. P. Smith and it fell ablaze near Bois de Hamel. On April 7, Richthofen claimed his last "double," an S.E. 5A which exploded in midair, and a Spad which, he reported, crashed to earth north of Villers-Bretonneux.

The Baron moved to his final airfield at Cappy on April 8. He was unhappy with the transfer. He had hoped to have J.G. 1 moved further northward along the plain of the Lys where the main thrust of the German offensive was being expended. The weather, too, was foul and gave the battle-scarred village of Cappy a most depressing appearance. While there was a good flying field nearby, the nearest town, Peronne, was more than ten miles away. In these, his last days, the Baron mostly kept to himself, devoting much of his time to writing a treatise on air fighting. It was a labor of love as it was meant to bring Boelcke's Dicta up to date.

The rain continued through April 19 and into 20. However, the skies began clearing late in the day of the 20th, and the Baron took off early in the evening, flying a new Fokker tripe, Dr.-1 425/17. With him were several selected members of Jasta 11. Spotting six Camels of C Flight, No. 3 Squadron, RAF, Richthofen gave the signal to attack. The Camels turned to meet the assault head on. The opposing aircraft whipped past each other with guns blazing. The Baron quickly banked around, however, and got onto the tail of Major R. Raymond Barker's plane. A few well-placed bullets speedily dispatched Barker's bus in flames.

Richthofen, without wasting a moment, turned quickly and

took after a Camel attacking a tripe. This latter Camel was flown by David Greswolde Lewis, who quickly recognized the identity of his adversary by the all-red plane he flew. Lewis twisted and turned to escape the Baron's fire. But in vain. Three minutes after Barker's Camel fell flaming to earth, Lewis' followed, also afire. Lewis' Camel crashed only fifty yards from where Barker's bus burned with the unfortunate major still in the wreckage. The impact flung Lewis from his Camel, and he escaped with superficial cuts and facial burns. He was taken prisoner. At this writing, he is still alive and residing in Salisbury, Rhodesia.

Lewis and P. J. Carisella have been correspondents for years. In a most recent letter, Lewis noted that "over the past years there appears to have been a revival of interest in Baron von Richthofen, a gentleman for whom I had the highest regard—not only for his personal qualities but naturally for his powers as a fighter pilot."

As for his own scrap with the Baron, Lewis told Carisella that "nobody can dispute the fact that I was the last man shot down by Richthofen for I know that Major Raymond Barker went first in flames for I saw him out of the corner of my eyes when heavily engaged with a German. I followed also in flames and Richthofen's official report confirms the two events . . ."

In their extensive correspondence, Lewis summarized his fight in the following account: "I only had a total of twenty-five flying hours in my logbook when I arrived in France and was posted to No. 3 Squadron, RFC. Poor flying weather prevailed most of the day on April 20, 1918, but at six o'clock in the evening it cleared sufficiently for two flights of planes, twelve in all, to take off. Some four miles behind enemy lines, at ten thousand feet, we sighted an enemy formation of fifteen Fokker triplanes. They were flying at right angles and above us. When we flew past them and turned to choose our opponents, I knew we had encountered Richthofen's famed Circus. The Huns were painted every possible color. Richthofen was out in front of the formation in his brilliant red Fokker.

"The fight had barely begun when I saw Major Barker's Camel explode on my left. An incendiary bullet must have hit his petrol tank. I went down on the tail of a bright blue triplane which crossed directly ahead of me. I was about to try for a shot when I heard machine guns firing behind me. Bullets splintered the carbane struts in front of my head. I quickly forgot about the blue triplane and began evasive tactics. Glancing over my shoulder, I saw that my adversary was Richthofen in his all-red triplane.

"I knew I couldn't compete with him so I concentrated on keeping out of his line of fire. At that moment, Captain Douglas Bell, my flight commander, chased Richthofen off my tail. The tripe slipped down below me and I found myself in a good attacking position. For a few seconds I even had visions of bringing him down. He had become fixed in my sights and I opened fire. My tracers seemed to hit several portions of his tripe. But Richthofen was a wily devil and gave me the slip by pulling up in a steep right-hand climbing turn. Once again I was the target.

"He quickly squeezed off a concentrated burst and set one of my petrol tanks afire. I switched the engine off just before the Camel started to fall to earth. I fought for control but couldn't bring the plane back on an even keel. All the time sheets of flames alternately billowed up from my feet and over my body. But I was too late. The Camel slammed into the ground and I was flung about sixty feet from the wreckage by the impact.

"I was severely stunned but lucky to escape without any broken bones. Major Barker's plane was blazing fiercely some fifty yards distant. I stumbled over to it but there was nothing I could do for him. He must have died in the air when the craft exploded. I went back to my own flaming bus and was watching it when Richthofen dove down to within one hundred yards of the ground. He waved at me and I waved back. I then walked over to some German soldiers and surrendered myself. I was nineteen at the time and spent the rest of the war as a prisoner."

Manfred was delighted on scoring his eightieth victory. He liked the sounds of the number and the nicely rounded look about it when written out. Accepting the congratulations of his flying men, he exulted, "Gentlemen, eighty, now that is really a decent number." He left it unsaid but it was implicit in the tone of his voice that it was a number no flier would overtake for a long time to come. Now he could truly rest on his laurels for a while without fear of any ambitious flier running up a score anywhere near his eighty.

After celebrating with his jubilant aviators, he left them to go over the final arrangements for a leave that he was to take in two days' time. He and Joachim Wolff had been invited by the late Werner Voss's father to be Herr Voss's guest in the family hunting lodge in the Black Forest. The fliers' travel orders already awaited them in the adjutant's office. It would be good to get away, the Baron thought. Cappy was a hole. The weather was awful. He thought again about his eighty kills. It was a good solid number. He could take leave for a few days in good conscience. He was tired of hunting men and being hunted by Allied fliers eager for the glory that would be theirs for shooting down Germany's ace of aces.

At midmorning of Sunday, April 21, 1918, Baron Manfred von Richthofen roared aloft from the airfield near Cappy, France, accompanied by members of his beloved Jasta 11. As always the trim tripes rose smartly into the blue. They hardly seemed to move any distance along the grass runway when left wingtips were hooked into the air to shoot the small craft vertically upward. Several British reconnaissance planes were over the front near Hamel. It was the Baron's mission to intercept them.

Imperial Germany's leading ace of the war with eighty confirmed victories never returned from that patrol. His loss inflicted a devastating blow on the morale of the German nation. The mysterious death of the "golden youth of adventure" added fuel to the legend of the Red Baron. All that was known was that he participated in a dogfight south of Sailly-le-Sec, chased a Sopwith Camel up the Somme Valley, and landed atop Corbie Hill behind the Allied lines. Front-line observers on the German side of Morlancourt Ridge reported that the pilot did not vacate the aircraft. The Baron was dead, but the question as to who killed him set off a controversy that has lasted to this very day. The answer to the question is to be found in this book. The authors ask only that their readers keep an open mind and weigh the evidence objectively and without any preconceived opinions.

✠　✠　✠

Chapter 3

DEATH OF THE FLYING UHLAN

*"Richthofen, like the old Romans, died fighting,
with all wounds to the front."*

COMMANDING OFFICER
14TH BRIGADE
AUSTRALIAN FIELD ARTILLERY

✠ BARON Manfred von Richthofen, Germany's great national hero, awoke slowly on the morning of the day he was
to die and ignite a controversy that has burned incessantly
for more than half a century. Always a clean-living gentleman, he loved to go to bed early and sleep late. Even when
he had the early morning patrol, he would descend and
return to his bed after flushing a quarry in the blue and
shooting it down. His strict sense of obedience to his Kaiser
and Fatherland kept his mind free of any remorse for the
men he had dispatched, possibly in flames, to their eternal
reward. It was important for the hunter that he garnered all
the sleep he could so his razor-sharp mind would be clear and
his eyesight keen when next aloft in the exhilarating pursuit
of prey.

The Red Falcon stretched lazily and through his slitted
eyes he tried to perceive whether the weather was suitable
for flying. It was the third Sunday after Easter, 1918. Attired
in silk pajamas of a grayish hue, with the threaded mono-

gram "MVR" on the left breast, his limited view out the small window only revealed what appeared to be another overcast day. He snuggled deeper into his blanket. How comfortable was the bed, still warm from the heat of his body. He cocked his ears but listened in vain for the patter of rain on the roof. Damn it, he thought, he would probably have to go up after the "lords" sometime during the day. As he listened intently, he could hear the muffled voices and laughter of some of his gentlemen. How could they be up so early on such a morning, he wondered. He supposed he might as well be up, too.

Slipping out of bed, he washed vigorously and the noises of the ritual bath quickly brought his batman knocking at the door. The Baron bade him enter and they exchanged curt "good mornings." His uniform was laid out for him, but the Rittmeister decided instead to put his flying suit on right over his pajamas. If they didn't fly, he could quickly doff his flying gear and hop right back into bed. He loved his sleep.

The hunter, slim and straight as usual, stalked out of his sleeping quarters. He smiled slightly when greeted by the damp fog and gray ground haze that swirled across the aerodrome at Cappy. The dismal aspect of the field suited his lazy mood. Hopefully, the mist would thicken and he could keep his gaily painted buses grounded daylong. The two kills he had gotten yesterday evening had raised his score to eighty. A most respectable figure, he thought. One that should go unchallenged for a long time. He would not object if he and his gentlemen did not get off the ground that day. The hunter had had his fill for the time, fill, that is, of the two-legged variety. Now the four-footed type, that was something else again.

He walked, almost strolled, across the grass toward the officers' mess. What an awful day to be about. Cappy certainly was about the most depressing field from which he had ever flown. With a bit of luck they could finish up the business that had brought them there and move further up the line to Flanders Front. As he walked along, he felt again the lingering pain from his head wound. At times he became giddy and nauseous as a result of it. But he was determined not to use those symptoms as an excuse to be taken off combat flying. The war, despite the early successes of the March offensive, was not going well. He could not deny that

Richthofen playing with Moritz, his dog, shortly before takeoff on April 21, 1918.

fact to himself. He was needed at the front. There could be no thought of asking for a rear-echelon post or a ground appointment.

Besides, he would be off in two days on leave with Lieutenant Joachim Wolff for a shooting holiday. The father of Werner Voss had invited him and Wolff to stay at the Voss's hunting lodge deep in the Black Forest. The Baron, visualizing the peace of the forest and the pursuit of evasive woodcock, smiled thinly again. Too bad, he thought, about young Voss. The boy's death was a great blow to J.G. 1. Voss had been one of its brightest stars. But his foolhardy spirit had been his undoing. Imagine a lone tripe attacking a host of S.E. 5A's. Voss must have been insane, he thought.

The Baron again studied the mist billowing up from the lowland adjacent to the Somme Canal. Was it his imagination, or did it seem to be dissipating ever so slightly? The sun, too, seemed to be making a heroic effort to break through the cloud cover. He breathed deeply. The soft moist air was edged with the rich full smell of spring. It was good to be only twenty-five and alive and healthy, well, fairly healthy, after three years of air fighting.

He had a lot to live for, of that he was sure. He was the brightest star in the German firmament; the toast of the nation, truly the most fortunate of men. He had been received and applauded by the Kaiser and his wife; the Commander-in-Chief personally had praised him; the people idolized him beyond anything he had ever dreamed possible when as a young Uhlan officer he had ridden off to war. The hunting had been superb; the relics to be treasured forever when he returned to Schweidnitz after the war. He mused about that: would there be an after the war for him? He couldn't be sure, but then who could? It would be good to survive if Germany triumphed. But he would not care to live in a defeated Germany.

After a light breakfast of tea and hard rolls, the Baron appeared outside the officer's mess. Again he sniffed the air. He raised his strong chin. Strange, the wind was picking up and was blowing out of the east. It very seldom blew out of the east and in the direction of the Allied lines. He would have to watch it, if they got into a scrap with the "lords." Before you knew it, the wind would blow your machine far

Richthofen chats with his comrades for the last time, April 21, 1918.

over the enemy lines, an advantage usually enjoyed by the Germans as the winds mostly prevailed from the west.

The Circus Master sauntered along to the flight line where he was greeted exuberantly by a group of his gentlemen. The Baron echoed their greetings in a jovial mood that was rather unusual for him. Usually, he was aloof and reserved in the manner of his land-owning class. But that morning of the day he was to die, he apparently felt very chipper and gay. Like himself, his airmen, all personally selected and examined by him, were clad in their flying suits and waiting near their neat line of triplanes to hear whether the weather would be favorable for patrol duty.

Richthofen spoke a few words with his cousin, Wolfram von Richthofen, reminding the fledgling pilot that he was to duck out if they went aloft and became engaged with any of the Britishers. His conversation with Joachim Wolff was more animated as it concerned their impending leave. Aware that even then their train tickets to the Black Forest awaited them in the adjutant's office, they happily discussed the prospects of bagging woodcock. The men, whose mood was usually attuned to that of the Rittmeister, became even more boisterous as they quickly detected his lighthearted outlook. As he passed among them, they made small jokes and were delighted to hear their leader laugh aloud. How good it was to hear the great hero let himself go for a few moments.

Spotting Lt. Richard Wenzl, one of the more recent replacements, relaxing with his eyes closed on a stretcher, the Baron quietly drew near, and with a loud huzzah, upended Wenzl. Wenzl smiled sheepishly. What else could he do? Another pilot righted the stretcher and stretched out. Again the Red Baron kicked out one of the supports and the unlucky pilot plopped to the ground to the roar of laughter from Richthofen and his watching birdmen. The gentlemen all agreed that they had seldom seen their admired Geschwader commander in a more ebullient spirit.

The wind had become even more brisk from the east. The clouds began to break. The Baron stood around with his men, with all agreeing that they more than likely would be receiving orders for takeoff before long. Something brushed against his thigh. The Baron turned to find his huge Danish hound, Moritz, nuzzling him. The two pilots had gotten their revenge in a roundabout fashion—fastened to the dog's tail was a length of rope attached to a wheel chock. The Baron laughed lightly. Nothing could change his mood. He untied the rope and lovingly patted Moritz.

When it was almost noon (10:30 A.M. British time), the sky showed large patches of blue. His men began to move toward their tripes, but the Baron signaled for them to hold up. "Let us wait for a few more minutes. The 'lords' will soon become overconfident and fly across the lines. It will be easier then to get them in our gunsights. Let me warn you again not to permit that stiff easterly wind to drift you over the enemy line."

The German birdmen milled about. At that moment a mechanic, with a postcard in one hand and a camera in the other, shyly approached the Circus Master. The erect aristocrat listened good-naturedly to the nervous enlisted man's request. Smiling, he autographed the postcard and posed briefly for a photograph. "Couldn't this have waited for my return?" he asked with amusement. "Or can it be that you are not expecting me back after this morning's work?" The mechanic assured the Baron he had no such thought, made his thanks, and hurried away to help with the aircraft, arrayed wing tip to wing tip with Prussian precision on the flight line. Richthofen, unlike many German fliers, disdained superstition. He was aware that Boelcke and many others had failed to return after being photographed at the last moment, but he refused to believe that his fate could be influenced by any such mundane activity.

Then at last a telephone operator dashed from the communications shack with a message. The Baron grabbed it from his hand and quickly read it: "There are several English planes at the front." The Rittmeister sighed. There would be no respite for him that day. He signaled his men to prepare for takeoff. He hurried to his own blood-red tripe. (Dr.-1 425/17), attached his parachute, one of the first ever worn in combat, and gave his mechanics, Sergeants Pickel and Lange, his final orders. The mustachioed mechanics quickly removed the chocks as the triplane's engine burst into a throaty roar. The Baron made a final check of his equipment. He looked down the line of aircraft and signaled for takeoff. A final wave to the usual coterie of fliers and nonfliers who liked to hover about the great hero and his tripe began rolling forward. Within seconds the Red Baron's plane was off the ground. Then, as usual, he hooked the left wing slightly and his plane sprang into the air and headed for the Front, followed by his men. Along with him flew his cousin, Wolfram, Vizefeldwebel Edgar Scholz, Lieutenants Hans Weiss, Paul Wenzl, Hans-Joachim Wolff, and Emil Karjus, a one-handed flier. Airborne they were joined by the Albatroses and tripes of Jasta 5, temporarily assigned to J.G. 1.

As Richthofen approached the front, west of Hamel, at seven thousand feet, accompanied by the tripes of Jasta 11 and the Albatroses of Jasta 5, he spotted the two reported "lord" reconnaissance aircraft about one thousand feet below, despite the mist and low cloud cover. The two-seater R.E. 8's were from No. 3 Squadron, AFC, and had taken off from Poulainville airfield about 10 A.M. on a routine mission to photograph the corps front. The Australians in that sector had been warned several days earlier that the Germans had massed strong air units opposite their front with the hope of regaining air superiority in the sector. The R.E. 8's arrived at their designated position about 10:20 A.M. and began their photographic mission, with the number two machine, piloted by Lt. T. L. Simpson and with E. C. Banks observing, nearest to the approaching German buses, and the number one machine flown by Lt. S. G. Garrett and his observer, Lt. A. V. Barrow, on the Australian side of the line flying north.

The Red Baron, in his usual manner, carefully studied the situation. The R.E. 8's looked like "easy meat" but they could be bait to lure his men into a deadly ambush by RAF Camel and S.E. 5A aircraft. His scrutiny revealed no signs of any ambuscade in the clouds and he gave the signal for four of his men to follow him down after the R.E. 8's while the others remained above to keep an eye out for any RAF machines that might have escaped his sharp eyesight. Eighty was a nice round number but eighty-one would push him that much closer to the magic "century" mark, which he had so often referred to in moments of introspection. To shoot down one hundred enemy aircraft would raise him forever beyond the reach of any other competitors in the race for everlasting glory.

As the tripes swept down, the Red Baron was confident that the "Harry Tates" were unaware of their impending doom. Surprise was his. Victory should be quick and com-

The Red Baron's Fokker Dr.-1 triplane. Slow (about 106 mph top) but maneuverable and a great climber (10,000 ft. in 6 min.). Voss made the Dr.-1 famous.

plete, and then home to the airfield near Cappy. But the onrushing tripes had not gone unseen as is reported in the following hitherto unpublished account of the fight by Lieutenant Banks, the observer and gunner aboard the number two R.E. 8.

"Some six photographs had been taken by each machine when we saw a close formation of triplanes heading directly toward us," Banks told the authors. He and Barrow signaled each other, double-checking to make sure each was aware of the approaching Germans, and then manned their Lewis guns. "The leader was a red triplane." Writing in the third person, Banks continued: "Each time a triplane tried to maneuver onto the tail of an R.E. 8, our pilot turned his machine around and the procedure started all over again. Our machines kept together and protected each other.

"This fight lasted about six to eight minutes while von Richthofen and his mate were always under fire. The fight was at close range and the airmen could see each other clearly. Suddenly, the red triplane turned over and fell away rapidly."

Banks wrote that he and Barrow then concentrated their fire on another triplane. "He took a bad battering and after splinters were seen to fly from his wings [he] pulled out of the fight and dived for home. This fight occurred a few minutes before the recorded time when von Richthofen crashed and was precisely above the pinpoint on the military map where his plane landed. The mosaic diagram of our photographs prepared in the mapping section of the squadron clearly shows a gap in the sequence around the crash point. With the combat finished, the two R.E. 8's continued their photographic program."

That was a "wild day" for the two R.E. 8's, as Banks described it. "About half an hour later, they were again confronted by a formation of some Albatros planes flying at seven thousand feet. As this armada approached, Simpson and Banks, now separated from the other plane, assumed the big formation was a squadron of their own machines and flew over to take a photograph.

"Their amazement was complete when suddenly they could see a mass of Maltese Crosses and wildly gesticulating German airmen in the cockpits. Fight was out of the question as their ammunition [the R.E. 8's] was almost exhausted.

British R.E. 8 flying machine of the type involved in Richthofen's death.

Simpson put the R.E. 8 into a steep dive and passed through the Germans so closely that their faces were clearly visible. The long dive continued for about six thousand feet while the whole German formation broke and followed like hornets. The Australian machine was riddled, and broken control wires streamed out behind, but at two hundred feet, Simpson pulled out and hedgehopped home.

"The reports of these adventures were written and recorded by our four officers in the Squadron headquarters before it became known that von Richthofen had been shot down. The four officers [including Banks] were overwhelmed with congratulations by the commanding officer and staff officers of the wing."

All witnesses and records agree that the R.E. 8's put up a stiff fight. One Fokker triplane was shot down, apparently from Jasta 5 as J.G. 1 reported no loss in this air action. The tripe, in any case, could not have been the one flown by the Red Baron, despite Bank's lifelong belief that fire from the two R.E. 8's dispatched the Rittmeister to his reward. The site of the battle was at least two and a half miles from the location where the Red Baron's plane crashed, and that's as the crow flies. Additionally, the mortal wound suffered by the Circus Master precluded any possibility of his having been able to fly his bus to the spot where it finally put down beside the Bray-Corbie Road. It can be easily understood, however, that in the excitement of the day, Banks could have confused the downed tripe as that of the Rittmeister. The opposing aircraft flashed by each other at more than two hundred miles an hour, and undoubtedly, any number of the German tripes appeared to be painted all-red and, therefore, that of von Richthofen.

In a letter to the authors, Banks, residing at this writing in Sidney, Australia, and the sole survivor of the R.E. 8 crews, said: "Many stories have been told regarding Baron von Richthofen's last flight and his final defeat on the 21st of April 1918. These accounts have mostly been compiled by persons other than combatants. They all differ so fundamentally, it is safe to say they cannot be true. My story of Baron von Richthofen's last battle has never been told publicly though I have had many requests to publish it. I could see no benefit by being involved in this evergreen controversy."

The authors, however, prevailed on Banks to make his

reminiscences available to them for the record. They salute him as a gallant air fighter, but have to state that they are in agreement with Lt. H. N. Wrigley, a one-time commanding officer of No. 3 Squadron, who wrote in *The Battle Below*, the history of No. 3 Squadron, AFC, that two aircraft of his squadron encountered the Richthofen Circus about the same time as Richthofen was shot down, "but they were not concerned in the actual shooting down of their celebrated enemy."

The Baron, angered by the resolution shown by the R.E. 8's and the loss of one of his men, disengaged. As he attempted to reform his birdmen, the R.E. 8's ducked into the cloud cover. Richthofen swept over the lines about a mile south-southeast of Sailly-le-Sec. The German buses now were in range of British antiaircraft guns, which quickly opened fire. The shells burst, with their telltale white puffs, among Richthofen's men. The exploding cotton balls were spotted by a formation of eight Camels. Rushing up, they saw the tripes regrouping and attacked.

The red-nosed Camels were led by Capt. A. Roy Brown, DSC, a Canadian from Toronto who had been commissioned in the Royal Naval Air Service late in 1915. Brown, on the morning of April 21, was in a state of exhaustion. Never physically strong, the constant strain of air fighting had taken its toll. Though victor in eleven aerial combats, the Canadian, at the time, was suffering intensely from indigestion and dysentery.

Raymond Collishaw, one of Canada's top aces of World War I with sixty confirmed victories, knew Brown well and reported the following incident to the authors: "Capt. Brown was a friend and when I heard that he was ill and that he was being invalided home from a nervous breakdown, I flew over to see Brown (at Bertangles) on April 20th. The day before the death of von Richthofen, Brown was definitely in a bad way, both mentally and physically, and he was both nervous and he had lost his nerve. He explained that he was being invalided home forthwith and I suggested that he certainly ought not to fly again on active service, until he had had a respite. He agreed and, not unnaturally, I was extremely surprised to hear about the von R affair."

Collishaw, commander of No. 203 Squadron, RAF, at the time of Richthofen's death, lived at the time of this writing in

West Vancouver, B.C. His views on other key aspects of the controversy will be found further along in the manuscript.

Brown had been scheduled to be off the ground from the airfield at Bertangles with his flight of five machines at 8:15 A.M., but the same swirling mist and fog that had delayed Richthofen's men, held up the actual takeoff of Brown's flight until 9:30 A.M. The Camels' mission was a routine patrol at twelve thousand feet over the front between Albert and Hangard. With Brown were Lts. F. Lomas, Francis J. W. Mellersh (later Sir Francis who died in a helicopter crash in 1955), William John MacKenzie, and Wilfred "Wop" May. May was an old Canadian school chum of Brown's. He almost didn't become a front-line pilot because he had been two days late in reporting to No. 209 (Naval) Squadron. It seems he was delayed by a wild party. The Squadron commander, incensed, had read him out and ordered him back to the pilot's pool. A chance meeting with Brown, as May moved red-faced and smarting out of the C.O.'s office, saved him. After hearing May's story, Brown intervened on his behalf. The C.O. was very high on Brown and agreed that May could stay, but only if Brown accepted him in his flight.

May was not a complete novice, as usually is reported, when he took off that morning with Brown. May's logbook actually shows that he had participated in two offensive patrols the day before, April 20. During one of those patrols, his flight had even tangled briefly with a German tripe. However, May, who had been assigned at "outside-left" on the April 21 patrol, was told by Brown to stay out of any fight that developed. May was informed that he could observe any action that occurred but to run for home if attacked by a German machine.

After takeoff of Brown's flight, two additional flights of five Camels each led by Capts. Oliver W. Redgate and Oliver Le Boutillier, an American living today in Las Vegas, Nevada, roared down the runway at Bertangles within a ten-minute period and zoomed aloft. Their machines joined Brown's, and the squadron headed for the front in an extended flight line of fifteen machines. As the squadron neared the southernmost point of the patrol line where it was to turn north and patrol along the lines, two Albatros C-type buses were spotted over Le Quesnel. Captain Le Boutillier's flight rushed to the attack, quickly shooting down one of the

The Richthofen controversy begins.

German two-seaters in flames while the second one scooted into the cover of a cloud. Le Boutillier's Camels scurried about seeking the elusive enemy plane.

Brown, satisfied that Le Boutillier's men had the situation in control, ordered the remaining two flights of ten Camels, with their cherry-colored noses, to turn northward toward Le Hamel. As they did so, two Camels from Redgate's flight signaled engine trouble and circled about to return to Bertangles. Left, then, with only eight Camels, Brown proceeded now in a northeastward direction. It was at that time Brown first saw the friendly antiaircraft bursts denoting the presence of German aircraft. He signaled his men to close up and head for the clearly visible white puffs and soon spotted Richthofen's Flying Circus, milling about at an altitude of some six thousand feet. May remained above at twelve thousand feet as Brown led seven Camels down against the Red Baron's men.

The Rittmeister, at that moment, spotted the RAF planes and signaled his men to face about and meet the attack. The tripes and Albatroses hustled to join up and present a united front. Too late, Brown's buses ripped into the Baron's men. A blue-tailed triplane, too slow in turning about, was hit by bursts of Vickers fire from the guns of Lieutenant Mellersh's Camel. The German bus dropped straight down but zoomed out at the last moment to try to make it back to Cappy. It didn't make it—crashing instead several miles short at Cerisy. As Mellersh followed the wounded enemy bird down, two Fokkers fastened onto his tail. Mellersh put his Camel into a spin in an effort to lose the tripes. He came out of the spin at fifty feet with the Fokkers still in hot pursuit. Sticking close to the ground, he began to hedgehop for home and eventually the German pursuers broke off. While rushing off, Mellersh observed a "bright red triplane" crash nearby and saw, overhead, "Capt. Brown's machine."

Richthofen and Brown's groups now were in the midst of a full-fledged dogfight—watched with the greatest interest by thousands of ground troops below on both sides of the lines. Tripes, Albatroses, and Camels darted at each other, trying to fix one another in their gunsights. They whirled and twisted, closing and firing split-second bursts. The air reverberated with the throaty roar of full-on engines as the opposing pilots fought for an advantage. Death watched anxiously for new victims to feed its hungry maws.

Right in the thick of the mass of milling aircraft was the Red Baron. He easily flicked off the attempts of any Camel pilot to fasten on his tail. Darting about in the fray, extending over an area half a mile to a mile and a half southeast of Sailly-le-Sec, he looked about for victim number eighty-one. The R.E. 8's had escaped his attack. He was determined to knock down one of the Camels as compensation. The Camels had been reckless in attacking a superior group of Germans and would have to be taught a lesson by Germany's ace of aces.

The first man from Brown's flight to leave the dogfight was MacKenzie. Fire from a tripe struck him in the back. Despite his agony, MacKenzie loosed a stream of Vickers fire at an enemy bus. The tripe reared up and fell away, the pilot fighting to regain control. MacKenzie then broke away and headed for Bertangles. On landing, an inspection of his Camel showed that the center of the fuselage had been ripped by Spandau bullets. A hit also had been recorded on one of the bearers[1] of his 150 h.p. Bentley engine.

As the dogfight raged below, May, faithful to Brown's orders, watched from above at twelve thousand feet. Constantly circling about in his Camel, he became ever more eager to take part in the action. For a few moments, one tripe offered him a beautiful target as it rose up to gain altitude and dived back into the battle. May was tempted to attack, but held back, remembering his instructions. Then, a second tripe came up out of the melee. The temptation was too much for May. The hell with orders. His buddies needed help. He flung his bus down after the enemy machine, fired, missed, and shot after it into the very middle of the midair struggle. May caught the tripe once again in his gunsights and triggered another burst of fire. The enemy plane staggered and headed toward the ground. May was sure he had scored his first kill and later requested confirmation. He received it despite the fact that reports of the battle say nothing about any tripes being shot down at this point. There is a possibility that this German machine was that of Wolfram von Richthofen, the Red Baron's cousin who rose to

[1] Now in Carisella's collection.

high command in Hitler's Luftwaffe before dying of a brain tumor in 1943. Wolfram, like May, also was a novice, with orders to run for home if attacked.

May later gave the following account of the fight. It is not his official combat report. "Capt. Roy Brown was taking me over the lines for the first time. He had warned me not to participate in any engagements for the first few times. Our squadron dived on some enemy aircraft which I did not see. I did not dive with the remainder, but I stayed up trying to see what it was all about. Finally, I discovered an enemy aircraft right below me, and it was too tempting a target. I missed and followed him down. I woke in a regular beehive of enemy aircraft. This was Richthofen's Circus of about fifty [sic] machines. The fight was at close quarters. Enemy aircraft were coming at me from all sides. I seemed to be missing some of them by inches and there seemed so many that I thought the best thing to do was to go into a tight vertical turn, hold my guns open and spray as many of them as I could. Through lack of experience, I held one of my guns open too long. It jammed and then the other. I could not clear them so I spun out of the mess and headed west by the sun for home. After I had leveled out, I looked around, but nobody was following. Feeling pretty good at having extricated myself, the next thing I knew I was being fired on from behind. All I could do was to try to dodge my attacker, which was a red triplane. Had I known it was Richthofen, I should probably have passed out on the spot."

It was Richthofen, indeed, eager as ever in the midst of combat to notch another kill on his victory stick. May obviously was "fresh meat" and the Red Baron was determined to finish him off quickly and scoot eastward for home. He had had enough flying and fighting for one day. Down he plummeted to close fast on the tail of May's Camel. Lining up his bus, he began firing bursts of Spandau fire. The Allied pilot was taken by surprise. Of that, the Baron was certain because of the way the Camel suddenly staggered in the air.

Though a novice, May instantly began evasive tactics as he swooped down and in a westerly direction away from Sailly-le-Sec. He cursed his predicament and his useless guns. He was going to be lucky to get out of this fix. Headlong up the Somme Valley the Camel roared with the German aircraft coming up fast from the rear. They now were over the Allied lines but the tripe gave no indication of breaking off the fight.

At this point, Brown, in the midst of the dance of death above, noted May's desperate plight. Engaged at the time with two triplanes on the fringe of the dogfight, he broke away and winged to his friend's rescue from a height of some two thousand feet. The Canadian quickly caught up with the two zig-zagging planes as they raced at some five hundred feet over the river valley. Their course paralleled Morlancourt Ridge that ran east to west from the German lines to its terminus atop Corbie Hill nearly two miles distant behind the Allied lines.

Brown coaxed every possible bit of power from his straining engine. He prayed he wouldn't be too late. Even as he watched, Richthofen was closing fast on May. Soon now, the German's fire would take effect. Brown gave his bus all the gas it would take. His Camel shot downward ever faster. As Brown angled in fast from above and to the rear, he fixed the all-red tripe in his sights and loosed one sustained burst of fire. He was sure he had scored. The German pilot had looked about on hearing the Camel's burst. Yet Richthofen, ever cautious was in the habit of constantly looking backwards when in pursuit of his prey. But Brown was sure his fire had fatally scored. From his viewpoint, the German pilot seemed to have slumped in his cockpit.

Because of the angle and speed with which he had swept in on the Baron, Brown's bus roared by the tripe. As he sought to flatten out, he shot across the Somme east of Vaux-sur-Somme, losing sight of the tripe behind a row of trees. He was confident, however, his machine guns had accomplished their work and continued westward to pass over Vaire-sous-Somme. Low on fuel and ammunition, he decided to fly on home to Bertangles.

Despite Brown's belief, the Baron continued his hot pursuit of May along the river valley. He fired repeatedly at May. The chase was at treetop level now. Ground troops at this point either were too startled to fire or fearful of hitting the Camel just in front of the tripe.

May, in his own account, stated: "I kept dodging and spinning down until I ran out of sky and had to hedgehop along the ground. Richthofen was firing continually and the only thing that saved me was my poor flying! I didn't know what I was going to do and I don't suppose Richthofen could figure this out, either. I started up the Somme Valley at a very low altitude with Richthofen close on my tail. I went around a curve in the river just near Corbie, but Richthofen beat me to it by cutting over a hill and, at that point, I was a sitting duck; too low down between the banks to turn away. I felt he had me cold and I had to restrain myself from pushing the stick forward and disappearing into the river. I was sure this was the end. Then, as I looked around, I saw Richthofen do a spin-and-a-half and hit the ground. Looking up I saw one of our machines directly behind. This I joined up with and returned to base."

To go back a bit, the Baron continued chasing May after Brown's burst. The pursuit was constantly along the north side of the Somme River and slightly south of Morlancourt Ridge which paralleled it. The Baron's tripe duplicated every move of May's machine. His Spandaus ripped repeated bursts of fire at the Camel but without telling effect.

When they approached the point where the Somme turns abruptly southward in the direction of Corbie, May banked his Camel to head north and roared up from the river valley to skim over the crest of Corbie Hill, the western end of Morlancourt Ridge. Here eager Australian ground gunners finally were able to get a clear shot at the tripe. Torrents of fire from the Aussie gun emplacements, notably those of the 24th Machine-gun Company and the 44th Battalion, laced the sky. As hunter and prey cleared the crest of the ridge, gunners of the 53rd Australian Field Battery opened up with their Lewis guns. Even riflemen took pot shots at the tripe.

The Allied fire scored. Pieces of the aircraft were seen to fly off from the forward section of the fuselage. The slugs thudding home snapped the Baron from his momentary obsession to add the Camel to his kill list. It was not like him to become so involved in the chase that he forgot about threats to his safety. He had even forgotten about the east wind. To get home, he would have to buck it all the way.

Still he remained fixed on the Camel's tail. At times only thirty feet separated them, as the Baron sought to find the decisive range. One more burst! Suddenly one of his Spandau guns stopped firing because of a broken firing pin,[2] and then

2Now in the Carisella collection.

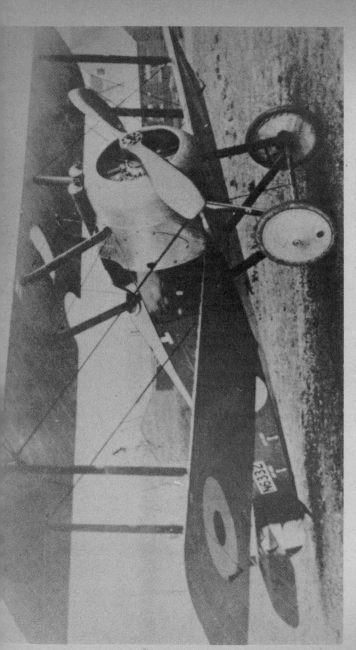

Sopwith Camel. With the Fokker Dr.-1, supreme fighter of World War I.

the other gun developed a number three stoppage. He was incredulous. He hammered his guns with his fist as he maneuvered to stay on the tail of May's craft. Again and again he pressed the gun trigger, but in vain. The guns failed to fire. It was definitely time to go home.

Cursing the loss of his fire power and with every weapon on the ground apparently trying to shoot him down, Richthofen broke off his pursuit of May and banked sharply to the east. As he did so, bursts of Aussie ground fire again ripped the forward section of his tripe. He put the bus into a sharper bank. The wing tips were almost vertical to the earth. Bullets thudded into the tripe. The German aircraft swerved, staggered as though hit hard. The air reverberated from the lashing of the Aussie weaponry.

The Red Baron's head was observed to jerk sharply backward. He reached up with his left hand and ripped off his goggles and flung them over the side. The tripe dropped into a sideslip, flattened out, and glided toward the ground. Down, down it fell on an even keel. Atop Corbie Hill it slammed into the ground, bounced about ten feet into the air and then crashed nosefirst into a pile of mangels just off the north side of the Bray-Corbie road. May continued to fly northward. Meanwhile Brown, who had swung westward around the bend in the Somme, turned directly north, well to the west of Corbie Hill. He and May hooked up near Heilly, about a mile north of the point where the all-red tripe crashed. The two Camels flew home together.

A somber picture of the hero after he was shot down on July 6, 1917. In the nine months left to him Richthofen never recovered fully.

✠ ✠ ✠

Chapter 4

THE CONTROVERSY

✠ ON the day that the Red Baron fell, the RAF issued this concise and stark daily communique: "The enemy's machines were seen in large numbers but were not aggressive. Eleven machines were brought down in air fighting and six others were driven down out of control. A hostile observation balloon was also destroyed. Our antiaircraft fire brought down two other hostile machines. Five of our aircraft are missing."

Of the German buses shot down on April 21, one was credited by the RAF to Brown, even though the ailing Canadian did not mention Richthofen by name in the following combat report he filled out on his return to the field at Bertangles.

"At 10:35 A.M. [British time] I observed two Albatros burst into flames and crash. Dived on large formation of fifteen to twenty Albatros Scouts D.V's and Fokker triplanes, two of which got on my tail and I came out. Went back again and dived on pure red triplane which was firing on Lieut. May. I got a long burst into him and he went down vertical and was observed to crash by Lieutenant Mellersh and Lieutenant May. I fired on two more but did not get them."

Brown's report appears to be logical up to the point where he did fire at Richthofen's tripe just east of Vaux-sur-Somme. But after that, his facts, as stated in the report, do not follow. Despite both his claim and that of Mellersh and May, Richthofen could not have crashed near Vaux-sur-Somme, as the Baron's machine was observed by hundreds of Australian ground troops to continue pursuing May's Camel up the Somme Valley, over Morlancourt Ridge (or Corbie Hill) to the point where it crashed nosefirst beside the Bray-Corbie Road. Brown's report becomes even more confusing because of his claim in the final sentence that he "fired on two more but did not get them" after he allegedly shot down the all-red tripe. Several ground witnesses agreed that after Brown got in one long burst of fire at Richthofen's machine, he flew his Camel directly to the west, past the point where the Somme River hooks sharply to the left in the direction of Corbie, and then swept in a wide curve northward on a path some half to three-quarters of a mile parallel to that of the Baron's and May's. Neither Brown nor any other credible witness reported that Brown closed again with the Baron's plane before it was seen to crash. In fact, Brown, apparently believing that he had rescued his school chum from the Baron's clutches, headed as quickly as possible for home. He was suffering intensely from stomach cramps and had no choice but to return to Bertangles or risk the possibility of losing control of his aircraft. In fact, just before going into the hangar tent of No. 3 Squadron, AFC, at Poulainville the next day to view the Baron's body, Brown told several airmen that he had to break off the fight after the long burst because he was in agony from dysentery. At the time, he also said that the RAF higher-ups were already pushing him to state unequivocally that the tripe he had claimed to have downed was that of Richthofen.

In a five-part article "My Fight With Richthofen," published in the late 1920's, Brown was quoted as saying about the battle: "I was in perfect position above and behind. It was a mere matter of straight shooting. Neither plane (Richthofen's or May's) was aware of me. ... I had dived until the red snout of my Camel pointed fair at his tail. My thumbs pressed the triggers. Bullets ripped into his elevator and tail planes. The flaming tracers showed me where they hit. A little short! Gently, I pulled back on the stick. The nose of the Camel rose ever so slightly. Easy now, easy. The stream of bullets tore along the body of the all-red tripe. Its occupant turned and looked back. I had a flash of his eyes behind the goggles. Then he crumpled—sagged in the cockpit. My bullets poured out beyond him. My thumbs eased on the triggers. Richthofen was dead. The triplane staggered, wobbled, stalled, flung over on its nose and went down. The reserve trenches of the Australian infantry was not more than two hundred feet below. It was a quick descent. May saw it. I saw it as I swung over. And Mellersh saw it."

Dramatic copy but obviously so much humbug. Brown was not a professional writer; the above report is written in the colorful slick manner of the hack writer of the period. With his manner and temperament, Brown would never have described the fight in such words; and more specifically, he never at any time said that he was the author of such a piece. As a matter of fact, he stated in 1935 that he never even read the publication in which the article was found.

The newly formed RAF, of course, was most anxious to gain credit for the end of Germany's great hero, even to the point of insisting that Brown gained the kill. In its summary of April 22, 1918, 5th Brigade, RAF stated: "About 11 A.M. yesterday morning Captain Brown, D.S.C., whilst on high offensive patrol, near Vaux-sur-Somme, dived on a red triplane which was firing on Lieutenant May. It had followed Lieutenant May down to about five hundred feet. Captain Brown fired a long burst into it and it went down vertically and was observed to crash by Lieutenant May and Lieutenant [sic] Brown."

Brown, in his combat report and until his death in 1944, was never so positive. A modest and courageous flier, who ended his fighting days within a few days after the Baron's death, he maintained only that he had shot at a tripe and that May and Mellersh had seen it crash.

May's report of the famous fight was even more confusing than Brown's. He stated "I was attacked by a red triplane which chased me over the [Allied] lines, low to the ground. While the triplane was on my tail, Capt. A. R.

Brown attacked, and shot it down. I observed it crash [*sic*] onto the ground near Vaux-sur-Somme."

So reads May's report filed the day of the Baron's death. But later, in recollecting the deadly chase, May wrote the following: "I kept dodging and spinning down until I ran out of sky and had to hedgehop along the ground. Richthofen was firing continually and the only thing that saved me was *my poor flying!* I didn't know what I was going to do and I don't suppose Richthofen could figure this out either ... I started up the Somme Valley at a very low altitude with Richthofen close on my tail. I went around a curve in the river just near Corbie, but Richthofen beat me to it by cutting over a hill and at that point I was a sitting duck, too low down between the banks to turn away. I felt he had me cold and I had to restrain myself from pushing the stick forward and disappearing into the river. I was sure this was the end. Then as I looked around, I saw Richthofen do a spin and a half and hit the ground. Looking up I saw one of our machines directly behind. This I joined up with and returned to base."

Even a casual reading of this testimony clearly shows that May was in a near panic as the Baron closed in. The young Canadian says he even considered diving into the river to escape the lethal bursts of fire from Richthofen's Spandaus. How could a pilot, in his state of mind, especially flying a tricky Camel, possibly observe the maneuvers of a pursuing tripe?

Top Canadian ace Raymond Collishaw, in stating his views on the controversy, told the authors that "a Camel pilot flying at full speed very close to the ground cannot see anything to his rear, without altering his course forty-five degrees to both flanks." While May had been zig-zagging to avoid the Baron's fire, it is very unlikely that he would have constantly altered his course forty-five degrees to his flanks, thus losing headway just to see how the Baron was doing.

Note, too, that May, in his combat report of April 21, stated that he saw the Tripe "crash into the ground near Vaux-sur-Somme." This, of course, was impossible because it is an indisputable fact that the Baron's plane went down along the Bray-Corbie Road. That latter point is about a mile and half in a straight line from where May says the Baron crashed at Vaux-sur-Somme and a distance of some two miles in the circuitous manner in which May and the Baron covered it.

May, additionally, refutes his own report by stating in his later recollections that the Baron was still chasing him "around a curve in the river near Corbie." This statement coincides with that of the Australian ground troops and attests to the fact that Richthofen continued his pursuit of May for a much greater distance behind Allied lines than the point where Brown and May claimed his tripe crashed.

As to May's statement at the end of his later recollections that he looked up and "saw one of our machines directly behind," this undoubtedly was correct. The machine was more than likely that of Captain Brown, who had completed his wide swing and was heading north—above and to the left of May—between Bonnay and Heilly. May's flight path, immediately after the Baron's crash on Corbie Hill, would have had him bisecting that of Brown's nearly a mile from the site of the crash and north of the point where the Rittmeister broke off their engagement and turned sharply eastward in a vain effort to gain the safety of his own lines.

Two other airmen also claimed to have seen Brown down a triplane: one was Lieutenant Mellersh, a member of Brown's flight, and the other was Captain Le Boutillier who had led a separate flight of No. 209 (Naval) Squadron. Mellersh reported that, during the wild dogfight below Sailly-le-Sec, two tripes, flown by Joachim Wolff and Karjus, fastened on the tail of his Camel, and he dived to within fifty feet of the earth in an effort to save himself. He then headed for the Allied lines close to earth. "Whilst so returning," he wrote in his report, "a bright red triplane crashed quite close to me. As I looked up I saw Capt. Brown's machine." As for Le Boutillier, he tersely reported that he fired on a red triplane "which was shot down by Captain Brown and crashed our side of lines."

Quite obviously, from the reports of Mellersh and Le Boutillier, the attack on the above triplane occurred over "no-man's-land," and the German bus crashed in the forward positions of the Australian lines. While Mellersh and Le Boutillier undoubtedly believed they saw a triplane crash southwest of Sailly-le-Sec, it could not, under any circumstances, have been the Baron's. (They may have seen the machine of Wolfram von Richthofen in an evasive dive. The

Baron's cousin got into trouble and extricated himself.) The Rittmeister's plane, as has been stated, went down at least two miles from that point. Mellersh, too, cannot be considered a reliable witness because of the obvious state of his mind. Remember that he was fleeing for his life from the fire of two tripes and undoubtedly had no real opportunity to observe with any accuracy what Brown or anyone else actually was doing at that time.

II

On the other side, former Corporal J. Homewood of B Company, 44th Australian Battalion, AIF, a resident of West Australia, believes Richthofen was hit by ground fire. He describes what he saw this way: "In April, 1918 our battalion was billeted on the sharp slope of a hill in the Bonnay-Heilly sector. . . . my section was detailed to occupy an antiaircraft post on the brow of the hill. . . . our quiet game of cards was disturbed by the sound of approaching aircraft. On standing to, we saw two planes coming in low over the hill from the direction of the front line. The front plane (British) was closely pursued by a red German triplane. Before coming into range of our gun, (No. 7 Platoon, Lewis Gun section), the red plane turned back, banking sharply, seemed to stand still on a wing tip. Just then I heard the rattle of a Lewis gun from a position in front of us (I learned later it was an antiaircraft Lewis attached to an artillery battery). The red triplane immediately dived into the ground narrowly missing a 'flying fox' installation. Several of us ran over to the plane, approximately one hundred yards, and pulled the pilot out. On examining him we found he was dead, a bullet had entered his back. In the meantime somebody had 'souvenired' his watch, and by the inscription on this he was identified as Baron von Richthofen. When the Australian Flying Corps men arrived to take what was left of the wreck (the souvenir hunters got the rest) they removed his machine guns and left them in our gun pit while the plane was loaded on a tender. When they came to retrieve the guns some pilfering Aussie had pinched the gunsight and they were very upset. (I still have that sight.)"

The authors at this point would like to note that the Aussies refer to the western end of Morlancourt Ridge as both Corbie Hill and Heilly Hill; that is the section of the ridge where Richthofen's tripe made its last landing. Again, too, Homewood makes no mention of Brown's aircraft being in the vicinity when the Red Baron went down. Note also that he describes the fatal wound quite accurately.

Former Staff Capt. C. C. Hillary of Forrestfield, Western Australia, is also convinced that the Rittmeister was shot down from the ground. He told the authors several years ago that he holds this belief because "the Baron disengaged his self from the dogfight above (Sailly-le-Sec) and then chased an observation R.E. 8 plane up and down the Ancre Valley.[1] To avoid the Baron, this plane turned and twisted with the Baron in pursuit and they both came down near the ground. The next thing that happened the Baron crashed after a tremendous lot of ground fire had taken place."

Hillary said he was with Lt. Jock Fraser when the Red Baron crashed "a few yards from where we were standing watching the dogfight going on above." Another man nearby at the time was Warrant Officer Jock Inch of Homewood's 44th Battalion, according to Hillary. Inch wrote the authors the following account of the Baron's last moments.

"I was watching an air fight in the sky from the cover of the coppice on the slope of the Somme Valley. Nearby was Staff Captain Hillary also watching the fighting up aloft when I noticed two planes break away from the main group and from our vantage we saw a British scout plane being chased by a German fighter plane. As they came within our sight I noticed the German firing his machine gun, then he stopped firing as he came near the ground. By this time he was about a hundred feet from the ground and, in my opinion, this is the second he was shot. The British plane suddenly twisted at right angles and disappeared and the German plane came on and crashed about eighty yards from where I was standing . . ."

Taking strong opposition to the RAF claim that Brown killed Richthofen, is Douglas Campbell Tilghman, a former gunner with the 53rd (Australian) Battery, and now a resident of Berry, N.S.W. He wrote recently: "The claim made by the RAF that Captain Brown shot him [Richthofen]

---

[1]Authors' Note: Hillary, like most ground troops, confused the various types of aircraft viewed overhead.

down is false. On the date of his death, I was out minding mules, being then a gunner in the 53rd Battery. My battery was located on an eminence overlooking the villages of Vaire and Vaux, not far from the junction of the Ancre and Somme [rivers]. As we naturally had a lot more mules than drivers, some of us were detailed to help the latter, so that the animals could get a decent feed of green stuff.

"I saw a British plane being hotly pursued by a German one, painted a vivid red, so I suspected it must be the Baron, whom we called the 'Red Devil.' I called out to 'Snowy' Evans and his mate [Robert Buie], our two gunners who were playing poker. They raced to their gun and, as the Baron swept in low, they gave him a burst. The next I saw was the red plane turning over, and plummeting to earth. Those of us who were minding mules raced over, and found the Baron very dead.

"Evans and his mate were given special leave to England as a reward for their initiative. I remember feeling a bit annoyed, as the two gunners were so intent on their poker game that the Baron probably would have gotten out of range had I not yelled out to Snowy. We were so used to dogfights that no one paid much attention to them as a general thing. And it was exceedingly rare for any planes, ours or Fritz's, to fly so low as on this occasion. . . ."

Tilghman wrote again later to report that he had taken issue with Lt. Col. Tyrrel M. Hawker's claim in the book about his brother, *Hawker, V. C.*, that the Baron was shot down by Brown. Tilghman said that biographer Hawker gave Brown credit for the Rittmeister's death because "the fatal wound was in the back. I shall write him [Hawker] again," Tilghman reported, "and tell him that the Baron's plane was under perfect control until within a few seconds of a burst of machine-gun [Lewis] fire from my battery, and that what he [Hawker] says is probably correct [about the wound], but is accounted for by the fact that the two planes had passed over our Lewis guns, and Evans and his mate shot him from behind. Further there was not another plane in sight that morning for half an hour before the dogfight, and the Baron simply could not have flown his plane and fought his opponent had he been mortally wounded. . . ."

Remember the goggles Carisella obtained from E. E. Hardaker? The fact that the Baron ripped them off and flung

them earthward received substantiation in a communication
from Ray McDiarmid of Moruya, Australia. He was a mem
ber of the 11th Australian Field Artillery Brigade. It wa
Gnr. Robert Buie, of the neighboring 14th Artillery Brigade
who was credited by the commanding officer of the British
Fourth Army "for the destruction of Baron von Richt
hofen."[2]

McDiarmid wrote in part: "There was a good dogfight on
somewhere in front of Corbie. One of the RAF plane
dropped out and Richthofen got on his tail. I was a machine
gunner . . . and had a crack at him as he passed but did no
good. About ten seconds after I heard a gun on my lef
open. I saw the plane stagger and get out of control. Some
thing was thrown out of the plane, which proved to be
Richthofen's goggles, but I'm darned if I remember the bloke
who picked them up, although I knew in the 11th Brigade
My mate, Joe Hill, was one of the first on the scene and go
a chunk of the petrol tank. He gave me a piece and I cut it
into a map of Australia and made a dead meal ticket of it.
still have it.

"We were told in Corbie orders the next day that
Gunner Buie had shot down Baron von Richthofen. My diar
confirms this. The RAF tried hard to claim the victory. But
as an eyewitness, I'll swear to the fact that he was shot from
the ground. The only thing I'm croaked about is that I missed
him."

III

One of the most interesting reports received by the author
came from F. G. Sheppard of Brighton, South Australia, who
flew as an RAF fighter pilot in the United Kingdom, Malta
and the Western Desert during World War II. Sheppard
learning of P. J. Carisella's interest in Richthofen, got in
touch with former Pvts. Vern Elix and Jock Newell of the
44th Battalion and interviewed them concerning their remin
iscences of April 21, 1918. Here is his report:

"Privates Vern Elix and Jock Newell had been detailed to
'bury a line' across the Bray-Corbie Road. Vern recalled tha

[2]Authors' Note: Buie's account will be found further on in this sec
tion.

It was a pleasant sunny morning and they were working near a 'flying fox' which ran to the village of Heilly. The field telephone line was duly entrenched and the job completed. They were collecting their tools when they heard the sound of an aeroplane engine. Vern looked up and saw a British aircraft closely pursued by a red triplane—both aircraft were flying very fast and low. He also noted that they were gradually losing height. His assessment of their height was about three hundred feet. (I estimated this with Vern by comparing the height of our Post Office clock in Adelaide.) The ground over which the aircraft were flying was undulating. The aircraft were broadside on to Vern's line of vision and he states that no violent evasive action was being taken by the Camel, although he did observe slight evasive action. At no time was there any firing from the triplane. He could see the head and shoulders of the German pilot quite clearly and estimated that he was about five to six lengths behind the Camel. Vern knew that there were Lewis gunners in the vicinity—but not a shot was fired to his knowledge whilst the chase was on. He states that the aircraft were so close together that there would be danger of hitting the British aeroplane. Quite suddenly the triplane whipped into a steep right-hand turn and crossed the road. (The Camel flew on and he did not see it again.)

"A mere second or so after the triplane commenced its turn, heavy machinegun fire broke out about Vern Elix and was directed towards the aircraft. Vern and Jock were still watching when suddenly Vern yelled, 'Look out, Jock, the bugger is after us.' Vern states that he got an awful shock as quite suddenly the nose of the triplane was pointing straight at him. Jock took off down the road at a tremendous rate of knots and Vern dived to the edge of the road. There were no hedges, but he grabbed a drum of 'Don 23' cable, swung it over his back, pushed down his steel helmet over the back of his neck and crouched down with his arms folded—and then heard the crash.

"Vern was quickly on his feet and noticed that a small cloud of dust had risen where the triplane had crashed in a bordering field of wurzels. He was alone and all was quiet. He walked towards the crash. He did not run and states that he reached it in less than two minutes. Vern walked around the aircraft and looked into the cockpit. The pilot was

slumped forward and he noticed a bullet wound in his back
He assumed that the pilot was dead and did not touch the
body. . . .

"Vern learned later that the pilot was Richthofen. He
stated that at the time the pilot was just another dead
German and he had seen plenty of dead Germans in his time
He was against souvenir hunting and stated that his old steel
helmet (which was issued to him) was the only souvenir he
kept.

"I questioned Vern about another aircraft in the vicinity—
particularly another Camel. Vern stated that there was no
another aircraft to be seen, that Richthofen was obviously
alive before he commenced his right-hand turn as no gun
had fired before its commencement and that he could no
understand how the Canadian pilot 'had had the effrontery to
claim shooting down Richthofen.' "

Maj. Blair Wark of the 32nd Battalion, a holder of the
Victoria Cross, was adamant in his belief that Brown was no
involved in the chase past Vaux. He said, "I watched the
chase and beyond question there were only two aeroplane
present, one a British plane, being pursued, and a second a
red triplane which was following it, firing keenly. No other
plane was near. And there could be no possibility of the pilot
already having received a wound such as that which killed
him.

"This battery was bivouacked on the hills near Vaux on
the rising ground above the Somme Valley. Richthofen had
elected to follow on the tail of a British plane down into the
valley below the surrounding hills, and ran into ground fire
from the hills on all sides. My company's guns were lending a
hand at long-range. I consider that the fire from the ground
forced him to give the chase away, and he turned around in
the valley and, heading toward the German lines, began to
ascend to clear the hills on which the artillery battery men
tioned and my battalion, a little further behind, were sta
tioned. It was at this stage that the ground fire became the
heaviest and closest, the men firing direct with rifles as he
passed.

"As he neared the battery from the valley his machine
came level with the guns, and as he continued to climb the
guns were able to follow him up. I consider that it was in this
position he was hit. Within a few seconds there was a distinct

altering of the machine in flight and it swerved away to where it crashed against the mound three to four hundred yards away, in a spot under direct observation by the enemy and considered dangerous during daylight hours.

"I may have been concentrating on the chase so much that I failed to notice, as claimed, that another machine was following up in the wake of the Baron. If so, I did not see it, and from the courses followed by the pursued and the pursuer it is to my mind very improbable that another machine was in the chase. . . ."

Another eyewitness, R. H. Barron of London, England, wrote to say in part: "I know that Colonel [sic] Brown has more or less been officially credited with the 'kill,' but in my mind, I cannot conceive how he ever came into the picture at all!"

Barron said that in 1935 he was in contact with a Mrs. Reginald Denny, wife of the English actor, who was a personal friend of the Baron's mother and that he gave Mrs. Denny an account of his views for the Baroness. Mrs. Denny was on her way to Berlin to visit the Rittmeister's mother. Barron received an acknowledgment from the Baroness for making her aware of what he had seen on April 21, 1918. She told him that she always refused to believe that her son "could ever be 'bested' by another airman."

Here is Barron's report: "On 21st of April, 1918, the 110 Section, F.A.A. Battery, Royal Garrison Artillery, consisting of two 13/18 pounder mobile guns, was in action on the side of the Bray-Corbie Road. At the time we were attached to the Australian Division, having just come through the retreat from St. Quentin with the Fifth Army under General Sir Hubert Gough, and having been posted to the Fourth Army under Lord Rawlinson.

"The Australians were holding a line in front of a ridge of high ground, running parallel with the road, and about a quarter of a mile away. Australian Field Batteries were in position between us and the ridge. The day had been fairly quiet from a flying point of view on our sector, so that we were somewhat surprised to see suddenly a Sopwith Camel coming in from the German lines at full speed, and so low that it seemed only just to clear the top of the ridge. Immediately behind and sitting on the tail, was the red Fokker triplane flown by Baron von Richthofen. The Baron was putting bursts of machine-gun fire into the Camel with great impartiality. We immediately came into action, together with our Lewis guns, and the Lewis guns attached to the Australian field batteries also opened fire. After a few shots, the Baron executed an Immelman turn, and went down at a steep angle just over the ridge.

"Some accounts state that his plane made a perfect landing—but this was decidedly not the case, he crashed rather badly, although he was flying so low that he did not actually 'pile-up' his machine. The crash is confirmed by a German artillery observer (Lieutenant Schoenemann), who states in his diary that Richthofen 'came down at an angle of forty-five degrees, and it was impossible for any man to have survived such a crash.'

"The Baron was quite dead when we reached him. Until quite recently I have always considered that our guns shot him down, but I have since been assured by my section officer, who conducted the shoot, that he put up a barrage between the triplane and the Camels to try to save our men, and in this he was successful.

"Richthofen then apparently realized for the first time where he was, and turned away. In doing this, he was undoubtedly caught by the Australian machine gunners, and received his fatal wounds.

"One of the British pilots [May] visited our guns later in the same day, and thanked our C.O. and informed him that the machine guns on his Camel had jammed, and that was why he had not engaged the Baron."

Barron concluded his account: "It cannot be too highly emphasized that Richthofen was not, and could not, have been shot from the air. In the first place, no British plane—other than the Camel—was in sight at the time, and, secondly, even had the Camel's machine guns been in working condition, the fact that they could only fire forwards through the propeller, would have made it an impossibility, as the triplane was directly behind and slightly above the British plane."

W. A. Audsley of Sidney, who commanded the 108th Battery, Australian Field Artillery, AIF, sharply disputes the RAF's contention that Brown slew Richthofen. In several letters to the authors, Audsley said: ". . . at the time, our position was on high ground overlooking the Somme near

Vaux. We had, as antiaircraft defense, Lewis machine guns mounted on poles on each flank of the gun position. These were always kept loaded with double drums ready for instant action.

"On the day in question, we observed a dogfight going on fairly high in the air in front of us between a mob of our Sopwith Camels and about an equal number of German planes. Suddenly two planes peeled off and headed toward us, the German plane in pursuit of our Camel. By the time they reached us they were only about one hundred feet or so up and our machine guns were blazing hotly at the German plane. Suddenly he went up in the air, looped over to the right and dived into the ground about two hundred yards from us. I, with others in the battery, rushed over and pulled the pilot out of the wreck.

"Thus ended the career of Richthofen and his famous Circus, which had been a thorn in the side of the Allied air force fighter pilots during World War I. Quite a controversy arose as to how he was shot down, but it is my belief that he flew directly into a hail of machine-gun bullets from the ground and that the fire from the Lewis guns of the 108th Battery played no small part, as he was flying very low and the range was very close.

"Records give credit to a Canadian named Brown who was flying the Camel for shooting down R.[3] I cannot agree with this as Brown could not have fired towards the rear which he would have to do while being closely pursued by R. The guns on a Camel could only shoot through the prop. I am still firmly convinced of the opinion, R was shot from the ground."

IV

Dr. F. C. Florance of Sidney, Australia, also reports that he never saw a second Camel chasing behind the Baron. At the time, Florance was attached to the 30th Australian Infantry Battalion, which was resting in a quarry along the Somme River near Vaux.

His account follows: "... in the morning of that day, a red triplane with the black cross of Germany flew very low

[3]Authors' Note: Audsley also confuses Brown for May.

overhead coming on us suddenly in close pursuit of a British plane, the latter evidently trying to escape. He was flying very low, perhaps in order to help ground fire to assist him to throw off, or shoot down his adversary. The Lewis guns, always mounted on swivels when in support or reserve positions against hostile aircraft, were being brought into action, but by this time the two planes had disappeared across the area of sky seen from the quarry, and shortly we heard that the red triplane had been shot down and was the plane of Capt. von Richthofen."

F. B. Hinton, a retired brigadier general and a patron of the Royal Australian Armoured Corps Association, wrote from Sidney that Brown "never, in my opinion, fired on Richthofen."

"At the time," he wrote, "I was commanding a machine-gun company with forward guns in antiaircraft positions, forward and up in the vicinity of Corbie Hill. I saw the whole fight and—while it has been written and many exaggerations have taken place—I am perfectly satisfied that the German ace was brought down by a burst of machine-gun fire, which was under the command of Sergeant Popkin of my company.

"The action, as I saw it, was out of the clouds far in the east and from a great height came a Camel with a plane right on its tail, which ultimately turned out to be Richthofen's. No fire was coming from the triplane, and no fire was coming from the Camel which seemed to be only anxious to get clean away. The dive was a steep one, and the climax came when the Camel came to within a few hundred feet of the ground and then flew over a steep ridge, and turned north, hurrying back to his base.

"On the disengagement of the two planes, the way was open for the machine guns to open up. They could not fire before May was out of the road. The Baron was diving in a direct line for the machine-gun commanded by Popkin. He opened fire immediately, and it was all over in a matter of seconds, when Richthofen wobbled and dived to the ground. Before the actual finale, everything that could fire in the way of light antiaircraft missiles was firing, and this included Lewis guns, which were attached to Artillery on the reverse slope of the ridge above Corbie."

"I was not in a position," the brigadier said, "to see what

happened to the plane, but within a few minutes I received word from my forward guns by telephone that Popkin had been successful in bringing down Richthofen. I immediately reported the action to the commander of the 4th Machine-gun Battalion, Colonel Murray, V. C., who I think discredited my statement, as his only reply was: 'That's good. Go on bringing them down.'

"I make this statement because I feel that, had Colonel Murray appreciated the situation at once, there would have been no doubt that the credit would have gone to Sergeant Popkin . . . [who] later lost a leg in the First War."

Confident, too, that Richthofen was felled by ground fire is J. A. Nugent of Melbourne, Australia. Nugent was attached to the Australian 10th Field Ambulance, 3rd Division, on April 21, 1918.

He wrote: "I was in close proximity to where it happened. A dogfight was in progress some considerable distance away. The Baron appeared to cut off one of our planes and followed it down at close range and putting frequent machine-gun fire into it. When it appeared from our position they hit a hill top because of the angle they were flying, our plane skipped the peak and, I think, the Baron, realizing he was so low and so far behind our lines, suddenly shot upwards, banked to the right, then dived to the ground.

"As no other plane was near the two of them, I feel certain he was shot down from the ground. I have often wondered if Captain Brown got a kill from the same fight on the same day, which may have happened elsewhere."

A key witness to the view that the Red Baron died from ground fire is retired Maj. Gen. L. E. Beavis of Victoria, Australia. In several letters to the authors, he gave the following account:

"As the officer commanding the 53rd Battery, 5th Division, AIF, I am intimately associated with the claim that one of the two antiaircraft Lewis guns of the battery was responsible for the destruction of Richthofen. I was a close eyewitness of the circumstances, and as I had Richthofen's body brought from the aeroplane to my dugout before it was called for by an RAF tender, there is no question of the identity of the airman.

"Briefly the circumstances were these. On the morning of April 21, 1918, we watched from the battery position, which was a very short distance on the western slope of the ridge which runs north between the Ancre and the Somme, the air fight in the vicinity of Sailly-le-Sec, some two miles to the east of the battery. . . . Whilst watching, a telephone message came from the battery observation post, situated near the stone windmill on the north side of the Somme, about mid-way between the battery and the air fight, that a British aeroplane and a red aeroplane, which was pursuing it, were flying in the general direction of the battery. In a very short time, the aeroplanes appeared in view flying low along the west-east valley of the Somme.

"Keeping on this general course brought them, owing to the right-angle turn of the Somme to the south, close to the crest of the transverse spur on which we were stationed. At the time I estimated their height as one hundred and fifty feet. The British Sopwith Camel was deviating to right and left for protection and the red plane was trying to keep dead on his tail. The Lewis gunners were standing to their two guns, which were mounted on posts and fitted with the A.A. ring sights. As soon as the Sopwith Camel was clear of the line of fire, the guns opened fire. Immediately, the red triplane turned sharply to the north, because somewhat un-steady in its flight, then went about northeast, and hit the ground about four hundred yards north-northeast of where the Lewis guns were.

"There was no third plane in the vicinity, certainly not within a radius of at least two thousand yards. In fact, there were none to be seen nearer than the fight still going on over Sailly-le-Sec. . . . As is known, corroborative medical evidence is to the effect that one bullet entered on the right side of the back, was deflected by the spine, and exited on the left side in the vicinity of the heart. With such a wound, Richthofen could not have continued to pursue his intended victim, so it is plain that the wound was received just before the crash.

"The junior Air Force medical officers who examined the body were of the opinion that the wound could only have been sustained from the air. This, which might be called circumstantial evidence, conflicts with the direct evidence disproving this theory, it would be difficult, if not impossible, to say whether a bullet came from the ground or the air, considering the inclination of an aeroplane, especially a small fighting aeroplane, on the turn, and the fact that a bullet may be deflected by striking a portion of the aeroplane before hitting the pilot, Colonel G. W. Barber, an Australian Medical Service physician, examined the body and he has placed on record that the wound 'was just as would be sustained as result of a bullet from the ground while the machine was banking.'

"In his official report of the occurrence," the retired general continued, "Captain A. R. Brown says he 'dived on large formation of fifteen to twenty Albatros Scouts, D.V's and Fokker triplanes, two of which got on my tail and I came out. Went back again and dived on pure red triplane which was firing on Lieutenant May. I got a long burst into him and he went down vertical.' This report indicates, that the aeroplane attacked was brought down near the main fight, since Captain Brown says he 'went back again dived on the enemy machine.' Actually, as explained above, Richthofen crashed some two miles west of the main fight, which was in the vicinity of Sailly-le-Sec. The statements that he 'went down vertical' indicates a spin, or nose dive, or something of that sort. Actually, as stated above, the triplane was only about one hundred and fifty feet up, and on ceasing to pursue the Camel, it only lost height gradually since it struck the ground about four hundred yards away.

"The conclusion to be drawn from this is that Captain Brown somewhere near the main 'mix-up' fired on some other plane which was pursuing a British plane and brought it down 'vertical.' His official report gives no indication of the locality where he shot the aeroplane down, beyond being near Vaux-sur-Somme, and it would also appear that he presumes the identity of the enemy pilot. Besides Richthofen, at least one other red triplane was brought down in the neighborhood of Cerisy and no doubt Captain Brown brought down this one or one of them—and has made a mistake in regard to place and identity of the enemy pilot. . . .

"The manner in which Richthofen met his death may be historically unimportant, but what is important is that no doubt should be cast on the accuracy of the official history. If by chance the official history says that an RAF pilot shot the great German aviator down, the tendency will be to doubt the accuracy of other narratives of events, at least in the minds of the hundreds—possible thousands of eyewitnesses—who could see with their own eyes, that Richthofen was not shot down by one of our fighters.

"I have in my possession messages of congratulations from headquarters, Fourth Army, headquarters, Fifth Australian Division, and most important of all, headquarters, 9th Infantry Brigade, Third Australian Division, which occupied the sector and placed a guard on the wrecked machine a few minutes after it crashed. The 9th Infantry Brigade, with its hundreds of eyewitnesses would not have given the credit to a ground unit, incidentally of another division, had an attack by a second British aeroplane taken place, and cast doubt on the claims put forward for the Lewis gunners."

V

F. L. Carter, now living in Katunga, Australia, but a member of the 42nd Battalion, AIF, in 1918, sent along the following account to the authors: "The event is loosely stated to have taken place over the Australian lines. In actual fact, it was a few miles behind. My unit . . . had been withdrawn from Sailly-le-Sec to a position behind the crest of a ridge known to us as the 'Whistler Ridge' near Corbie, the ridge gaining its name from a tall brick-kiln chimney there, with so many shell holes through it that it resembled that particular instrument. Before is the country sloped down to the 'line.' . . . Over this area, the apex of the German March push, aerial activity was frequent and we had erected scores of Lewis guns on improvised shoulder-high turrets 'just in case.'

"One day a plane, flying low from the direction of Sailly-le-Sec, skimmed the top of the ridge and there was a rush for the gun posts. There were cries of 'She's right. One of ours!' and 'Must have been hit!' Then almost at once, 'There comes a Jerry!' The second plane was a German and obviously in pursuit of the first. It was unfortunate for him that the first plane had flown straight over us, presumably on his way to his aerodrome, for which we were in a direct line, and had so caused every gun to be manned.

"As the German plane came over the ridge, at not more than a couple of hundred feet, he 'copped the lot.' He went into a brief climb and then banked sharply to the right—we could see right into the cockpit—falling away into an almost vertical dive into the ground. Cheers went up and a lot of fellows went off to see the plane. ... I was shortly afterwards detailed to go with a party to the town of Daours where we were told later that the airman shot down was von Richthofen."

Malcolm Moore of Queensland, Australia, held the same view, as noted in the following account he forwarded:

"... I was as were many others an eyewitness to the occurrence, and there is no possible doubt that the Baron was shot down by machine-gun fire from the ground. The only two planes in sight when the Baron was shot down was [*sic*] Lieut. May's going for his life a few feet off the ground and Richthofen right at his tail. Directly the two planes reached the 53rd AFA battery, with its antiaircraft battery attached. The antiaircraft fired a burst and Richthofen's plane veered away and crashed in a gully in front of 53rd Battery's gun positions. Some of the troops ran to the crash, but I didn't ... I was a corporal in the 53rd Battery at the time. We were right on the spot when the plane was hit and there definitely was no other plane in the sky at the time. Gunner Buie was given the credit for shooting Richthofen down. ..."

Another ground observer was W. J. Lawler of Brisbane who hotly disputes the RAF contention that Richthofen was shot down from the air.

"... I was facing the German lines and out to my left front there was a dogfight going and we all stood up and watched it, and the next thing two planes came away from the flight and flew toward the ground and we could see that it was one of Richthofen's red planes chasing a British plane. They were both at the rear of our front-line trench.

"I was in the 53rd Machine-gun Company in the rear of the boys that were in the trenches and the plane came down between their position and ours. I heard Richthofen give a small burst into the British plane and when they got a couple of hundred feet from the ground two machine guns opened up. Being a machine gunner myself, I could tell the difference of the two guns. One was a Lewis gun and the other was a Vickers. Which one of the two got him I could not say. But to be fair, I would say they both got him. ... I can assure you there was no other within firing range of Richthofen and the British plane he was chasing. That is what I saw and I don't see what good I would get out of it by telling you lies about it. . . ."

E. M. Barker, writing from Cottesloe, Western Australia, said: "At the time I was lieutenant in the 38th Australian Infantry Battalion . . . near the small town of Heilly in France.

"There was a dogfight going on between British and German planes fairly high up and we suddenly saw a British . . . plane coming towards the ridge, apparently looking for a place to make a forced landing. Diving on it from the rear was a red German triplane whose pilot was trying to shoot down the plane before it got away. As it got to the ridge, the triplane flattened out just as a Lewis gunner dug in there, opened fire on it at short range. The triplane swerved to one side and crashed.

"We were three or four hundred yards away, but did not go to the crashed plane because of the idea that the Germans might shell the area to catch the troops there. In my mind there was no doubt that the Lewis gunner shot the triplane down. I do not remember seeing another British plane behind the German plane and within range of it. Many years later I read a claim that the plane was shot down by another diving on it from behind, but I did not pay much attention to it."

R. N. Bodington, formerly of the 10th Australian Field Ambulance and now living in Melbourne, wrote to say this about the Baron: ". . . I actually saw him shot from the ground by an Australian machine gunner about two hundred yards from where I was. I was delivering a dispatch to one of the battalions and walking along the top of the high bank on the side of the Somme River when I stopped to watch a real good air fight over the front line about two miles away.

"About five minutes later I was surprised to see one of the planes break away and come in my direction and closely followed and plastered by a Fritz plane. They continued to come directly towards me and when they were almost above me a machine gunner on my left opened up and immediately the plane shot straight up into the air for about five hundred yards and then nosed dived into a brick kiln approximately quarter of a mile away.

"I walked over to the gunner who was a member of an Australian machine-gun company and told him that he had shot the plane down and he agreed with me. There was no other gun firing and there was no other plane visible in the sky."

P. A. Penny of Cairns, sent along the following report: ". . . my rank, bombardier, 49th Battery, 13th Field Artillery Brigade, 5th (Australian) Division. We were on the Somme at the time not far away from Bonnay, to be correct, between Bonnay and Vaux-sur-Somme. On a very fine morning of the 21st April 1918 our air scout of spotter, a gunner by the name of Ack Young blew the whistle for all to get under cover as German planes were in sight. I had three Lewis machine guns mounted for antiaircraft work. My gunners were Gunner A. Barker and Gunner Lech Lee and myself. Well, when Ack blew the whistle we stood to, and believe me, we did not wait long when coming right at us, about eighty feet in the air, was the red plane. We gave him all we had. We were firing one armour-piercing bullet every four and one tracer bullet in every two, so you see three Lewis guns firing at the rate of about four hundred and fifty to five hundred a minute must have done some damage. Of course, my guns were not the only ones firing at this plane. Vickers and Lewis guns must have caused a lot of damage . . ."

VI

R. B. Oliver, Glenside, South Australia, wrote that he "well remembered the occasion of the death of Baron von Richthofen. At the time I was a sergeant serving with the 11th Field Battery, R. A. Engineers, AIF, and had been in France since October 1916. On the day in question, I was returning to our advanced position in the line from a visit to our headquarters when suddenly I saw away to the east a dogfight going on between British and German airmen. . . . Suddenly two planes singled out from the melee and headed straight in my direction (westward). As they came above me . . . the leading one (British), trying to get away from the German, turned south with the German in hot pursuit. Just after both planes had turned south, I heard a Lewis gun open up not far away from me. . . . My opinion was then and still is that Richthofen's plane and himself too were hit by bullets from the A.A. Lewis guns . . . I cannot see that the pilot of the British plane would claim that he had shot down the German ace. He was too busy trying to get away."

R. B. Zimmerman of East Brisbane, Australia, said: "... about the Red Baron, or the Red Devil, as we called him, a cobber and I happened to be going up to our (42nd) Battery with pack ammunition and were on a ridge facing another ridge when we heard a plane coming. We got off the road under some trees and over the ridge opposite one of our planes came first and then the Baron behind him and he gave the chap in front of him a burst. Our plane dived toward a gully at the right. The red plane banked to turn back and as he did so a machinegun on our left opened up and gave him a burst, in fact, two bursts and he dived into a gully on our right. We both said, 'Well that's the end of the Red Devil.' That was the only two planes in sight at the time ... and so far as I'm concerned it was the machine gun on our left that brought him down."

Dr. R. A. Money of Bellevue Hill, N.S.W., Australia, reported that he "was on duty at the guns of my battery, the 107 Howitzer Battery, on the ridge of Morlancourt on the eventful day, and I think the paragraph which I marked in the attached photostat copy of a letter, sent to my brother on that day, will let you have the information you desire. In case you cannot read it clearly, it runs as follows:

"One of our M.G.'s brought down a Boche aeroplane today. The pilot was the famous Baron Richthofen. We read it on his identity disc. He had two bullets through his heart."[4]

The following is the report of former Lt. George M. Travers, M. C., of Balranald, Australia. It is a duplicate of the one he handed in to the commanding officer of the 53rd Battalion.

"I had no idea a Canadian had claimed the victory over Richthofen. Where was he? Like the snow-shoe rabbit of Canada, I suppose. Invisible. . . . That's why I couldn't get him focused into my glasses. And I was on top of Corbie Hill and could see for miles around on either side. There wasn't another plane ... except Richthofen's and Wop May's. May, if he is still alive, will tell you that his guns jammed in the fight that morning over the German lines. That was why he left the fight. . . .

[4]Authors' Note: Richthofen's wound was so extensive that many men who saw it thought more than one bullet hit the same spot.

"My runner, Private Webber, was with me. I had the two planes in view, coming straight toward us for two or three miles. They came straight along the line of the Somme to Corbie Hill. Richthofen was very close to the tail of the other plane and firing at it when he was within a few hundred yards of us. Just then a machine gun, down below us, fired three or four bursts and Richthofen's plane seemed to turn on its side, right itself again, then swerve sharply to the right and swoop gradually to the ground and land half a mile away."

John Brake of Mont Albert, Australia, related how he heard the sounds of airplanes approaching and looked out from the headquarters' dugout of the 11th Australian Infantry Brigade. The location was also the headquarters of 8th Australian Field Artillery Brigade. Brake said, ". . . our range of view was very limited—actually only to skywards, owing to the trees of the wood in which the dugout was located. We saw R right overhead and turning northwards . . . R then circled round and crashed out of our views, whilst May broke away in a westerly direction. I am certain there was not any plane behind R as we emerged from the dugout (on the west side of Corbie Hill)."

A very descriptive report of the Baron's death was received from R. A. Wood. He wrote: "I was a '2 Star Artist' and with my platoon was occupying a switch trench, which in case of a German attack was to be occupied by my battalion— the 51st—which was in billets in Corbie. Mine was a self-contained little 'show' even to the extent of a cooker (field kitchen) because the battalion was approximately four miles away.

"I was idling away the time in my own 'possie' when I suddenly heard yells from the cooks to the effect that they were being fired upon and that the cooker had been hit and damaged. It was then seen that there were three planes flying low and chasing each other; the center plane was a red triplane and occupied by Richthofen. He was firing at the first plane, and was in turn being fired at by plane number three.

"As soon as the planes had passed overhead my platoon opened up with rifle fire and two sets of machine or Lewis guns on my left opened fire. Richthofen was seen to crash soon after one of these bursts. It was not much of a fall as he was flying very low, in fact it seemed as tho' he carried on and eventually the plane hit the ground. He fell about three hundred to four hundred yards from my position. I at once called for a section of my platoon to mount guard and with them rushed over to the machine. . . .

"As far as I can remember one bullet wound was noticed but this I could not be sure of as the Baron was fully clad. This is corroborated by General Barker and the statements of French medicos . . . and entirely backs up my contention that one of my platoon was responsible, because if a machine gun had caused the death, either fired from the ground or the air, then I should think that there would be more than one bullet wound in the body.

"I am fully convinced that all the third plane 'hit'—in which must have been Capt. Brown—was the cooker belonging to the 51st Battalion, and which resulted in the men losing half of their lunch. My platoon also was certain that this is what happened as evidenced by the loud 'moanings' against the pilot at lunch time."

Certain that the ground gunners shot down the Flying Uhlan is seventy-four-year-old O. E. Smith of Brisbane, Australia. He described the events of April 21 this way: "I was a private with the 44th Battalion, AIF, and I was with a party filling water tanks for the cooks by bucket brigade up the sloping banks of the Somme River. It was about 10 A.M. when we heard the whirr of engines, and we saw two planes flying north from the Villers-Bretonneux area. They were flying unusually low, no more than two hundred feet, parallel to and about a mile from the front line."

"As they approached," Smith said, "we identified them as a British plane being hotly pursued by a German plane. None of us had any idea it was Richthofen. It was just another German plane, just another dogfight. The British plane was taking frantic and evasive action, but the German was right behind him, duplicating every bank and roll. The German plane had the British plane in his sights all the time, but at no time did he use his machine guns. We reckoned he must have run out of ammo, and was trying to force the British plane into the ground by pure devilry.

"The British plane flew up over the ridge of Corbie Hill. Australian ground gunners from the 11th Brigade allowed the British plane to pass, and then opened up on the German.

Half a dozen of our blokes all fired at once as the German sailed overhead. Up until then there had not been a shot fired by anyone. And there definitely was not a third plane in view. It was obvious that the ground fire hit the German. His plane suddenly lost speed, wavered, and then slid slowly and gracefully down like a child's paper plane. It seemed that the pilot still had the plane in his control and was guiding it to a crash landing. He dipped out of view so I didn't see the actual crash. But we heard it. And you wouldn't believe it, there was hardly a cheer. To us it was just another German shot down, and we went on with our job of filling the water tanks. If only we had known we had bagged the mighty Baron, you would have heard the cheering for miles."

Smith continued: "The whole dogfight had been in my clear view and I was close enough to it to hear any shots. The German didn't fire any; the British pilot did not get a chance. And there was definitely no third plane. But I did see and hear the ground gunners, so the claim for the coveted kill must be split up among the six or so Australian ground gunners."

Of all the ground witnesses who saw Richthofen's fall, no one undoubtedly was in a better position to watch it than George Ridgway of Lang Lang, Australia, who is still corresponding with P. J. Carisella at this writing. Here is his report as he wrote it for this work:

"I was a signaler in the 29th Battery, 8th Brigade, 3rd Division, 1st AIF. At approximately 11 A.M. on April 21, 1918, in company with another lineman, I was repairing broken lines on the crest of the (Corbie) Hill, about one hundred yards from the Heilly chimney stack, when we heard aeroplanes firing above us and the spent bullets fell near us. Looking up we could see that three [sic] planes had broken away from the formation of a dozen or so, that were fighting about two miles up over Sailly Laurette in the German lines and were heading for us at an angle of approximately forty-five degrees. When about three quarters of a mile up, we could see that the first plane was British, the second a red German triplane, and the third plane British and about one hundred yards behind.

"The first plane began flying up and down—wavelike—to escape the bullets of the German who was only about one hundred feet behind, and maneuvering wavelike also he fired desperately at his quarry. We had a side view of them as they passed on our left about one hundred yards away and about two hundred feet up. Just before passing us, the last plane flew away to the left, and the other two carried on down the gully below us right above the wagon lines of Australian artillery and infantry camped in the gully.

"Machine guns opened fire from every direction about seven seconds after the last plane piloted by Capt. Brown turned to his left and left the chase. If Lt. May and Richthofen had carried straight on they must have flown into the side of the hill. The first plane then turned to the right. Richthofen turned to his right below the treetops and was lost to our view for about three seconds behind the trees, and then came up on the end of the hill, just skimming the ground, and making straight for the German lines, his flying angle approximately forty-five degrees.

"As he banked, we could see him sitting up quite clearly. When passing us on our right, about three hundred feet away and about three hundred feet up, we saw his head fall over to the left, and immediately the plane turned to its right and nosedived to the ground about one hundred yards in front of us, sending splinters and dust everywhere. It hit on its wheels and propeller and bounced about fifty yards into a heap of pitted mangels.

"We ran up and could see that the pilot was dead, his face was flat. He was dressed in a bearskin grayish flying suit, with only the face showing. He had no hat, helmet or goggles on[5] and his head was flattened, face upwards on the back of the plane. When the plane bounced it did not turn over. It rose about ten feet into the air and nosed onto the heap of pitted mangels. When they lifted him out of the plane, we could see a patch of blood below his right shoulder.

"The plane crashed a few yards from the Bray-Corbie sunken road in full view of the enemy. As hundreds of Australians ran up for souvenirs, the Germans began shelling. The plane was then dragged into the sunken roadway. I picked up a piece of splintered wood from where the plane first hit and it had the number plate on it, "MILITAAR FLUGZEUG FOKKER DR. 1425/17," which evidently was the plane's number.[6]

[5] Australian souvenir hunters beat Ridgway to the plane.
[6] Now in the Carisella collection.

"I consider that Richthofen flew at least a mile after Brown left the chase and that there was no aeroplane within a mile when he crashed. I think I can claim that I am the only person alive now who saw the crash. I am the only one who mentions the crash and bounce. All the wagon lines were in the gully, and the height of the hill from the Somme Valley to crest would be approximately three hundred and thirty feet as shown by contour of one hundred meters: Army map of Amiens 17.

"From the start of the battle, when we were getting spent bullets, until the crash, Richthofen flew approximately three and a half miles, which at one hundred and twenty miles per hour[7] would take one hundred and five seconds. Brown left the chase opposite Heilly [sic] at approximately seventy-five seconds. That is why many witnesses only claim there were two planes in the fight. It is incredible that out of the thousands of bullets fired at his plane, the only one that hit him was the one when his head fell over to the left. In another twenty seconds he would have been over his own lines.

"My regimental number was 22974. This is a true report by me, Councillor George Ridgway. J.P.M.M., Pioneer Road, Lang Lang, Victoria, Australia."

VII

No chapter dealing with the controversy itself would be complete without the inclusion of the reports of the ground gunners who actually claimed to have shot down the Red Baron. While any number of Aussie ground troops fired at the Baron's tripe as it swept up over Corbie Hill, including a number of riflemen, Australian authorities usually cite the following group as having had the best opportunity to score: Sgt. Cedric Bassett Popkin and Gnr. Rupert F. Weston of the 24th Machine-gun Company, 4th Division; Gunners Robert Buie and W. J. Evans of the 53rd Battery, 5th Division; and Sgt. Alfred G. Franklyn, F Battery A.A., Royal Horse Artillery, attached to the Australian Imperial Forces.

Carisella has corresponded for years with both Popkin and Weston and here is a compilation of their writings, first from

[7]120 mph is high; 100 mph was top for the DR-1.

Popkin, who actually fired the Vickers machine gun, and then from Weston, who handled the belt.

Popkin wrote: "I was in charge of four Vickers guns on the bank of the [Somme] canal between Sailly-le-Sec and Corbie and had a gun mounted for antiaircraft defense. About eleven o'clock a British and a German squadron started a battle in midair. Presently, two planes separated from the rest and headed for our lines, flying over Sailly-le-Sec. They came straight along the canal towards my gun. I immediately got into position and waited.

"On came the planes, the Britisher in front and about sixty feet in the air. They were so close together that I had to wait for the Britisher to pass. Then I opened up on the German machine—a red triplane. I fired about eighty rounds and he immediately turned at right angles to my position[8] and banked to clear the top of the ridge on the left of the canal looking towards the line. He then turned and I gave him another eighty rounds. The plane started to dive, described a half circle, and crashed into the ground on the top of the ridge near a quarry and facing Bonnay.

"I immediately rushed up the hill and on arrival a couple of minutes after the crash found the wrecked plane surrounded by infantry officers, who would not allow anybody to touch it. However, I stepped in and wrenched a piece off one of the wings for a souvenir. About an hour later an intelligence officer [Capt. Donald L. Fraser] of the 11th Brigade came and took my regimental particulars and told me who I had shot down. About six o'clock the same evening a liaison officer of the 52nd Battalion, with his report written out, saw me and he also took my regimental particulars to support my claim. The colonel of the 52nd also supported my claim, but owing to the report from company going in a week after the incident, I am afraid I got very little consideration."

Weston, who was Popkin's mate on the Vickers gun, forwarded these extracts from his diary for April 21, 1918:

"Our gun mounted antiaircraft, Sgt. Popkin, self No. 2 handling gun, witnessed a dogfight between a number of planes, ours and Fritz's. One of our scout planes was singled out by a Fritz triplane. Our plane at the mercy of the pursuing plane. Both planes came directly towards our gun

[8]About a mile west of Vaux-sur-Somme and half a mile north of the bend in the Somme.

position. The pilot of the all-red Fokker was continually firing bursts at the pursued plane to within about one hundred to one hundred and fifty yards of our position. It was at this point that we opened fire (Sgt. Popkin doing the actual shooting). A burst of about eighty rounds being directed at the German plane. This in my opinion did some damage and made the pilot aware of his danger. The plane was unsteady at this point. But the pilot was still in charge, for instead of continuing the chase, he doubled on his tracks to return home.

"Sgt. Popkin once more opened fire as the airman turned for home. This in my opinion proved fatal as the machine was at once out of control, gradually losing altitude and crashing into a dump where it came to grief. There is not a shadow of doubt in our minds that our gun was responsible for Richthofen's end. And I am quite certain that if we had not got him, he would have gotten away. I should say he was some three hundred feet up. It was only a matter of who fired first. Our gun was situated on hard ground in the open, with no protection of any sort.

"A British intelligence officer[9] some little time later came over to our gun and inquired as to who were the men who had handled it. He took Sgt. Popkin and my name, rank, etc. and told us that it was not possible for anyone else to claim the bringing down of that plane, as he himself had witnessed the whole thing. Many of the 5th Division, who witnessed the whole thing, also gave us the credit. During the day many congratulations were offered by different officers, including Lt. Col. J. Murray and Major F. B. Hinton. Major Hinton was asked to report on the matter. This he did. We believe that he received information to the effect that they (headquarters) could not give the credit to anyone in particular as another claim had been submitted and they feared international complications. To here from my diary."

Weston also forwarded Carisella an unusual clipping from an Australian newspaper, *Newcastle Sun*, to back up his claim that Richthofen was shot down by Aussie ground gunners. The report found in the newspaper following the war was supposedly written by a one-time German spy.

"At the time of the occurrence, I was attached to the

---

[9]Lieut. Fraser, who was Australian.

[German] army corps which was defending our front against the Australians, and as I was a good deal behind the enemy [Aussie] lines, you do not need much imagination to know what I was. I was seeking information about the Australian artillery that day when I spotted a plane flying very low, closely followed by another. And there was a third plane, but it was too far away to be in the fight. And Baron von Richthofen was too good an air fighter to be caught like that with another on his tail. Another thing that bears out my point [sic] is that when he was examined the bullet that killed him penetrated his back. As far as I can remember it was the 55th Battery. I was the one who reported his [Richthofen's] death to the [German] high commander. And in my report, I stated that the Baron had met his death from bullet wounds inflicted by Australian machine gunners. . . . For obvious reasons I am not disclosing my identity, hoping that your readers do not bear any animosity toward me. I do not, for I used to take my hat off to the Aussies. One always had to be so particular when you were behind their lines; they used to ask so many questions."

VIII

Next we come to the actions of Gunners Buie and Evans on the day the Flying Uhlan fell. Their deeds are reported only by Buie as "Snowy" Evans died shortly after the war.

Buie begins his account thus: "At 10:45 A.M. on April 21, 1918, near Villers-Bretonneux, a squadron of our planes was intercepted by the Richthofen Circus.[10] Two planes were shot down and a third corkscrewed from the melee and fell towards the ground. Suddenly, however, the plane flattened out and made for home over our lines. A German plane gave chase and was gaining rapidly on our plane firing short bursts all the time. They were both flying at a very low level and were the only two planes in the vicinity of Vaux-sur-Somme.

"Then Major Beavis, our C.O., received a telephone message. It came from a forward observation post. It said the two planes were flying directly down the valley towards us. I cleared my Lewis gun, which was post mounted for antiaircraft use. It held a pannier of forty-five .303 caliber bullets,

[10]Buie died on Anzac Day, 1964.

four of which were tracers equally spaced at every tenth spot.[11] We had orders to fire at any time. But I was prevented from firing immediately because Lt. May's plane was almost in a line with Richthofen's. At the time Major Beavis and Lieutenant Doyle were on my right and left respectively. Both were about thirty yards away. Capt. Ellis, to my front, shouted to me: 'Fire on that plane, Buie!' Still I had to hold my fire out of fear of hitting May.

"Snowy Evans, manning the other Lewis gun to left forward, got his clearance first and opened fire. The range was just over three hundred yards. The triplane was only about sixty feet behind and some ten feet above May and firing short bursts at the Camel. My finger was on the trigger and I was eager to fire. My chance was coming. I had my peep sight directly fixed on the Baron. I can still remember how he looked. His face was mostly covered by his helmet and goggles. He sat hunched. It appeared that every time he fired a burst he leaned forward in deep concentration. I am sure he was not aware of the danger of his position or the proximity of our guns.

"I finally opened fire when he was about two hundred yards distant. I gave him steady bursts. His tripe was flying frontal and just a bit to the right of me. I could see my bullets striking the right side and forward section of his machine. Fragments could be seen flying off. But the Baron came right on, both his guns firing at May. Just as my last shots blazed out at a range of forty yards, the tripe's guns stopped firing. It was then that I was certain that I had hit him.[12] There was a sharp change in the triplane's engine sound as it passed and flew fifty feet over our gun position. We were posted on some rising ground, a couple of hundred yards in front of the crest of the peninsula between the waters of the Somme and the Ancre.

"While we watched the German machine lost speed and the propeller began to slow down. The machine still appeared to be under control though. The tripe swerved a bit to the right and then to the left. It lost height gradually and crashed near an abandoned brick kiln, some four hundred yards

[11]Authors' Note: So Buie stated, although the Lewis gun drum held 47 rounds, 97 rounds in a double-drum.

[12]Evans, too, had been firing.

distant on the Bray-Corbie Road. His plane did not fall to earth in a heap as some suggest. It came down as if he was bringing it down, although on landing the wings and fuselage were damaged fairly."

Buie remained by his gun, along with Evans. Within a few minutes, several Aussies brought back the word that the dead pilot was Richthofen. Buie's mates crowded around him and offered their congratulations. The gunner first saw the Baron's body about half an hour later at the headquarter's dugout of the 53rd Battery. Major Bearis had claimed the body for the battery and had it brought back on a stretcher.

Buie also makes the interesting statement that Captain Brown visited his post in the early afternoon. He said that Brown was accompanied by Lieutenant Colonel Cairns, the Wing Commander of No. 209 Squadron. Buie said he and his mates were amazed to hear that Brown claimed to have brought Richthofen down. Brown appeared to be sincere, but Major Beavis and the other battery officers would not buy any part of his contention. Buie vehemently contends that Brown's Camel was not in the vicinity when the Baron was downed: "No planes pursued Richthofen. There was only Lt. May chased by Richthofen. Two planes only! There was no third plane in my line of vision when I saw the two planes crossing the front lines two miles away."

Buie notes that he was still up front a month later when British Army Headquarters finished its inquiry and announced its official decision. A dispatch from General Rawlinson, commander of the British Fourth Army, was forwarded to the 53rd Battery and to Buie and apparently gave them the credit for shooting down the Baron. Buie said that the findings of the inquiry stated that "after careful consideration and the weighing of all evidence, it has been proved beyond a doubt that No. 3801, Gunner Robert Buie, 53rd Battery, was responsible for the destruction of Baron von Richthofen."

Buie felt that "surely that should be enough to settle the statement that General Rawlinson's thanks and congratulations were addressed to the 53rd Battery. Soon after the telegram came, three other generals visited the battery and congratulated the gunners. They were Generals Sir William Birdwood, Bessell-Brown and Hobbs. I met them all personally and General Birdwood said to me: 'It was a great pity that such a good man as Richthofen was shot dead. It would have been splendid had he been only wounded and taken prisoner. Nevertheless, he is better out of the way as he was very destructive towards our men.' These were his own words. I told him that I was proud to have been the man who brought him down. General Birdwood nodded and touched me on the arm. His last words to me were: 'Good luck and good-bye. Keep on bringing them down, Buie.' I saluted and told him that I would do my best.

"When General Hobbs spoke to me he asked about the gunsight. I told him that it was a makeshift sight as our new ones had not arrived yet from Ordnance. He asked me if he could have it as a souvenir. I gave it to him and he sent me one from Ordnance. The makeshift sight was made by Fitter Bartlett of the 53rd Battery out of an eighteen-pounder shell case. After General Hobbs' death, the gunsight was placed on display in the Australian War Memorial in Canberra.

In a letter, years ago, to Carisella, General Hobbs wrote that he was convinced that the shot which killed Richthofen was fired by men of his command—i.e., Gunners Buie and Evans—"one or both, although the weight of evidence at the time seemed that Gunner Buie was really responsible." General Hobbs supplemented his letter by a report based on the evidence of eye witnesses presented to him immediately after the event.

The report mentioned Richthofen's pursuit of the British plane and adds: "He had now left the Somme Valley and come over the high ground north of Corbie, the machine not being more than one hundred and fifty feet up. . . . Richthofen was firing into the machine before him but it was difficult for the Lewis gunners to shoot owing to the British plane being in their line of fire. They accordingly waited until the British plane had passed.

"Richthofen's plane was not more than one hundred yards from each when they were able to fire directly into the person of the aviator. The plane turned NE being still under fire from Lewis guns. It was now staggering as though out of control. Further effective bursts were fired. Plane veered to north and crashed. The aviator was already dead . . . Richthofen was a great adversary. It was fitting that he should have fallen in the old Roman fashion with all wounds to the front. . . . The Lewis gunners who brought down the machine were: No. 3801 Gnr. R. Buie and No. 598 Gnr. W. J. Evans of the 53rd Bty., 14th AFAB, 5th Australian Divisional Artillery."

Asked what he thought of the Canadian claim and the suggestion that the diggers should go fifty-fifty with the Canadians in taking credit for shooting down the great ace, Buie disposed of them with one unprintable word.

Lieutenant Colonel Frank, the C.O. of the 14th Australian Field Artillery Brigade, which included the 53rd Battery, always contended that Gunners Buie and William John Evans were responsible for Richthofen's death. A witness of the event, he cites General Rawlinson's telegram to substantiate the claim of the 53rd Battery, along with the official report of the battery, which states:

"At about 10:30 A.M. on April 21, 1918, the distant rat-a-tat-tat of a dull and muffled nature that distinguished the sound of machine guns fired in the air from those on the ground drove us out of our dugouts to the ridge, on which our guns were situated, to locate the planes which we suspected would be *fighting*.

"A great battle was in progress. One enemy triplane, after circling around the fighting planes, suddenly singled out a British plane from a bunch. The attack was so direct that the British plane was driven towards the earth. We all thought the fight was over, but although hard pressed the Britisher, by some miraculous means, when almost on the ground, got clear of his relentless pursuer, headed west at top speed and came over the undulating tableland between the Somme Valley and the River Ancre directly toward us. He (the German) failed, apparently, to notice he had left his own lines far behind.

"On came the two mighty birds of prey—the triplane gaining steadily. We gazed fascinated as they flew over the wood on our left. A single machine gun fired by the 24th Australian Machine-gun Company spoke from the ground. The whirl of the machines came louder.

"Our antiaircraft Lewis gunners mounted on the rear of their guns trained on the advancing planes, which were one hundred and fifty feet from the ground. By this time the triplane was so close that the Lewis gunners had to wait until the British plane—a Sopwith Camel—had passed before fire could be opened.

"Our gunners opened fire at a range of not more than one hundred yards [sic] directly upon the body of the pilot. Both Buie and Evans were able to draw a bead sight upon the body of the Baron. After the first burst of fire the triplane staggered, but continued advancing, but further bursts caused it to veer northward. It crashed to the ground near the compound which housed German prisoners.

"A rush was made to the spot where the brave Baron had fought his last fight. The coolness and markmanship of Gunners Buie and Evans undoubtedly saved the British plane from certain destruction."

Buie was a small, dark man who was described by a friend, Gordon Allen of Calga, Australia, as "a quiet sort of chap. It was generally considered around these parts [Calga] that he could have shot down Richthofen. But he never boasted about it." Buie enlisted in the Australian Army in October 1916. He sailed for France in January 1917. On the night of August 8, 1918, his twenty-fifth birthday, he suffered a heart attack and was invalided home. A professional fisherman, he never fully recovered his health and was twice denied a war pension. Undecorated to the end, in 1964, he died of a heart attack while fishing. To the day he died, he insisted that the "honor of destroying Germany's top ace belongs to Australia."

IX

The final ground gunner, who still claims to this day that he shot down Richthofen, is Alfred George Franklyn of Leigh-on-the-sea, Essex, England. On April 21, 1918, Sergeant Franklyn of the Royal Horse Artillery was a member of the 110th Section, F Battery A.A., British Expeditionary Force, attached to the Australians. In 1913, he had joined the Essex County Constabulary and transferred to the Borough Force when it was formed on April 1, 1914. He returned to the police force after the war and served as a sergeant for seventeen years before retiring.

In his correspondence with Carisella, he recalled his actions on April 21, 1918, in the following manner:

"At the time I was a sergeant in charge of two antiaircraft guns stationed in a sunken road [Bray-Corbie Road] 880 yards east of Bonnay where Richthofen's Circus, as we knew them, were patrolling the line flying at a height of 10,000 to 15,000 feet. Whilst we were engaging them with our 13-18 pound antiaircraft guns Richthofen suddenly left his Circus and dived towards us.

"At the same time two of our Sopwith Camels were returning to their base, probably the aerodrome at Bertangles. The British planes were to the left of our gun position and we could not continue firing at Richthofen with our antiaircraft guns owing to his stunting and low elevation. This caused me to run for my Lewis gun which was fixed on a post on the bank of the sunken road.

"Whilst Richthofen was following the two [sic] Sopwith Camels I fired at him—one round in every four being a tracer bullet, so that the course of the bullets could be observed. He then crashed to the ground about two hundred yards away from my position, the gun crews of my section witnessing the incident. Standing at the side of me at the time were two Australian sergeants, one of whom remarked, 'You've got him, digger.' I replied, 'Yes, he is down all right.'

"Being in charge of the guns I could not leave the position so sent Corporal Benthem to the plane. Upon his return he informed me that the pilot was dead and handed me a piece of the plane which I brought home. The bringing down of the plane was reported to my H.Q. F. Battery, A.A. About an hour afterwards a large motor came to our position from the aerodrome with a high official of the RAF, also one of the pilots of the Sopwith Camels, who had been chased by Richthofen. They asked me how it occurred and both congratulated me. I asked the pilot why he did not engage him and he replied stating his machine guns had jammed. Later an RAF tender came up and took the body away.

"At the time Richthofen was brought down, the Sopwith Camels were retreating and therefore could not have engaged him. As I was a qualified aircraft spotter and rangefinder I knew every type of Allied and hostile machines flying on the front at the time.

"Since the war I have read several so-called reports by eyewitnesses as to how and where Richthofen was brought down. The accounts were ridiculous and I came to the conclusion that they knew little or nothing about it. Some of the so-called eyewitnesses even gave the wrong date and type of plane he was flying at the time of being brought down.

Many of the accounts I have contradicted, but up to now no person has done the same to mine which was published in the press some time ago."

In a letter to Carisella in the summer of 1968, Franklyn wrote: "I have had quite a lot of correspondence about Richthofen during the last fifty years and he was well in my thoughts during April this year. The correspondence that I have enclosed will probably answer all the questions in your letter . . ."

Franklyn noted that he was seventy-five years old this year and that he was feeling well except for rheumatism in his left leg. He is a grand old gentleman and a stout fellow who served his king and country well. However, Carisella believes that Franklyn is mistaken in his belief that he shot down Richthofen. The War Diary of the Fourth A.A. Defenses, to which Franklyn's battery was attached, states that an enemy plane was brought down by F Battery near the Somme. But the diary makes it vividly clear that the German bus was shot down on April 22, 1918, and not April 21, 1918. Franklyn, reading about Richthofen's death two days after the event saw the word "yesterday" in the account and thought it referred to April 21 when in truth it meant April 22. He thus believed the plane, which he undoubtedly brought down on April 22, was the Baron's, which had fallen the day before.

✙ ✙ ✙

Chapter 5

THE CRASH SCENE

✠ THE famed Red Knight of Germany was dead, his closely cropped head slumped forward against the butts of his Spandaus, the blue eyes opened and unseeing, his gloved hand still grasping the control stick. The watching Australians waited for a few moments for some signs of life from the all-red triplane. None came. The tripe sprawled alongside the Bray-Corbie Road, in the sunken ditch in the pile of mangels which were used for fertilizer by the French farmers. The Baron's bus had suffered little damage in his last landing. The propeller had been snapped off at one end, the bottom wings were slightly crumpled, and the wheels of the German craft were splayed outward.

Silence gripped the scene for a few more moments. The guns were stilled. The Aussie gunners were certain their well-directed and sustained fire had brought the Boche bus down. Confident that there was no immediate danger, a digger broke from his shelter and dashed to the side of the tripe. With one deft motion, he whipped the helmet off the

162

dead pilot's head and ran back to his cover.[1] Then a few more Australian ground troops headed for the plane. Like infantry men everywhere, they sought souvenirs of the incident, especially parts of the aircraft and strips of the parachute.[2]

One of the first men to arrive at the scene was Donald L. Fraser, the intelligence officer of the 11th Australian Infantry Brigade. In his report, he stated: "I ran out of the wood and over to where it [the plane] had fallen, about two hundred yards away, alongside the Bray-Corbie Road. . . . About six men reached the wrecked plane before me. I immediately undid the airman's safety belt, and got assistance to pull him from the wreckage, but he was quite dead and was considerably cut up about the face, and was apparently shot through the chest and body.

"As a large body of men were collecting [souvenirs], I requested Captain [G. L.] Adams, 44th Battalion, AIF, to place a guard over the plane to prevent looting and to disperse the crowd, as the spot was open to enemy observation, and I feared we would be shelled. A guard was duly placed over the machine, and the crowd dispersed.

"I searched the dead airman, taking his papers and personal effects, which consisted of a few papers, a silver watch, gold chain and medallion attached, and a pair of fur-lined gloves. I gave them to Captain C. C. Hillary of 11th Brigade Staff who took them down to our German speaker, Corporal Peters who, on investigation, gave the identification of the famous German airman, Baron von Richthofen.

"I reported this to General Cannan and 3rd Australian Division promptly. On General Cannan's direction, I went out to get particulars of the machine gunners who had brought the plane down, and found Sergeant Popkin of 24th Australian M.G. Company, at his antiaircraft M.G. at J.23.b.3.7 [approx.] Somme Valley.

"At this time I was not aware that any other M.G. had been firing at this plane. I congratulated Sergeant Popkin on his successful shot, but afterwards found out that two A.A.

---

[1]Moments later he was ordered to return the helmet to the crash scene, which he did.

[2]Authors' Note: General Bodenschatz wrote Carisella late in 1968 to confirm that the Baron wore a parachute.

Richthofen's plane nosed over in pile of mangels. Sketch from information given by Australians who visited the crash scene.

Lewis guns belonging to 53rd Battery, AFA, had also fired at this plane when it was directly over my head, but the noise of the engine prevented my hearing the shooting. The 53rd Battery Lewis gunners probably assisted in sealing the fate of this airman, as he apparently flew right into their line of fire. However, I am strongly of the opinion that he was first hit by Sergeant Popkin's shooting, as he was unsteady from the moment of that first burst. The airman's body was afterwards taken in charge by officers of the AFC and wrecked plane salvaged by them after dark."

P. J. Carisella contacted Gen. James H. Cannan in 1962 for his memories of the incident, but the then retired major general was unable to contribute any specific details as the following shows:

"I did not visit the scene of this crash. I never kept any private diaries. As I am now eighty years of age, my memories of 1918 are fading. . . . All I can say is that at this period I was in command of 11th Australian Infantry Brigade and doing my very utmost to prevent the Germans from reaching the Channel ports. This incident of Richthofen was of small account to me at that time. . . ."

Private Inch, who earlier gave his views of the shooting-down of Richthofen, added these further details of the crash scene:

"I at once ran across to the plane which was tilted forward at an angle to see if the pilot was hurt as he was sitting in the cockpit, but when I climbed up the side of the plane I could see that he was dead. On the right side of his back low down there was a bullet wound and when I lifted his arm there was no movement. His eyes were wide open (very blue) and his blond hair was close cropped and he did not have helmet or goggles. As I could see nothing more I had a look at the plane and noticed the propeller had broke off at the boss, one blade stuck in the ground and broken and the other blade looked as if it had been hit by a bullet. I pulled the propeller out of the ground and took it to our headquarters where it was sawn [sic] up as souvenirs.[3]

"I then went back to the plane with others, which included Captain Adams who was put in charge of the plane by Captain Hillary. We then removed the body of Richthofen.

[3]A piece of this propeller is in the Carisella collection.

Then Captain Adams removed his wallet with his air force history. It was then we found out who the pilot was. . . ."

W. A. Audsley, who commanded the 108th Battery, and was quoted earlier in this work, had this to report about the crashed plane:

"I cannot recall who was with me when we rushed over to the crash. There were only a few of us and could not stay long as our guns were in action and we had to get back to our battery position. When we left, others had arrived at the scene. . . . I did not see any chest wound although this may also have been a possibility. The wound I saw in his forehead may have been caused in the crash. As I said before, I had to get back to the gun position and was not interested in souvenirs.

"My recollection is that R did not have his goggles on, in fact, I think he was bareheaded. The plane was crashed up in the nose and undercarriage, but otherwise fairly intact when we left it. I remember that not long afterwards Fritz shelled the spot heavily and my gun position got a fair whack of the overflow. I think he tried to destroy the plane and probably smashed things up a lot."

Jack Hocking, a former member of the 108th Howitzer Brigade and a resident of Bannerton, Australia, also was one of the first diggers at the crash site. He reported that "he came down close enough for our battery personnel to be first on the spot, that two of them souvenired his gloves and the clock out of the aeroplane. I further know the bloke who got the gloves spoke a bit loud, with the results that the gloves were confiscated so much so that the man with the clock kept his mouth shut. He kept the clock and later sold it to another member of our battery, who many years later returned it to a German named Dr. Becker, who said he would hand the clock back to the German government 'and this would bring about a more friendly understanding between the British and German nations.'[4]

"Incidentally, any further souveniring of this plane was stopped because Fritz shelled it. . . . In talking about the many stories of this battle Capt. Brown must be the most inaccurate. He says that he [Richthofen] 'went down vertical.' Well I would say he was flying almost horizontal with

‘Authors' Note: The man who took the clock was the late Len Wincey of the same battery.

engine throttled back, trying to keep behind the fugitive he was chasing. . . . It was then that the Red Baron took off as if he had fallen over his engine throttle, for the plane engine roared at full throttle in a semicircle and dived into the ground at an angle not much short of horizontal. . . ."

P. J. Carisella attempted to contact Wincey but was informed by Att. Garry M. Blumer of Griffith, Australia, that Wincey "died in May of 1962. Unfortunately, he never married and his nearest relatives are two nieces living in Adelaide, South Australia. Whether they will be able to help you or not we cannot tell."

Blumer went on: "Mr. Wincey did have as a souvenir of the war, the watch from the cockpit of Richthofen's plane but some time in 1936 or 1937 during a visit of the German Consul General to Griffith that the watch was handed by Mr. Wincey to him and by him returned to the German Air Ministry, the late Mr. Wincey receiving a personal letter of thanks from Reisch-Marschal Hermann Goering. . . ."

In another letter, Attorney Blumer reported that he "knew the late Mr. Wincey for a period of thirty years. Prior to 1938, I used to visit his home quite a lot when I was a boy and heard the story of the clock from Baron von Richthofen's plane on numerous occasions. The story told me by Mr. Wincey was that he was in the artillery of the Australian forces and one day he saw a German plane flying very low over his battery.

"He later found that the plane had crashed and he immediately went to look at the wreckage. Whilst he was there he purchased from one of the soldiers the clock which had been removed from the plane. It was later found that the pilot of the German plane was Baron von Richthofen. Mr. Wincey could not throw any further light on the controversy which exists as to whether he was shot down from the ground by an Australian soldier.

"The clock was an aircraft clock and had been removed, as previously stated, from the instrument panel of Richthofen's plane. This clock and the pieces of canvas from the plane were kept by Mr. Wincey until the German Consul for Australia heard of their existence. He paid a visit to Mr. Wincey at Griffith and after much persuasion Mr. Wincey gave him the clock to be sent back to Germany where he

Richthofen crashed in area shown in foreground of photograph.

was informed the clock would be placed in the War Museum.

"When Mr. Wincey had not received any reply or letter from Germany with regard to the arrival of the clock, he wrote on several occasions to the Consul in Sydney and finally, just after the last war had started, Mr. Wincey received a letter from General Goering, or rather his secretary, acknowledging receipt of the clock and thanking him for same stating, 'that it was such gestures as Mr. Wincey's that binds the ties of friendship between the two nations!' "

Lt. R. B. O'Carroll of B Company of the 44th Battalion, quoted earlier, added this about the crash scene: "Colonel Clark of the 44th Bn., who was watching called to me to collect a few men and put a guard on the pilot's body. I collected some men and ran towards the plane. As we neared the plane, we could see the pilot slumped over the right-hand door apparently dead. By this time several men arrived on the scene and the pilot's body was moved from the plane. Capt. Fraser, the intelligence officer of the 11th Brigade, who had come up, started to open his suit. I noticed he wore a fine flying suit of leather with a fine suit of silk underwear. He had a large square head with close cropped blond hair. He had a large silver identity disc suspended on a chain. Both were of solid silver. Opening the shirt disclosed a bullet wound on the left breast.

"Capt. Fraser knew from the identity disc who he was but did not say publicly. While this was going on a sergeant in the crowd started souveniring. I had Richthofen's large black flying gauntlets in my hands. Turning to the sergeant, I said, 'Sergeant you ought to be helping me, not showing a bad example.' He replied, 'Sir, I shot the bastard down so I ought to have something.' I handed him the gauntlets, saying, 'Sergeant, you have these. That was a mighty fine shot.' "

H. M. W. MacPherson, the gunner with the 108th Howitzer Battery, added that "about four or five of us dashed up to the crash, but even then we were not the first on the scene. About twenty yards from the wreckage we met a British soldier, Royal Engineers, I believe. He had already 'souvenired' the small brass clock from the dashboard—a very handsome little 'souv.' A gunner in my battery, Leonard Wincey, who was acting as medical details, offered the British soldier ten francs for the clock, which he accepted. Wincey took the clock back to Australia. . . .

"To return to the story, we reached the road to discover a . . . small triplane at an angle and not covering the road, as it was so small . . . the plane was standing on its own wheels and except for the wing appeared intact. A few small pieces of broken wood were lying about, apparently broken struts. . . . The plane had a good deal of red about . . . Richthofen's body was lying between the wing and the plane, flat on his back and straight out. He looked very short and blocky, but this may have been due to his clothes, as he was well rigged up in a fur coat, boots and gloves. He had a bullet hole across his chest and a chip off his chin. He looked well [sic]. . . .

"We proceeded to look for souvenirs ourselves when we were interrupted by a young Australian officer, Lt. O'Carroll, who commanded all gunners to return to their batteries. A young signaler from my battery who had procured Richthofen's fine fur gauntlet gloves and had stuffed them in the front of his tunic cheekily replied, 'Yes, while you rat him.' 'Yes, and I'll start with those gloves. Please hand them over,' which the Sig did. The officer then told us that they had reason to believe that the airman was a very important German leader, which was confirmed a few days later when word drifted back that it was, indeed, Richthofen and that he had been buried with military honors by an Australian unit. I forgot to remark that he was wearing a light gray shirt of fine material and carrying a small coronet and a cipher on his chest."

Fred C. Hyder of Boyanup, a member of the 51st Battalion, recalls that he and his "cobber, or buddy as you Americans would say, ran over to the plane and there finding the Baron quite dead, removed the altimeter, which was suspended by three springs to the stay wires of the wings of the plane. It was nothing more than an aernoid barometer. Unfortunately, I have only the face plate left as I pulled it to pieces for souvenirs for my friends. It bears on the obverse the maker's inscription and on the reverse an inscription I had done in London after being wounded. . . .

"My friend, the first man to the plane, I was ten feet behind—removed the Baron's gauntlets, but he was only allowed to keep them for five minutes. As the first officer on the scene took charge of them and I believe they were afterwards sent to his widow [the Baron's]."[5]

The widow of Cpl. John Bernard Cunningham of the 44th Infantry Battalion wrote to say that he "was one of three men who guarded his [the Baron's] body after he was shot down and until the proper authorities took over. . . ."

Mrs. E. W. Cunningham, writing from Kalgcorlie, Western Australia, added, ". . . I do remember him telling me about the airman. He said that he [Richthofen] was a fine specimen of a man, and as far as he could see, there wasn't a mark on him. My husband took the airman's belt[6] for a souvenir and I still have it, if you would like it. I could send it to you. It's just a plain leather belt with no markings on it. . . ."

As the Baron's body lay sprawled beside the wreckage, swarms of soldiers continued to appear. They literally hacked the red triplane to pieces, unfortunately, destroying all traces of bullet holes in the fabric. Within minutes, despite the entreaties of the padre of the 8th Field Artillery Brigade and several other officers, the Fokker bus was almost stripped in several sections to the framework.

One of the officers participating in the "souveniring" was Lt. James A. E. R. Daley, a native of Jamaica, B.W.I., and then a pilot in No. 24 Squadron, RAF. Daley was at the Front on foot because of some stunting he had done the previous day over a battery position. His wing commander, to punish him, had ordered him to go forward and personally apologize to the battery officer. While en route, Daley saw the downed triplane and helped himself to a souvenir.

Retired Air Force Lt. Col. W. C. Lambert of Ironton, Ohio, wrote to say that Daley "was one of my best friends in 24th Sqd. He was not shot down and killed; he was killed in an accidental crash. Yes, he was at the scene of Richthofen's death, and brought back some material. I have a piece of the plane fabric in a frame . . ."

The "souveniring" then had been going on for a little more than fifteen minutes under the watchful and anxious eyes of the Germans who had a clear view of the scene from their lines on the eastern end of Morlancourt Ridge. Fearing that the Allied troops might be assaulting the Baron, who they

---

[5]Richthofen, of course, was a bachelor.
[6]Now in the Carisella collection.

View of the Bray-Corbie road showing line of crash dive and crash site.

thought at the time was still alive, the Germans laid down an artillery barrage in a boxlike fashion around the plane. The sounds of the very first salvos sent most of the Aussies scrambling for cover. The body of the Baron was left lying on its back between the fuselage of the tripe and the road. German shells burst around the remains but did not touch them. However, some shards of shrapnel were believed to have pierced the machine. Damage caused by this fire helped to obliterate any possible evidence that might have been uncovered in trying to determine whether the Baron had been shot down from the air or from the ground.

P. J. Carisella learned during his extensive correspondence with Australians that the Baron reportedly wore a bulletproof vest. While he has never been able to substantiate this claim,[7] the following letter undoubtedly will be of interest to the reader. It was forwarded on July 15, 1968, by Lew J. Harvey of Glenelg, Australia, and reads as follows: "I have received your communication of 5th July and in reply desire to answer some of the questions which you are asking. (1) I was a member of the 43rd Infantry Battalion, AIF, serving as a signaler. (2) There was a third plane. (3) Approximately eight hundred yards distant. (4) I have a small portion of the Maltese Cross which was removed from his plane by a comrade who divided the whole cross up into small pieces for souvenirs and gave a number of us a piece. This was a cross painted on the aircraft. The aircraft was a triplane painted red. . . .

"Another point of interest to you is the fact that Mayor (C. W.) Anderson has a small piece of bulletproof steel which was taken from a bulletproof vest worn by the late Baron during his flights. One other member of our battalion living in this area, Mr. W. Hillam . . . has another smaller piece. I have asked Mayor Anderson to contact a third party who may be able to throw some further light on the bullet-proof vest. . . . Conferring with Mayor Anderson, I agree entirely with his statement that Baron von Richthofen was brought down by a machine gunner from an Australian unit of the 11th Infantry Brigade who was stationed at the time in the Australian Artillery wagon lines."

[7]Authors' Note: Karl Bodenschatz, Richthofen's Adjutant, wrote in late 1968 that Richthofen was not wearing such a vest on the day he died.

Major Beavis, the C.O. of the 53rd Battery, denied, in correspondence with Carisella, any knowledge of photographs taken of Richthofen's crashed plane. He wrote that "the use of cameras was forbidden except by official photographers."

He went on to relate that the Germans shelled the general area of the crash scene shortly after Richthofen's fall, "probably about twenty to thirty minutes later. I don't remember exactly, but it did not prevent diggers from trying to 'souv' the plane. One of my officers, Lieut. Ellis, and a number of gunners ran across immediately after the crash. Ellis brought a souvenir with MVR on it. That was the first indication I had that the dead pilot might be Richthofen.

"I reported the crash and the holding of the body to H.Q.—14th Artillery Brigade. Later a tender or truck from No. 3 Squadron, Australian Flying Corps, came along and picked up the body. The officer with it said Richthofen had been shot down by an R.E. 8 of their Squadron, which of course was ridiculous."

The officer who came forward from No. 3 Squadron with the tender was Lt. W. J. Warneford, of Sidney, Australia. As the R.E. 8 Squadron's equipment officer, under Capt. Roderick Ross, he had been ordered by Major Blake, the C.O., to take a salvage party from the Poulainville airfield and proceed to the crash scene.

Warneford's role in the drama was recalled by Joe Knapp, of Ashgrove, Australia, in a letter to Carisella during the summer of 1968.

Knapp wrote: "Lt. Warneford was the equipment officer of No. 3 Squadron and it was part of his duties to attend to the recovery of No. 3 Squadron and all other machines, which for any reason landed in the sector controlled by the Australian Corps. As we were the Corps squadron, there's no doubt that he was in charge of the recovery detail. The detail sergeant was Dick Foale from South Australia, and the driver of the motor vehicle was Mick Worsley—the names of the others I have forgotten.

"They left for the area where the plane was down late in the morning. Warneford and Worsley arrived at the squadron with Richthofen's body at around sundown. And after the body was taken to the medical building, which was in charge of Corporal Ted McCarty, Warneford told me that they couldn't get the plane out as the Germans were ringing it with artillery fire, but now that darkness had set in, he was hoping that they [the Germans] would discontinue these tactics, and if so, he hoped to return with the plane around midnight (which he did).

"Before going I remember him asking me what I wanted as a souvenir, and I told him that souvenirs did not interest me. He then said that he was going to get the 'joy stick' for his personal souvenir. He did, however, bring me several spark plugs. What happened to them I don't know, as I did not bring them from France. Neither can I find the pieces of fabric which I had. When the machine did arrive I put a guard on it; mainly composed of keen souvenir hunters, and this gave them an opportunity of selecting just what they wanted. I can assure you that I did not have any difficulty in obtaining the men to mount this guard. . . .

"Please yourself what you do about the names of the men of this detail, but believe me, my version is correct. How do I know? I was Warneford's flight sergeant, and did arrange some men from my section and obtained the others from other flight sergeants to comprise the recovery crew."

The names of other members of the recovery crew were obtained by Carisella through a contact with J. K. Kitts of Melbourne, Australia. Kitts said that besides the men identified by Knapp, the others were A. A. Boxall-Chapman, an Englishman from Spalding, Lincolnshire; Colin Campbell Collins of St. Georges, South Australia; Joseph Waldron; R. Foale, and himself.[8]

With Mike Worsley driving the tender, Warneford's group drove to within half a mile of Corbie Hill and dismounted, proceeding on foot towards the Bray-Corbie Road and the shell-pocketed crash scene. There they contacted Major Beavis who pointed out the downed tripe. Enemy shells still were exploding sporadically about the aircraft.

Kitts wrote: "I am quite sure when we got to the scene of the Baron's plane his body was partly on the ground, half held up by his harness. There was also quite a lot of markers from troops around the supports, I think from memory the 53rd Battery. I think Lieut. Ellis of the 53rd Battery ordered all his troops back, that was when we arrived.

"Then Jerry started shelling and as it was no-man's-land. They must have known of his crash. . . .

[8]Authors' Note: Also A. J. Porter.

Remains of Richthofen's triplane at Poulainville aerodrome. Souvenir hunters accounted for most of the damage.

"E. J. McCarty was our first-aid man. He may have the bullet[9] still from the Baron's body because he was not with us out there, but he laid out the body in the hangar for the special inspection.

"One other thing that I did not mention. He had a big white parachute in the plane. It was not strapped to him then. It was the first I had seen and I cannot say what became of it. . . ."

Kitts also was kind enough to forward a sketch of how the Baron's body was laid out in the canvas hangar at Poulainville.

It might well be of interest to include at this point Lieutenant Warneford's recollections of the day's events.

He wrote: "At the time Richthofen was brought down, I was attached to the 3rd Australian Flying Squadron. Under instructions from Major Blake, I went to the spot where the German officer crashed, with instructions to salvage the machine and to recover Richthofen's body. The German's body was taken to the 53rd Battery lines.

"Capt. Brown, who claims to have brought down Richthofen, came and interviewed some of the officers of the 53rd Battery, and quite a lively argument followed. Major Beavis refused to accept his claim. I remember Beavis said that he was certain his men had gotten Richthofen. However, Beavis had also said that 'it is possible some other shot from the ground got him, although Richthofen was a perfect target for our guns. Buie claimed him, but it could have been Buie or Evans.'

"From all the battery personnel which gathered around at the time and from an examination of the remnants of the German machine, we concluded that Richthofen's guns had jammed, and that Richthofen, being a very smart pilot, still kept in the tail of Capt. Brown's[10] [sic] machine. When the two machines came directly over the 53rd Battery, the Lewis Gunner Evans, who was on duty, had to wait until Brown's plane had gone by, before he could put a burst into Richthofen's machine.

"Richthofen's body," Warneford continued, "was taken to

[9]Authors' Note: The bullet which killed Manfred von Richthofen was found by No. 3 Squadron Medical Orderly, E. J. McCarty. This information has never previously been published.

[10]Authors' Note: Obviously, Lt. May.

our aerodrome at Poulainville, and was examined by the army corps doctors ... and they all concluded that Richthofen had been shot in an oblique angle through the right shoulder, the shot coming out of his breast. There was only one wound in the German airman's body. The description of this wound and all other evidence made it clear that Richthofen had been brought down from the ground."

When he wrote the above, Warneford quite obviously had changed his mind about who had shot the Baron down. On first approaching Major Beavis, he claimed the kill for his own squadron's R.E. 8's. Apparently, however, after listening to the ground troops, he quickly changed his mind.•

The first man to venture forward through the heavy enemy shelling to the Baron's plane was Colin Campbell Collins, an air mechanic with No. 3 Squadron. Collins, who died in October 1965 of cancer, had written Carisella this report:

"I crawled out sixty feet in front of the trench (where the other members of the party were waiting)—I had the end of a long rope I fixed around R's body after making sure he was dead, (he was cold), and the men in the trench had the other end of the rope and they hauled the body back very slowly a foot or two at a time so as not to draw attention from Germans who were shelling the position very heavily to prevent the rescue.

"Prior to moving the body, I saw Richthofen's helmet lying on the ground—I stuffed it into my jacket, then I cut buttons from his shoulder straps ... I removed the locks[11] from both guns and intended keeping these things myself. I then gave the signal to haul away the body. I later placed a rope around the plane and that was also recovered. I was told by an officer of our squadron that a small amount of German money and a ring containing a stone was given to various officers. Nobody mentioned a watch.

"I lost one lock which is now in the Museum of Canberra, Federal Capital.[12] I retained the other lock, the boots I put on the tender intending to get them when we returned to the squadron. Those were stolen from me and I later saw a paper cutting [clipping] stating that the boots had been sent to R's mother."

As a humorous aside, Collins told P. J. Carisella that he

[11]One lock is in the Carisella collection, along with broken firing pin.
[12]Not so, according to authors.

suffered a blow on the head while crawling out to the plane and thought initially he had been hit by a shell fragment. But it turned out to be a flying piece of potato displaced by a shell. For his heroism in exposing himself to enemy fire on April 21, 1918, Collins received the Military Medal.

Another member of the party, A. A. Boxall-Chapman, did not make the initial trip forward under fire with Collins but did go up to the plane on Collins' second foray. He recalls that as the group neared the vicinity of the Bray-Corbie Road, "the Germans were firing a few gas shells. We put on our gas masks. The red plane could be plainly seen. Myself and another (C. C. Collins) volunteered to go forward to the plane. We walked to within a hundred yards and crawled the remainder of the way. We found the body was out of the cockpit, lying full length, head towards our own lines, under the lower wing on the right-hand side of the plane, looking from the tail of the plane.

"The plane was lying on its left wings. The bottom wing was damaged and partly buried in a mound of earth, which looked like what is called in England a potato pie (where potatoes are heaped up and covered with earth for storage). The plane was lying at a steep angle, with its right wings high in the air, nose facing towards the German lines (home).

"The body was too heavy for we two, so my mate went back for a length of rope. Whilst he was away, I removed R's identity discs—there were two—one read 'Calvary Captain Manfred, etc.' and the other 'Baron von Richthofen etc.' I examined the bullet wound. I then examined the controls. The engine was off. This was R's habit. He always switched off his engine in an emergency in case of fire in a crash. . . . I then removed the cartridges from the breeches of his guns. There were two Spandaus lying side by side on the ground.

"I then searched the cockpit for the bullet which hit him. I thought it might have lodged in the cockpit. None was found. With the arrival of my mate with the rope it was passed around the body. . . . In doing this, it was noticed there was a large bruise on R's chin, doubtless when the plane hit the ground he was thrown forward against his guns. . . . Having fastened the rope around the body—we went back to the remainder of the party, who had come forward to the end of the rope, and the body was hauled back. The body was carried on a stretcher to the Howitzer battery of Major

Beavis and laid on the ground. An English officer arrived. He discredited that we had R's body. I gave him the identity discs. He put them in his pockets and I never saw them again.

"We left the body and we all, except for the R.S.M., returned to collect the plane. The Germans were shelling the plane but did not find the range. They were going well over, but we decided to wait for nightfall. We manhandled (the plane) back to the transport where it was loaded and taken back to the airfield. It was near midnight when we arrived. We did not stop on the way back. The plane was placed in front of H.Q. office. Tuesday morning I was detailed with others to dismantle it for dispatch to England, and we found that one gun was missing. It had been taken overnight. The plane was dismantled. I removed a small piece, about six inches square, of the fabric from the damaged wing. It had been painted blue (sky) under the red. . . .

"The only proof that both the lock and cartridges belonged to R's gun is that Mr. Collins and myself removed these items ourselves as there were many Spandau guns and cartridges about and they were all alike.

"I have more than the average knowledge of firearms and ballistics and spent a lot of time instructing in both subjects. I removed the charges and made a careful examination of both cartridges at the request of my C.O., Capt. Anderson. I gave him one. Both cartridges were 'dud' faulty primers. Both cartridges showed signs of having been snapped many times by hand-cocking in an effort to get them to fire, as the primers were driven well below the surface of the cartridge base. The ident [sic] of the firing pin was clean and regular. Constant snapping without point support often will break a firing pin, and it usually breaks at the base of the pin. If the pin had broken at the previous discharge, the cartridge in the breech would not show any pin mark, or at least a very small irregular dent. This was not so."

In 1937, at the request of the German government, Boxall-Chapman sent the cartridge to Germany where the Luftwaffe ran a series of tests on it. In a report returned with the cartridge, the Germans said that the bullet was Spandau ammunition and of a type used by Richthofen. The report stated that the cartridge had a defective primer cap. Boxall-Chapman said the cartridge later was stolen from his desk while he was serving as a civil engineer at an RAF station during World War II.

Boxall-Chapman later recalled that he noticed a dark ring around the Baron's neck. It is doubtful what caused the circular mark since the medical reports made no mention of it. There is the possibility that the ring was made by a loose wire whipping around Richthofen's neck as he descended to the ground.

The Englishman wrote in his last letter to Carisella that he believed Richthofen's plane went to Australia.

In truth, Carisella believes that the dismantled skeleton of the aircraft was dumped down a gully behind the hangars at Poulainville and just rusted away in the passage of time.

From other witnesses tracked down through the years, Carisella also has been able to put together more details of the facts concerning the recovery of the Baron's body and tripe. Such details are not to be found in any other published work.

R. E. Douglas of Brisbane, Australia, recalled in his correspondence that "I was a member of the 3rd Squadron, Australia Flying Corps as a car driver. The type of car being a forerunner of the panel van and instrumental for towing planes and taking mechanics about, etc., to crashes and the like work. At the date 21-4-1918 our squadron was stationed close to the railway station at Bertangles. (Poulainville and Bertangles abut and No 3 Squadron, AFC, and No. 209, RAF were separated by little more than a country road at the time.) Our squadron was equipped with English planes (R.E. 8) reconnaissance. . . . The unit also carried a photo and wireless section, carpenters, riggers, etc.

"On April 21 another car driver (Mick Worsley from Victoria, I think) asked me to come and see what he had in his car. This proved to be Baron Richthofen's body, fully dressed. Mick had been detailed to salvage a German triplane from near the front line, which proved to be Richthofen's. Owing to being under direct observation from the Germans, it was a tough job. However, a rope was attached to Richthofen's body, which was dragged to the safety of the trenches and then carried back to our unit. . . ."

In another letter, Arthur D. Craven of Victoria, Australia, a motorcycle dispatch driver for No. 3 Squadron, wrote:

". . . You may be wondering where I came into the picture

Members of No. 3 Squadron examining the triplane at Poulainville.

and how I collected this knowledge.[13] Well, perhaps a small personal story might be of some interest. . . . It was the job of our squadron to salvage the wrecked plane and also to bring the Baron's body into our aerodrome at Poulainville, where the inquest was being held to try and determine the cause of his death.

"Now the body was brought to the aerodrome in a light tender (a kind of a utility car). The officer in charge was one Lt. Warneford and the driver was one Private Mick Worsley. Coming back to the drome in the late afternoon from a dispatch run, I met this small cortege and also a request from Mick to give him a lift with the Baron. We were then pulled up outside the army medical tent. I was, of course, quite at a loss to know what he was talking about till he invited me to inspect the Baron who was lying on the floor of the tender."

Craven continued: "Then when I realized the whole position, I was only too anxious to help. So using a sheet of galvanized iron as a stretcher, Mick and I carried the Baron into the medical tent for the inquest. While the body was lying on the floor we, and by now quite a few others as the news spread, had a good opportunity to inspect it properly. He appeared quite young, about twenty-seven, had close cropped hair—probably now called a crew cut—also he was clothed in a fine suede leather jacket and leather knee-high flying boots. We heard later that the jacket, in an inner pocket, contained quite a considerable sum of money in francs. He was apparently 'catering' for the day when he may be taken prisoner.

" . . . The triplane was also salvaged and brought to Poulainville, and placed under close guard. But not so close that some of us were not able to remove the spark plugs and a fair selection of its fabric. The plug is rather a neat little Bosch."

[13]Authors' Note: In preceding paragraphs Craven had provided some details about the preparations and funeral of the Baron, which will be duly noted in the next chapter.

✠ ✠ ✠

Chapter 6

AUTOPSY AND FUNERAL

✠ IT was shortly after 9 P.M., Sunday, April 21, 1918. Baron Manfred von Richthofen had been dead approximately ten hours. His body lay on the section of galvanized iron in one of the hangar tents of No. 3 Squadron, Australian Flying Corps at Poulainville. The heavy ropes which C. C. Collins had placed about the corpse at the crash scene still bound the Rittmeister. Two guards watched over the remains. One stood near the body and the other kept guard at the entrance. They hardly spoke. On the Western Front, seven miles distant, the massed guns seemed strangely silent.

About that time, Maj. D. V. J. Blake, C.O. of the squadron, walked into the tent in the company of Sergeant John Alexander and several other noncommissioned officers. After quietly studying the body for a few moments, Blake told Alexander to take several photographs of the dead German ace. "Headquarters wants them to prove to the Fritz brass that the Baron is really dead," the major said.

"Very good, sir," Alexander replied. "We'll get right to it."

After Blake left the hangar, Alexander ordered Cpl. Ken McLeod and Cpl. E. T. Grant to lift the body and prop it against the main tent pole in the center of the hangar. McLeod and Grant grasped the edges of the iron slab, nodded at each other to signal each had a good grip, and then picked up the body, which at that time, still had not been prepared for burial. The pair of Aussies carried the body a few steps, put down one end and raised the other to prop the Baron's body against the pole.

Lewis O. Gyngell of Sidney, Australia, who was the squadron's orderly sergeant at the time, told Carisella, "Before Richthofen was buried we stood his body against a sheet of galvanized iron and took his photo. Where the photos all went, I do not know. . . ."

Alexander then began taking a series of photographs of the body. As he did so, the word somehow quickly got around the squadron and soon, despite the lateness of the hour, six other photographers, several of whom flew aboard the decrepit R.E. 8's, slipped into the hangar and took their own personal shots of the dead Baron. Alexander voiced no objection.

Cpl. E. T. Grant of Slade Point, Australia, was one of those photographers who took unofficial pictures. In a letter to Carisella, Grant said he took his pictures "from practically the same viewpoint as the official one, taken for identification in case the Germans denied his death." Grant said he did not personally know whether any pictures were taken of the Baron's wound. However, he added, " . . . some other member of the 3rd Squad. may have done so as the majority of the photo section had pocket cameras." Grant also said that he and another man undid the ropes and opened the Baron's flying suit to inspect the chest and abdomen area. There was only one "rather big hole in the front of his left chest . . . we lifted the body up and found a small hole under the right shoulder in the back." He also informed Carisella that the squadron armorer "told me that Richthofen's guns had jammed."

Grant forwarded Carisella a copy of the head shot he took of the body and a sketch of the wound.

Sgt. L. F. Cooper, an air mechanic with No. 3 Squadron, for years claimed that photographs of Richthofen's wounds had been taken. However, he died in 1951 before Carisella could contact him. But undaunted, Carisella tracked down his son, Ronald F. Cooper of Ryde, Australia. Cooper, a member of the Australian Aviation Historical Society, wrote that "at one time my father had a photo showing the actual wound [Richthofen's] but both the negatives and the only prints were destroyed in an ammonia explosion at the Boggatine Power Station in the early 1930's, so that I cannot remember much about it."

Sergeant Alexander, the official photographer, died in 1957. His son, John S. Alexander of Auckland, New Zealand, continued, however, to correspond with Carisella. In April 1967, he wrote to say, "I have found my father's war diary and for your information enclose a copy of the extract relating to the funeral. You are quite welcome to use this in any way you like. I regret that I cannot send you the diary itself."

Here are Sergeant Alexander's observations for April 21 and 22, 1918:

"Splendid day for flying, we are very busy. Great excitement our pilot [E. C. Banks] returned saying he had brought down a fast red G. Machine. Then the telegraph told us that it was the great German pilot Baron von Richthofen the leader of German Circus. After a long fight he had crashed down between the lines. At night our boys brought in his body and we sent a party up to salvage the machine. The papers found on him proved his identity. His body arrived at our drome awfully cut about. He was shot through the chest, chin, heart and legs [sic]. His bus was bright red and very light rotary engine single prop. We all got something as a momento [sic]. We photographed the body and he was buried that afternoon at 4:30. They obtained a coffin. Harold [Edwards] engraved the following inscription in plate for his coffin.

CAVALRY CAPTAIN MANFRED
BARON VON RICHTHOFEN
AGED 25
KILLED IN ACTION (AERIAL COMBAT)
NEAR SAILLY-LE-SEC SOMME
FRANCE
21/4/1918

"There were three wreaths from 5th Division H.Q. with German colors and the card read—'To a worthy and valiant foe.' Then another from the H.Q. Royal Air Force and one from our own 3rd Squadron, each having the German colors. We supplied a firing squad of twenty-five men. He was given a full military funeral. Oh, we had all the heads here—quite a dozen officials, reporters and a cinematographer from the War Records Department. Of course it seemed a down right shame that such a fuss should be made over an enemy airman. No doubt he was a brave man. They all are. But unless they have proof that Germany treats our good pilots in a like manner I would be one to pass him by like they are known to treat our boys. On the morning of his fall Germany was sending out to the world news of his eightieth victim, but our men say he always fought fair. We stood at attention as six of our pilots carried him out to the car. He was buried at Bertangles, a French village, but, oh, such a dirty forsaken hole . . . "

In a letter to Carisella, Mrs. Alexander, the widow of the photographer, said that one of the photographs brought home by her husband after the war "showed a picture of Richthofen and his bride of six weeks.[1] He had taken photographs of the body." This photograph, according to Mrs. Alexander, was destroyed in 1957 shortly after Sergeant Alexander's death. His widow, unfortunately, decided at the time to burn many of her husband's personal effects, including "his large collection of war photographs."

Corporal McLeod wrote in May 1968 to report his reminiscences: "You ask if I was there when the pictures were taken of Richthofen. Yes, I was. His body was laying in a hangar. Our photographers of No. 3 Squadron took photos. The body was hoisted up on a sheet of tin. These were sent back to Germany to let them have proof we shot him [Richthofen] down."

The subject of Richthofen's alleged marriage also was touched upon in a letter Roderick Ross of Melbourne, Australia, wrote to Carisella in May 1968. Ross, an engineer, noted that: "Our No. 3 Squadron, Australian Flying Corps (which was for a time known as 67 Squadron, Royal Flying

---

[1] Authors' Note: Again, Richthofen never married. It is believed he must have been carrying a photo taken of him with Nurse Katie Otersdorf at St. Nicholas Hospital in Courtrai.

Richthofen in death. Baking soda whitened the battered face.

The Baron's body was lashed to a piece of corrugated iron and set upright for the photographer.

Corps), went to Poulainville when we were sent down south in a desperate hurry at the time the Germans made their great push forward in the early part of 1918. And it was from the aerodrome at Poulainville that we and a Royal Air Force Squadron[2] of fighter planes worked during the operations which ended with stopping the German advance at Villiers Brettoneux [sic]. This, as you doubtless know, was the last advance the Germans made in World War I.

"We were operating from the aerodrome at Poulainville at the time Richthofen was killed. As you doubtless know, Richthofen was not shot down from the air although at the time of his death he was engaged in one of the greatest dogfights that ever took place during World War I. . . . In those days, the artillery had Lewis machine guns mounted on posts and all the evidence tended to show that Richthofen had been hit by a bullet from one of those machineguns belonging to the 53rd Battery of 4.5-inch Howitzers belonging to the Australian Field Artillery.

"Later that same day, a party from our squadron went to his forward artillery area and collected Richthofen's body and his plane. The officer in charge of this party was a Lieutenant Warneford who was one of my officers.

"When Richthofen was brought to our squadron, his body was placed in a hangar and placed on a sheet of corrugated iron so that it could be better photographed; the photographs having been ordered by the British Commander in Chief, so that copies of the photographs could be dropped over the lines.

"When Richthofen's body was being set up for photographing, it was noticed that very little blood was apparent on the front part of his body, which was incomprehensible if he had been shot down from the air [sic].[3] He was . . . a relatively small man, both in build and height and from the few documents found in his wallet (which our boys overlooked when they 'ratted' the wreck of his plane), he had been married approximately only six weeks before he was killed. . . ."

The photographing completed, the body of the Baron was stretched out again on the floor. Alexander and his crew,

[2]Authors' Note: No. 209 Squadron, next door in Bertangles.
[3]Authors' Note: Not at all so.

along with the group of unofficial photographers filed out
the tent. The guards once more were alone with the body.

Lt. Norman Mulroney, a wartime pilot with No.
Squadron, recalls in extensive correspondence with Carise
that the body of the Baron was placed on what he describ
as a "trestle." Here are excerpts from several of his lette
during the period October 1964 to late June 1968:

"As regards to Richthofen, I was on Dawn Patrol th
day, and on photographic reconnaissance at midday. I d
not see one enemy aircraft on either patrol, but when
landed fifteen minutes after leaving the lines I was told th
R had been shot down.

"Our equipment officer, Lt. Warneford, went up to t
front line with a tender, C. C. Collins crawled over the t
and tied a rope to his [Richthofen's] parachute harness an
pulled his body in. He retrieved the Fokker triplane in t
same way later on. The body of R lay on a trestle in one
our hangars all night and ... our M. O. conducted
autopsy. It was found that ONE [sic] bullet entered his bo
beneath the ribs on the right hand side and traveled
through his heart. He was dead when he hit the ground. A
aircraft capable of performing this miracle[4] would have h
to be underground and firing upwards from the side; a rath
difficult feat.

". . . the body of Richthofen lay on a trestle all night
one of our empty Besneau hangars and I saw it the next d
and had official photos taken of it, full face and side fac
. . . As far as I know the autopsy was carried out and then
was given a military funeral. I do not know about a chur
service. . . .

"R attacked two or three of our aircraft in the dogfight,
one of these was Lt. E. C. Banks an observer who fired
long burst at him as R dived at him and then went on dov
after another bus. Capt. Brown in a Camel dived at R wh
he was chasing another Camel at treetop level. He [Brow
really believed he got him, but I think it is evident that
was shot down from the ground, and that by a cook of
people, with a Lewis gun.

"When we heard that Brown had claimed him, our Sq
claimed him on account of E. C. Banks whom I have n

---

[4] Authors' Note: i.e., shooting down Richthofen.

seen for eighteen years when he did a survey for me. As regards the Bible[5] this is the first I have heard of it.

"He was buried with full military honors and we sent the firing party. His body by the way was dressed in pyjamas over which he wore a fur-lined flying suit. Sewn into a pocket of that suit was a 1000 franc note, worth a bit more than L40 at that time. This had not been souvenired.[6] I have a photo of R's grave with one of our four-bladed propellers over it. Three of the blades are cut short to form a cross. . . ."

When replying to queries about the color of Richthofen's plane, Mulroney wrote: "I notice that one of your cover [sic] is explained on inside page that R's bus was not all red. This might have been so when delivered to him but he had it painted. I have some of the three-ply and fabric. When the red cracked off it was sky blue underneath. His bus was ALL RED [sic]."

As the evening of April 21 slipped away, Cpl. E. J. "Ted" McCarty, mentioned by Kitts in the preceding chapter as probably possessing the bullet that killed the Red Baron, entered the hangar. A squadron medical orderly, McCarty had been ordered to clean and prepare the body for the autopsy requested by the RAF in an effort to prove Richthofen had been shot from the air. With the help of the guards, the orderly untied the ropes and lifted the body onto several planks placed between two wooden horses.

While the guards stood back, McCarty unbuttoned the Baron's outer fur-lined jacket. Then with the help of a guard, he slipped it down over the shoulders and arms of the corpse. He then undid the buttons of the Baron's inner flying jacket. As he struggled to slip that jacket over the shoulders and arms, he saw a large wallet tucked into a left breast pocket. McCarty quickly tugged the wallet out of the pocket, with a wink at the guard. When he did so, a spent bullet popped out with it and fell into the lining of the jacket. McCarty snatched up the slug and stuck it into his trouser pocket.

He and the guard looked at each other. "Not a word about

[5]Authors' Note: Carisella had asked Mulroney whether he knew of a report that Richthofen had a Bible or black book on him when he arrived at Poulainville.

[6]Authors' Note: Later removed by a squadron cook still alive at this writing.

it, mate. Make me a nice souvenir. We best leave the walle
alone," the orderly said.

McCarty then slipped off the Baron's coveralls and the to
of his silk gray pajamas. He tugged both down over the wais
of the body. That work done, McCarty took his first goo
look at the Baron's features. They certainly were smashe
up. He figured Richthofen must have taken an awful batter
ing when his tripe slammed down.

McCarty was sure the Baron's jaw and nose had bee
fractured by the impact with the bar connecting the twi
Spandau machine guns. The orderly dipped a large cloth int
a pan of warm water, laced with alcohol, and began washin
the Baron's face, with its half-opened eyes. As he did so, th
jaw dropped, forcing open the mouth. He was then able t
see that the Baron's three front upper left teeth were missing
and that the three front upper right teeth were pushe
inward. McCarty, an old hand at preparing bodies for pos
mortems and burial, reached into the Baron's mouth an
pulled the teeth forward, aligning them as neatly as possible
He shook his head. The Hun must have taken an awfu
wallop on the head. McCarty was convinced that if the bulle
wound had not killed the Baron, the impact on crashin
would have done so.

McCarty then inspected the Baron's wound. With the we
cloth he cleaned the small wound in the Baron's back. Th
body had been rolled over on its left side. The wound wa
small, clean, and obviously an entrance wound. It was lo
cated, according to McCarty, on the right side toward th
armpit.

In a letter to Carisella, Neville Hewitt of Canberra, Aus
tralia, a member of the Australian Society of World War
Aviation Historians, wrote to relate in detail an interview h
had had with McCarty. Carisella had written to McCarty fo
years to get his views, but the former Aussie medical orderl
was not much of a letter writer and never personally re
sponded. Hewitt, however, at Carisella's request, was able t
meet McCarty, who then agreed to give him his recollec
tions. McCarty understood that Hewitt was conducting th
interview on behalf of Carisella.

In one of the letters describing the interview, Hewit
wrote: "The bullet held by McCarty was lost in 1935 whe
his mother died and he burned all sorts of papers and th

bullet was lost in the debris. He [McCarty] had repeatedly said to me if he knew such an interest would be taken in the future, he would never have destroyed anything.

"Apparently R was in terrible shape when McCarty saw him. He put his finger in his mouth and pushed R's teeth straight and generally cleaned up his face. McCarty says if the bullet had not killed him instantly, he would have died of concussion. He says also that the bullet made a clean hole just below the ribs on the right side and went clean through the apex of the heart. It then left the body and lodged in the back of a wallet, but did not penetrate the flying jacket.

"When I mentioned your name to him [McCarty], he asked me if I would write on his behalf as he doesn't feel up to writing now."

R. Radecki of Carlton, Australia, who served with the 5th Division and saw the Baron shot down, also helped Carisella locate McCarty. In one of his letters, Radecki, who had written many articles for *Reveille*, a veterans magazine in New South Wales, wrote: "He [McCarty] told me he had in his possession at one time the bullet that brought Richthofen down. His story if he tells it to you will be interesting."

P. L. Bulluss, the air mechanic with No. 3 Squadron, noted in one letter: "Sorry to hear you are unable to trace the man that has the bullet that killed R. I am writing this with the faint hope it will help you. I don't remember his name[7] but the man who helped the doctors at the post mortem on R was the squadron's medical orderly, which means he attended to casualties. . . . I feel sure he would have the bullet. I feel he was the type that would keep and value the bullet. I am absolutely certain that he assisted the doctors and I feel sure he would have been the most likely to get the bullet. . . ."

McCarty then rolled the body over on its back and examined the exit wound, which was located about two inches below the left nipple. He grimaced at the sight of it. He had seen a lot of combat wounds, but the Baron's was ghastly. The bullet had punched a big hole in the breast as it came tumbling out of the body. McCarty told Hewitt that the bullet must have ricocheted off the spinal column and tumbled, as it bore a sharp indentation and caused a tearing type wound on exiting. McCarty said the bullet apparently did not

[7]Authors' Note: Carisella is convinced that Bulluss was referring to E. J. McCarty the man who said he did recover the bullet.

Possibly this photograph was carried by Richthofen when he died; this might explain the legend of his "bride of six weeks." Nurse is Katie Otersdorf of St. Nicholas Hospital, Courtrai.

ricochet off anything before entering the back, as the entrance wound would not have been so clean and neat. He said the exit wound was about an inch and a half long, slightly curved, the edges jagged and puckered outward.

The medical orderly dipped the cloth in the water, wrung it out, and washed around the exit wound. Satisfied that he had done all he could to prepare the body for the autopsy, McCarty, with the help of the two guards, replaced the Baron's clothes and did up the buttons. His work completed, he picked up his utensils and left.

More minutes passed. The guards again were alone with the body. It was after 10:30 P.M. Suddenly the guards heard muffled noises at the foot of the tent behind the body. They investigated and found one of their Aussie mates trying to slip under the canvas hangar.

The intruder was a squadron cook, still alive today in Australia. He said, "Matie, I understand he's got some valubles on him. If we don't get it, the high brass will. Let me go through the body."

One of the guards said, "Make it fast. Some of the brass are expected to come by soon to inspect the body. McCarty's already got it ready for them."

The cook slipped under the tent and went to the body. He unbuttoned the outer jacket, found nothing, and unbuttoned the second jacket. Quickly rummaging around, he found a hidden pocket in the back of it. His fingers felt a large packet of paper. He pulled it out and saw that it was a large amount of French francs. Later when he counted the money, it totaled two thousand francs. The Baron had intended to use the francs to bribe his way back to German territory in case of a crash landing.[8]

Suddenly, one of the guards whispered, "Cookie, you better scram. I think the brass are coming. Off with you!"

The cook hurriedly redid the buttons, ducked under the canvas, and dashed back to his own tent. It was a false alarm. Several flying officers, not the medical officers, entered the tent and silently studied the Baron's body by the dim light of a kerosene lamp. Then they, too, left.

Just before 11 P.M., the guards again heard someone at the

[8]Authors' Note: It is interesting to note that Richthofen's wallet was removed from his body on the night of the 21st. Any number of men could have taken it as many men entered the tent to view the body.

back of the tent. "Must be another one of our mates," one said. The mate turned out to be Cpl. A. J. "Joe" Porter, one of the group which had gone out to recover the body. He had become aware during the ride on the Crosley tender that the Baron possessed many valuables worthy of souveniring.

Porter asked for a "crack" at the body. The guards shrugged and told him to be quick about it. Porter went through the Baron's clothes but could find nothing. Even the small diamond ring, which the Baron wore on his right hand, had been stolen by that hour. Disgusted, Porter was about to go away empty-handed when he spotted the Baron's leather high boots. Taking one off, Porter tried it on for size. It fit perfectly. Porter then took off the other boot and put it on. As a quid pro quo, he placed his low cut shoes on the Baron and neatly tied them.

As a footnote here, Porter walked around the base for the few days telling his mates that he was wearing the Rittmeister's boots. Porter survived the war and returned to Queensland, Australia, with the boots. In 1937, on a trip to Europe, Porter visited the Baron's mother at Schweidnitz and offered her the boots. The Baroness refused as she could not be convinced that the boots were those of her son.

In correspondence with Carisella, any number of witnesses recalled Porter's souveniring of the Baron's boots, including Arthur Craven, R. E. Douglas, and Joe Knapp, a trio quoted in Chapter VI about other aspects of Richthofen's death.

Craven recalled that "one rather gruesome incident occurred, which is perhaps worth mentioning. His flying boots were 'souvenired' by a Corporal Porter and later taken home to his [the Baron's] aged mother some years after the war by the same Joe Porter. I understand his body was also later transported home."

Douglas, who became a physician after the war in Brisbane, remembered that "one of our transport sergeants, Sgt. Porter, salvaged his highly polished high boots (leather). Some years after Sgt. Porter returned these to Baroness Richthofen in Germany.[9]

Knapp wrote that Porter, "who was my corporal dispatch rider . . . wanted Porter's army gum boots. Some years ago I read in one of our newspapers that Porter (who was an

[9]She did not accept them.

English lad) was going home on a holiday and wrote to the Baron's mother saying he had the boots and would be pleased to deliver them to her for the Baron's museum. Whether Porter returned them or not I am unable to ascertain."

Air Mechanic Frank R. Rawlinson of Clayton, Victoria, Australia, wrote to tell how he souvenired Richthofen's coveralls, the steel step from his airplane, a piece of fabric, and a section of machine-gun belt,[10] along with some ammunition for the twin Spandaus. Rawlinson, who helped dismantle the Baron's tripe, said he gave all his souvenirs "to the War Memorial at Canberra years ago. I was there recently," he noted, "and none of them were on display."

The initial and official postmortem on the Baron's body was held at about 11:30 P.M., April 21, 1918. It was requested by the RAF in an effort to fully establish Captain Brown's claim of having shot the all-red tripe down from the air and to quash the reports of claims from E. C. Banks of No. 3 Squadron (R.E. 8's) and the Australian ground gunners.

The medical officers were led by Major Blake into the tent housing the dead German pilot. There were four of them: Col. Thomas Sinclair, consulting surgeon of the British 4th Army; Col. J. A. Dixon, consulting physician of the British 4th Army; Capt. Norman Clotworthy Graham and Lt. G. E. Downs, both of the Royal Army Medical Corps and attached to the RAF.

E. C. Banks, the R.E. 8 gunner who believes to this day that he shot Richthofen down, recalled in a letter to Carisella during the summer of 1968 that "there were about twenty officers, including myself, medical men and orderlies present at the examination. Its purpose," according to Banks, "was firstly to determine whether he carried any important papers and, secondly, the manner of his death.

"From bleeding, it was known that he was wounded in the chest and his clothes were carefully cut away. When his shoulders and chest were exposed, it was apparent that the fatal bullet entered his body at the rear and slightly below the right armpit. It passed through his chest and emerged again from the left side about four inches below the armpit.

"The unanimous[11] opinion and verdict of all present was

---

[10]Carisella also had similar souvenirs in his collection.
[11]Not so; there was no unanimous opinion either way.

that he must have been shot from the air by a bullet from the right side of his plane. Most of his possessions were quickly souvenired by those present. ... I have no knowledge whether Richthofen was taken to a church after the examination but this could have been possible as I did not see the body again until the next day when we joined it on the gun carriage as pallbearers. ..."

The senior medical officer nodded to Lieutenant Downs who quickly stepped forward and used a knife to cut off the buttons from the two outer jackets. The buttons flew right and left, falling to the floor where they were snatched up by the onlookers. McLeod, one of the photographers, was among those who grabbed a button as a souvenir. Downs then took a pair of scissors to snip open the coveralls. This done, two orderlies stepped forward and pulled off the Baron's (Porter's) shoes and stockings. The Rittmeister's clothing, including his silk pajamas, next were peeled from his body so that he lay nude on the examining table of wooden planks. The clothing was tossed to one side and was to disappear, except for the pajamas and shoes, shortly after the autopsy ended.

As the doctors performed their work, the officers and men formed a hushed circle about them. The autopsy only took a few minutes as the body was not opened with any surgical instrument as is the usual procedure in attempting to determine cause of death. Rather the entrance and exit wounds were probed with a long, thin instrument resembling a knitting needle.

Edward T. Grant of Slade Point, Queensland, Australia, recalled the incident briefly in a note to Carisella in the summer of 1968: "Re your question, 'what went on?' I didn't get close enough to see whether he used a probe or not. From where I was the doctor appeared to be rolling Rich. over to look at his back. I am nearly certain Richthofen's body was not taken into Bertangles church. ..."

With their examination ended, the physicians returned with Major Blake to his office and there wrote their reports, the only ones they ever submitted.

Colonels Sinclair and Dixon, the British army doctors, issued this report:

"We have made a surface examination of the body of

Captain Baron von Richthofen and find that there are only the entrance and exit wounds of one rifle bullet on the trunk. The entrance wound is on the right side about the level of the ninth rib, which is fractured, just in front of the posterior axillary line. The bullet appears to have passed obliquely backwards through the chest striking the spinal column, from which it glanced in a forward direction and issued on the left side of the chest, at a level of about two inches higher than its entrance on the right and about in the anterior axillary line.

"There was also a compound fracture of the lower jaw on the left side, apparently not caused by a missile—also some minor bruises of the head and face.

"The body was not opened—these facts were ascertained by probing the surface wounds."

The two RAF officers submitted the following report on their findings:

"We examined the body of Captain Baron von Richthofen [sic] on the evening of the 21st instant. We found that he had one entrance and one exit wound caused by the same bullet.

"The entrance wound was situated on the right side of the chest in the posterior fold of the armpit, the exit wound was situated at a slightly higher level nearer the front of the chest, the point of exit being about half an inch below the left nipple and about three-quarters of an inch external to it. From the nature of the exit wound, we think that the bullet passed straight through the chest from right to left, and also slightly forward. Had the bullet been deflected from the spine, the exit wound would have been much larger.

"The gun firing this bullet must have been situated in roughly the same plane as the long axis of the German machine, and fired from the right and slightly behind the right of Captain Richthofen [sic].

"We are agreed that the situation of the entrance and exit wounds are such that they could not have been caused by fire from the ground."

Graham and Downs, the two air force members of the medical board and junior in rank and experience to the physicians of the British 4th Army, thus rule out the possibility of ground fire killing the Red Baron.

In their report, the two colonels express the belief that the slug struck the spinal column. Graham and Downs, the RAF doctors, did not agree, maintaining that the exit wound would have been larger if it had ricocheted off the spine.[12]

Colonels Sinclair and Dixon, unlike the RAF officers, offered no opinion as to whether the bullet that killed the Baron was fired from the air or the ground. However, the implication of a semifrontal wound seems more favorable to the possibility that the lethal missile was fired from the ground.

Meanwhile, McCarty and another medical orderly redressed the Baron's body. They shrugged their shoulders when they found so many items of the Rittmeister's clothing missing. "C'est la guerre," they figured. McCarty had the bullet so why should he complain. After slipping the silk pajamas and Porter's shoes on the Baron, they left the body alone with the guards; the only illumination being several kerosene lamps.

The examination of the Baron's body, however, was not over. Early the next morning, Col. G. W. Barber, deputy director of Medical Services, Australian Corps and Maj. C. L. Chapman, Australian Medical Services, accompanied by Major Blake and Captain E. G. Knox of No. 3 Squadron, entered the tent. The Baron was again quickly disrobed.

Colonel Barber, later Major General Barber, C.B., C.M.G., D.S.O., V.D., director general of medical services to the Commonwealth Military Forces and the Royal Australian Air Force, later wrote this account:

"I was at the time deputy director of Medical Services to the Australian Corps, and one morning went to an aerodrome in France . . . to make an inspection. When I arrived I saw an orderly washing the body of a dead aviator. When I learned that it was the body of the famous German 'ace' Richthofen, I made an examination of the body.

"The report that it was riddled with bullets is absolutely incorrect. There was one bullet wound only and this¯was through the man's chest. The bullet had passed completely through the heart and chest and, from its position, I formed the conclusion that it was fired from the ground and struck the airman as he was banking his machine, because the point

---

[12]Doctors, of course, were unaware that McCarty had recovered the bullet which bore a sharp indentation.

of exit of the bullet was three inches higher than the point of entry."

As for Chapman, he was later quoted as saying that "the bullet came out about an inch higher than it went in and might quite well have been shot from the ground." Blake and Knox also expressed the belief that Richthofen was shot down by ground fire.

Shortly before midnight, Lieutenant Warneford and his crew returned with the remnants of Richthofen's plane aboard a Crosley tender. It was unloaded right beside the tent containing the body of its last pilot.

E. C. Banks recalled that "while the [first] autopsy was in progress in the hangar, a number of busy Australians, probably about twenty, were working on R's plane and it rapidly assumed the appearance of a skeleton. My share of the souvenirs was a brass wire strainer, a piece of chain drive and a piece of red fabric of which you [Carisella] already have a small portion."

Joe Knapp, Warneford's flight sergeant, recalled that "when the machine did arrive I put a guard on it, mainly composed of keen souvenir hunters, and this gave them an opportunity of selecting just what they wanted. I can assure you that I did not have any difficulty in obtaining the men to mount this guard."

Harold Edwards, an air mechanic with No. 3 Squadron and a native of Bendigo, Australia, forwarded his original diary pages for April 21 and 22, 1918. On Monday, April 22, he wrote this: "The party succeeded in salvaging the bus last night after dark and brought it back about midnight. It is a red machine and was a three-decker though one would not know that in its present state. Pretty well every squadron in the vicinity is claiming the bringing down of Manfred the Baron aviator, but I think we retain the honor. . . ."

Arthur Craven, the squadron motorcycle dispatch rider, remembered that "Richthofen flew a blood red triplane powered by a seven [sic] cylinder Le Rhone engine, I understand a copy of the British one. The fabric, as I said, was blood red, and I have a small piece of it among my souvenirs today, and to make it more interesting it has a bullet hole through it."

It was Craven who, with others, removed the tripe's remaining spark plugs and a "fair selection" of its fabric.

Members of No. 3 Squadron, AFC, precede the Baron's body with arms reversed.

Roderick Ross, the squadron's engineer, wrote to say that "it fell to my lot to examine the wreckage of Richthofen's plane and prepare a report on it, which was forwarded and accepted by the Air Ministry in London. Richthofen was flying a Fokker triplane [*sic*] fitted with an Oberusel Rotary engine which was a copy of the French Le Rhone engine. The machine was fitted with two Spandau machine guns both fixed and firing forward between the propeller blades. As it is well known, Richthofen's plane was painted red. . . . In closely examining the wreckage of Richthofen's plane, I found only one bullet hole and this was in the lower front portion of the fuselage which again gives strength to the idea that Richthofen was killed by a bullet fired from the ground. . ."[13]

Former R.E. 8 pilot Norman Mulroney wrote that "when his aircraft reached our Squadron, there was not enough of it left to see bullet holes. There would only have been one in any case."

During the rest of the night and all the next day the remnants of the Baron's triplane were distributed among No. 3 Squadron personnel, with souvenirs going to any and all officers and men who visited from other units. Guards assigned to protect the wrecked aircraft made little effort to halt the wholesale vandalizing of the aircraft. Collectors on the night of April 22 even stole the two Spandau machine guns. They were last seen propped against the fuselage.

Carisella wrote to Ross to try to pinpoint the whereabouts of the machine guns. Ross, in his reply, wrote: "I am afraid I cannot help you in your desire to obtain one of the guns from von Richthofen's plane. The guns, together with the remains of the plane, were handed over to the British Authorities (RAF Headquarters, France) and, for all I know, have probably been destroyed long ere of this. The possibility of these guns being in the hands of a private individual is so remote as to be hardly worth considering."

Carisella does not agree with Ross that the guns were forwarded to rear-echelon authorities. That might have been the intention, but there is no record extant to show they were ever received by such authorities.

Norman Mulroney, the No. 3 Squadron pilot, wrote that

---

[13]Plane had been hit by German artillery fire and badly stripped by souvenir hunters before Ross made his examination.

"his guns are in the War Memorial Building in Canberra.[14] There is a photo there of myself and two other officers of the AFC holding them and examing them."

Lewis Gyngell, the squadron's orderly sergeant recalled an incident concerning the wreckage. He wrote: ". . . whilst the machine was there a Capt. Brown, a Canadian flying a Camel with the RFC, came down with two companions to see the Fokker, and in my presence remarked: 'What rot! An R.E. 8 could not shoot down a plane like this. I am going to claim it.[15] I was in combat with the German Circus earlier . . . but had to leave off as I had an attack of dysentery. . . .' We members of the 3rd Squadron are fully convinced that it was [E. C.] Banks whom should be given the credit of shooting down the Baron. . . ."

Gyngell, in another letter, recalled that Captain Brown came by the hangar containing Richthofen's body "sometime on the 22nd." Gyngell claimed in a letter to Carisella that he overheard Brown tell several flying officers that the "RAF higher-ups have been after me to put in a claim for the shooting down of the Baron because I shot down a red triplane." And, according to Gyngell, Brown said he intended to, but the records show that he never did. Then, Gyngell wrote that Brown went into the hangar to view the Baron's body. He said Brown came out a few minutes later and was nauseated after seeing Richthofen laid out.

P. L. Bulluss, the 1st class air mechanic, from Brighton, South Australia, said the Baron's tripe was dismantled by a work party led by a Sergeant Nicholson "for delivery to a destination unknown to me."

E. T. Grant recalled that "English soldiers who came to collect the triplane told us that they were taking it to their salvage depot where it would be stripped of engine, guns, and gears etc. and each examined by experts, to see if they could find any 'ideas' or inventions that would be of use to our side and any metal that could be used in the war effort would be sent to England, as England was extremely short of all war materials in 1918. It was probably abandoned then. . . ."[16]

Fred P. Lienert of Broadview, Australia, who was ordered by Major Blake to make Richthofen's coffin, wrote this about

---

[14]Baron's machine guns were never received at Canberra museum.

[15]Brown, at the time, already had filed his combat report.

[16]Carisella is convinced the remnants of the tripe were stripped for any useful material and dumped outside the Poulainville Aerodrome.

the airplane; "Sorry you were disappointed about the turn-buckle. I couldn't give you better information as I cut six of them off the Triplane myself at Poulainville. So I can assure you, it is a genuine turnbuckle off Baron Richthofen's plane. I was a little disappointed at you doubting me over the color of the bracing wire. If you write to the Fokker people, I think they could tell from their specifications, the colors they were. The plane was dismantled and brought in by AFC mechanics from Sailly-le-Sec to No. 3 Australian Flying Corps at Poulainville. I can't know what became of it after but think it went to Dept. of Inspection. . . ."

Again in regard to the Spandaus, Lt. Raymond Watts, an American who served with No. 84 Squadron, recalled a conversation he had with an armament officer of No. 3 Squadron. Watts quoted the Aussie officer as saying that one of the Baron's guns was jammed by "a separated case" and that the other "had a broken firing pin or something of that kind, which did not permit the gun to fire more than one or two rounds and then stop."

Ronald Cooper, whose father had been an air mechanic with No. 3 Squadron, and who is himself a member of the Australian Aviation Historical Society, reported: "One interesting point I do know is that an examination of Richthofen's guns found one to have a separated cartridge in the breech, which constitutes a No. 3 stoppage which would be almost impossible to clear in the air, and the other gun had a broken firing pin which would only allow the guns to fire single shots so that at the time of his death he would have been 'out of action.'

"One eyewitness the Society interviewed, who claimed to be one of the first to reach the crash, described how as he [Richthofen] came down low he 'exposed the whole side of his body,' and I [Cooper] feel that this would have been conducive to an attempt to clear a gun stoppage. The person who gave this account, however, was not aware of the state of his [Richthofen's] guns so I would say his report is quite genuine."

An interesting report also was forwarded by Lt. Malcolm Sheehan, an R.E. 8 pilot, shortly before his death in February 1963. Sheehan wrote Carisella: "Our squadron salvaged Richthofen's machine . . . and the body was brought back to the Sqdn. I was not in the dogfight in which Richthofen was shot down, but two of our 3 Sqdn. machines were taking photos at the time—about 11 A.M. I think—six pilots of 3 Sqdn. including myself—Lt. Warneford and Pickering and I forget the others acted as pallbearers.[17] Frankly, there was no particular rush for the job, just pilots who were available. We regarded Richthofen as a good HUN [*sic*]—better when he was shot down. However, a brave and distinguished pilot and so we honored him with the honors due to a distinguished officer, and that was that. It was years after that all the fuss was made.

"I don't know who got all the bits you refer to, but as the body was always under guard and a postmortem was carried out, I have little doubt that most of his personal effects were duly returned to next of kin.[18] The whole job was all under control. The guns of his machine went to an armory and most of we fellows took a piece of fabric—but we were not very interested. . . ."

The morning of April 22, 1918 was an exceptionally busy one for Major Blake, C.O. of No. 3 Squadron. The Baron was dead but the war was still on. After his quota of R.E. 8's was off the ground for photographic reconnaissance, other squadron duties were fulfilled; he then turned his attention to Richthofen's funeral. Corps H.Q., just across the road at Bertangles, had told him to go ahead with the arrangements.

Major Blake filled out Army Form W3314, the only red tape necessary to release the body of the Baron for burial. Blake then called for Corporal McCarty,[19] the medical orderly; Sergeant Gyngell, the orderly sergeant; Fred Lienert, the flight carpenter of B flight; and Air Mechanic Harold Edwards. McCarty was told to prepare the body for burial. The day was clear and sunny and the major decided to hold the services at about 4:30 P.M. Sergeant Gyngell received orders to draw up the funeral party and the necessary cross for the grave. (Richthofen was a Lutheran.) Lienert was ordered to make the coffin. Edwards was informed that he was to prepare two enscribed plates, one to be affixed to the cross and the other to the coffin.

In correspondence with Carisella, Gyngell wrote: " . . . as

[17]Sheehan's report shatters another myth, i.e., all the pallbearers were captains and equal to Richthofen in rank.
[18]Lieutenant Sheehan gave part of one of the crosses from Richthofen's plane to Carisella.
[19]During this writing, word was received that E. J. McCarty passed away on June 24, 1968.

e propeller on Richthofen's plane was a two-blader, we got
damaged R.E. 8 four-blader prop. and made it into a cross
or his grave."

Private Craven also recalled how the cross was fashioned:
... at the head of the grave was a cross made in the work
ops of the 3rd Squadron, AFC. This cross was made from
four-bladed propeller, three blades of which had been cut
ort, and over the center boss was a beaten aluminum plate
itably inscribed."

Lienert, the carpenter, wrote: "I was detailed to make his
offin, which I did. We usually had a supply on hand but
idn't then. He wasn't too big a man and I quickly made it
om some packing cases. We lined it with cloth and painted
black."

The body of Richthofen was placed in the coffin by Jack
rawford, a warrant officer with No. 3 Squadron, and a
oung corporal named Will Scott. Crawford had been de-
iled by Major Blake for this duty. Crawford died before
arlsella could contact him, but his son, Jack Jr., responded.

Writing from Strathalbyn, Australia, the son quoted his
ather as saying that the Baron's outer "white, fur-lined
oots" ended up in the possession of Scott. Young Crawford
id his father always gave him this story about the boots:

"A few days after the funeral I called for a full-dress
arade of the squadron and upon inspecting the ranks I came
cross the young corporal, who was guard on the Baron's
offin, wearing a pair of boots that looked very familiar and
uch out of place for No. 3. I ordered him to my quarters
nd asked him where he got the boots." The corporal, ac-
ording to the senior Crawford, replied, "You know where
ey came from."

These outer boots had been placed on the Crosley tender
y Colin Campbell Collins, the man who had crawled out
rough the shellfire to recover the Baron's body. When
ollins returned hours later with the remnants of the tripe he
ound that the boots had been taken. Young Crawford claims
at the boots were confiscated from Corporal Scott and
handed into headquarters. What happened to the corporal I
ever heard."

After the war one of these fur-lined boots was on display
the Australian War Memorial in Canberra. Carisella
ound, in 1964, that the second boot was in the possession of

Richthofen's coffin is lowered into the grave at Bertangles.

Mrs. William V. Herbert[20] in Australia. Prior to her death, two years later, Mrs. Herbert gave the second boot to the Australian War Memorial.

The extract from Air Mechanic Edwards' diary for April 22 read in part: "He, the Baron, was put in a coffin after being subject to two post mortems. I had to engrave a large aluminum plate with both English and German to place on his coffin. He was accorded full military honors and four wreaths were sent from various squadrons. Many officers including some of the staff were in attendance. Cinema pictures were taken. Our officers were the pallbearers and some of our lads were the firing party. Two thousand Francs were found on the body before being interred. . . ."

Pressed for more details, Edward wrote: "A large plate of aluminum was engraved and placed on the coffin, and another one was put on a propeller cross. I had to do the engraving, and while at it found myself wishing it were for the Kaiser. It would afford me great pleasure, and I am sure would make a thoroughly good job of it. Some of the French people were very vexed that we did the fallen foe such honor. I suppose they find it hard to fathom the British, but in this case I think we are but reciprocating the honor they paid one of our great airmen, Ball, whom they brought down. I hear that they buried him [Ball] with military honors and placed flowers on his grave once a month and sent his mother a photo each month. The Baron was said to be twenty-five years of age. If this is correct, then he was brought up in a very stern school.

"This is a copy of the engraving I made on the plates:

CAVALRY CAPTAIN MANFRED
BARON VON RICHTHOFEN
AGED 25
KILLED IN ACTION (AERIAL COMBAT)
NEAR SAILLY-LE-SEC SOMME
FRANCE
21/4/1918

"Then followed the same inscription in the German language."

Edwards noted that "a Church of England chaplain, decorated with the D.S.O., officiated at the funeral."

[20]Lt. William V. Herbert was a member of No. 3 Squadron.

It is interesting to note that Carisella's research disclose the fact that the group of photographers and cinema re men recording the funeral for posterity included an Austra ian photographer by the name of George Hubert Wilkins. wartime photographer, Wilkins later was knighted for h work during several polar expeditions. Sir Hubert also was pioneer explorer by air and headed an Arctic submarin expedition in 1931. He died in 1958.

Sir Hubert later wrote that "the most striking aerial event witnessed was the death of the German ace of aces, Baro Manfred von Richthofen. I was on the way up towards th front in a car when we stopped to watch an aerial dogfigh There were some thirty or forty planes in that whirlin battle, split roughly into three groups, and they were fightin at such an altitude it was difficult to distinguish the Allie planes from the Germans, except by the character of th attacks.

"One plane seemed to be lagging, then went into a nos dive and came down. As it approached we saw that it was a Allied plane. A German swooped in pursuit, and as it cam down on our plane's tail we saw that it was all red, th distinctive coloring of Richthofen's plane, of which we ha all heard. Our man plainly was in difficulty, diving straigh for the ground. The machine in the lead came out of its div just as it neared the ground, zoomed steeply, banked, an went out of sight behind a hill. Richthofen followed th maneuver exactly in pursuit. There was the sound of just on machine gun firing. Over the very top of the bank we coul see Richthofen's red plane apparently go out of contro sideslip and then it also disappeared. I didn't see the actu crash, but it was evident that the red plane had been h when we lost sight of it.

"From a Colonel's headquarters nearby, I called up flyin corps headquarters and was told that von Richthofen had ju been killed. I drove to the scene as soon as I could and b that time the body of the German ace had been carried t British RAF headquarters. I did not go to view the body bu photographed his wrecked red plane and then went back t develop my pictures.[21]

"Later I heard there was a dispute as to who had kille von Richthofen. The report had come in that Roy Brown,

[21]Sir Herbert was definitely at the funeral as he forwarded a photo graph of himself, carrying a camera, and watching the cortege.

anadian flyer, had attacked the famous German during the
ght and the English maintained that one of his bullets had
een fatal. But the Australian troops on the ground had seen,
I did, that von Richthofen's plane came down in the
osedive under perfect control. An Australian machine gun
ew claimed that one of their men brought it down, firing at
from the ground as it banked. That was my impression
o. The machine gunner was stationed on the hill, and
parently in a lucky burst he had got the red plane as it
nked steeply in an upward climb."

Roderick Ross, the squadron's equipment officer, wrote in
is regard: "The burial of Richthofen was carried out by
ur Squadron and the funeral was carried out with full
ilitary honors, because the British Service took the view
at even if Richthofen was an enemy, he was a brave and
norable one. Quite a lot of flowers were received from
fferent British formations (including Australian) right up to
e headquarters of the Royal Air Force and Field Marshal
arl Haig's general headquarters in France."

Sholto Douglas, later Lord Douglas of Kirtieside, wrote in
s book, *Years of Combat,* that the Baron was buried with
ull military honors in the local cemetery at Bertangles,
ongside the airfield. The escort and the final salute were
ovided by the Australians, who were claiming that their
ople had shot down Richthofen from the ground.

"It was with mixed feelings that I watched the burial of
e great German ace, for it was impossible not to feel a
tle emotional about it. Richthofen was the most successful,
actual scoring, of all the fighter pilots of the First World
ar. I thought about what he had achieved, and I wondered,
I have many times since, just what sort of man he was.
ichthofen was undoubtedly a gallant pilot, although he
ways fought with the utmost caution except for his very
st scrap—and he never hesitated to avoid a fight or pull out
one if he thought the odds against him were too great.

"We were all glad enough in our hearts, that Richthofen
as out of the way. He had been a thorn in our sides, it
emed for such a long time."

It was almost 5 P.M., April 22 before all the arrangements
ere complete. At that time, six officers of No. 3 Squadron
ted the sealed casket containing the body of the Baron and
sted it on their shoulders. The pallbearers then made their
ay out of the tent and proceeded toward a waiting Crosley

Bush-hatted Australians fire a salute over the Baron's grave

nder. As they approached, the firing squad presented arms.
he coffin was gently placed on the rear platform of the
uck and slid forward. Four wreaths, three of them bearing
e Imperial German colors, then were put on the casket.
he wreath from the 5th Australian Division bore the in-
ription: "To our gallant and worthy foe."

Cpl. R. E. Douglas, the driver of the tender, then moved
f to the measured tread of the slow march on the command
the senior British officer, who wore a black mourning
mband. An officer, with his walking stick tucked under his
ft arm, led the way down the tree-lined road and off the
oulainville airfield. Right behind, in two files, came the
ring party, with their rifles reversed. The tender bearing
e body of Richthofen followed. The pallbearers walked at the
ar of the tender. Next came an infantry platoon and the
ar was brought up by a scattering of individual officers and
en who were off duty and realized the historical significance
the occasion.

Private Craven recalled that "on the day of the funeral I
as one of the outriders that led the cortege to the cemetery
Bertangles. It was quite an impressive affair and the
rench population turned out rejoycing [sic] and in all their
nday finery ..."

As the cortege passed slowly along the country road,
undreds of soldiers saluted. At the entrance to the small,
nclosed cemetery at Bertangles, the procession turned onto a
arrow lane and halted. The firing party moved to open
rder to permit the pallbearers, carrying the coffin, to pass
etween them. As the casket approached, led by the chaplain
ading the Holy Bible, the firing party presented arms.

The pallbearers passed through the entrance gate, turned
the left and placed the coffin down next to an open grave
st inside and under a huge hemlock tree. There, after the
uneral party had closed around, the chaplain read the simple
d impressive Church of England service, the pallbearers
wered the coffin by ropes into the grave. A sergeant then
lled the firing party to attention. In a sharp voice he called
ut quickly, "Load, present, fire!" Three volleys rang out. The
unds of the volleys were still echoing across the countryside
hen a bugler blew the plaintive notes of "The Last Post."
he military men, with the ceremony over, formed up and
oved out at the quick march. A few officers and men.

however, remained behind to pay their individual respect
Some even saluted out of respect.

The Baron was dead and buried, but he was not to kno
any peace, at least not right away. Shortly after the sun ha
set and darkness pervaded the cemetery, French civilians li
ing in Bertangles and nearby, slipped into the cemetery an
vandalized Richthofen's grave. The cross fashioned by th
men of No. 3 Squadron was tipped over and the inscriptio
made on the aluminum plate by Harold Edwards was rippe
off and flung away. The wreaths were torn apart and th
flowers strewn throughout the cemetery. The grave itself wa
even partly dug up as though some of the French civilia
had hoped to reach the coffin and defile the corpse.

These facts, never before published, were brought to lig
by Carisella in his voluminous correspondence with Austra
ians, and his trip to Bertangles in 1968.

Private Craven, among many, attested to this incident. H
reported that "after the ceremony had finished and the esco
departed, the French desecrated the grave. They mistakenl
thought Richthofen bombed their villages by night."

Air Mechanic P. L. Bulluss also recalled: "R was given
burial with full military honors and the Germans flew ove
and dropped wreaths without being molested by our mer
You know from the photo of the grave how nice it looke
but perhaps you don't know that as soon as the service wa
over and the military moved away, the local civilians move
in and in a very short time had wrecked the grave and cros
and committed most disgusting acts."

Late the next day, April 23, 1918, a British pilot at th
controls of a Camel swooped low over the German lines an
tossed down a canister with streamers attached. Germa
ground crews raced to the metal container and quickl
opened it. Inside they found several photographs, on
showing the Aussies firing a farewell salute over the Baron
grave, and two showing the Baron in death. The canister als
included this message:

"TO THE GERMAN FLYING CORPS: Rittmeister Bar
on Manfred von Richthofen was killed in aerial combat o
April 21, 1918. He was buried with full military honors
From the British Royal Air Force."

✠ ✠ ✠

Chapter 7

THE GERMAN VERSION

✠ IT was nearly noon, German time, when the tripes of J.G. 1 returned to the aerodrome at Cappy. A keen observer of the aircraft as they soared in and put down on the muddy field was Oberleutnant Karl Bodenshatz, the squadron's adjutant. In his book, *Jagd in Flandern Himmel*, published in Munich twenty-four years later, Bodenschatz reported that he was not immediately aware that Richthofen was absent from the returning fliers. Bodenschatz, a personal friend of Carisella's and a long-time correspondent, has generously permitted the authors to quote extensively from his own official account of the death of the Red Baron.

He noted that it "suddenly dawned on me" that the Rittmeister had not returned with the squadron. Bodenschatz, shaken but refusing to believe that anything serious could have occurred, called to two of the returning birdmen, Wenzl and Sarius, "Where is Richthofen?"

Sarius was silent. But Wenzl, who had just clambered down from his tripe, replied, "I have a funny feeling . . . We

218

were just over the lines when we were jumped by seven Sopwiths with red spinners, members of that anti-Richthofen group. The dogfight started, but we were outnumbered [*sic*] and no one could really get in a good shot. The Rittmeister came into view, and then seven or eight more lords came in, and it really developed into a tremendous battle. We gradually lost altitude. Then, as best we could, we broke off the engagement and returned over our own lines. As we began to return, I saw a small plane on the ground to the east. I believe it was a red one."

Bodenschatz then felt his first sense of foreboding. Could the Baron actually have been downed? He had never thought it possible. He and Wenzl and Sarius stared at each other, each alone with his own premonitions but hesitant to speak.

The adjutant was the first to voice his fears. He relayed Wenzl's story to Oberleutnant Wilhelm Reinhard. The latter, who was slated to be Richthofen's successor as commander of J.G. 1, quickly ordered Wenzl, Sarius, and Wolfram von Richthofen (cousin of the Baron) to refuel and get airborne to search for the missing all-red tripe.

Within minutes the trio of J.G. 1 aircraft was racing down the runway and up into the sky. Once aloft they soon lost each other and made the search individually. Wenzl later reported that he headed directly toward Corbie Hill, dropping down to about six hundred feet to identify better the red plane he had spotted earlier on the ground. To his surprise, he said he then saw two such aircraft instead of one. Unable to see what had happened to the aircraft and their occupants, he swept across the enemy lines. Instantly, the sky about him was lashed by British antiaircraft fire. An enemy plane swooped down on his tail.

Wenzl reported to Bodenschatz that he successfully dodged the English archie bursts and shook loose the pursuing Camel. This done, he flew down to inspect more closely the downed German planes; but as he did so, three British Sopwiths roared down, their machine guns blazing. Wenzl desperately dove to near ground level; then he turned for home. The Sopwiths followed in hot pursuit. As Wenzl raced over no-man's-land, the British planes fastened on to his tail. The German dropped even lower. At sixty feet altitude he flew over an observation balloon, swooped down to the deck and hedgehopped unscathed back to Cappy. Crestfallen, he had to report that he was unable to supply any details about the fate of the Rittmeister.

Bodenschatz said that while the tripes were aloft seeking information, the news that the Red Baron was missing quickly passed from man to man at Cappy. The Germans stood about shocked. No one spoke. Each man was alone with his thoughts. Only Bodenschatz was finally capable of action. He got on the telephone and rang up every nearby aerodrome; however, none of their personnel was able to give him any further information. He then alerted all the division commanders in his sectors. Hurriedly, he repeatedly made the same request:

" . . . Jasta 11 has returned from its mission. Rittmeister Richthofen is missing. Members of the flight report him going down. Has a red triplane come down in your sector? Has a triplane been seen to go down in your area?"

Bodenschatz, his efforts unrewarded, made the same call and request to the headquarters of the various infantry and artillery units stationed on J.G. 1's front. "Have you any news at all about a red triplane going down?" At the other ends of the telephone, messengers were hastily sent scrambling through the front-line trenches. By note and by voice they relayed Bodenschatz's anxious question: "Has anyone seen a red triplane come down?" All eyes were fastened on the British front across the pockmarked earth. If the Baron is down, he must be helped at once!

After what seemed an eternity, Bodenschatz received his first reliable bit of information. It came in the form of a message from the general staff officer of the 1st Division. He told Bodenschatz that a First Lieutenant Fabian of the 16th Field Artillery Regiment had watched the air battle. According to Fabian, a red triplane had flown off northerly toward the Somme only to make a good landing. Fabian reported that British infantrymen had dashed from their cover and pulled the plane out of sight behind a rise in the ground. The pilot did not leave the aircraft.

Bodenschatz was stunned by the news; yet he was relieved. The Baron had been downed, but he had made a safe emergency landing. At the worst, he assumed the Baron was wounded and a prisoner of war. The adjutant relayed the information to the commanding general of the Imperial German Air Force. Bodenschatz then requested and received permission to go forward to the observation post of the artillery unit. It was his belief that the trained eyes of an airman (Bodenschatz had been with Jasta 2 before his transfer to Richthofen's squadron) might spot something overlooked by a ground officer.

At the front, Bodenschatz obtained the most powerful binoculars available. Then he began a minute scrutiny of the terrain where the red triplane was observed to have descended. For more than half an hour he scanned the shell-scarred slope of Corbie Hill. Inch by inch the ground was studied through the binoculars. It was useless. He saw no tripe. A downhearted Bodenschatz returned to Cappy shortly after two o'clock in the afternoon.

The reports of several front-line infantry officers came in, but their information was as scanty as Lieutenant Fabian's. By that time Bodenschatz said he felt nothing could be done to help the Baron. The adjutant said he was not even hopeful that the Rittmeister might have landed behind his own lines: at worst wounded, at best unwounded. It would not be the first time Richthofen had put down wounded behind the German lines. All this time the squadron's communications center was being besieged with anxious queries from various German headquarters.

According to Bodenschatz, Army Headquarters then took most unusual action. The commanding general, desperately anxious to know the fate of Imperial Germany's ace of aces, sent the following message to the enemy: "Rittmeister von Richthofen landed behind your lines—request news of his condition."

No reply was received as the afternoon passed. The sense of gloom and disaster deepened at Cappy. The east wind became even stronger and cooler. The Germans cursed the damned wind. Why did it have to be blowing out of the east?

Everything that could not resist was driven west over the British lines. Any pilot whose engine balked that day would be driven by the wind westward. Perhaps, Bodenschatz thought, if the wind had not been blowing easterly, Richthofen might have made it back to his lines. But then Bodenschatz realized such thoughts were only idle dreams. Evening was approaching on the Western Front. He knew in his heart that the Rittmeister was not going to return to Cappy. It was time to notify the family.

Bodenschatz said he felt that this sad duty should be his responsibility. An observation plane was rolled out. The adjutant took off from Cappy and flew to the aerodrome at Kortryk, which was commanded by Albrecht von Richthofen, the father who took such pride in the son who had brought so much prestige to the family name. On landing, Bodenschatz immediately requested permission to see Major von Richthofen.

The pair met in the twilight-lit room of the inn at Kortryk. The elder Richthofen walked erectly toward Bodenschatz. In a hushed, controlled voice, Major von Richthofen said, "I have a feeling that something has happened to Manfred." The adjutant, standing stiffly, caught the Major's eye. "Sir, I must report that the Rittmeister has not returned from a patrol. As far as we can determine, he is still alive." For a few moments, they stared at each other.

Bodenschatz said that the father quite obviously doubted, even then, his son was alive. He had been too long a soldier himself to believe otherwise. The Major appeared for an additional few moments to be lost in deep thought. Finally he said, in a voice that was soft and hesitant, "Then he has fulfilled his highest duty."

Their conversation ended, the Major returned through the gathering dusk to his room to mourn alone. Bodenschatz observed that it must have been a walk through the deepest dark for the old man. For himself, he returned that same evening to Cappy. There in the casino he heard some of the men promising revenge if it was proved that the Rittmeister had been killed on the ground after putting down. Bodenschatz put such talk down to their grief and dismissed such thoughts himself. Out on the tarmac, he saw other pilots still watching the sky as though expecting momentarily to see the return of the Red Baron, who would explain away his late return as a huge joke.

But Bodenschatz's sad duties were not over yet. He realized that the Baroness and Lothar, the latter still convalescing at Schweidnitz, must be informed of the day's events. He carefully prepared and sent the following telegram to them: "Manfred has not returned from patrol, and from present reports landed unharmed behind enemy lines."

This done, Bodenschatz dropped wearily into a chair in the mess, but just as suddenly bolted up again. He had just remembered something. He went to the squadron office and unlocked a strongbox, drawing out a gray folder which was fastened with the J.G. 1's seal. He recalled that he had performed the same sorrowful task once before at Le Cateau, in the preceding year when the Rittmeister had been gravely wounded in the head and had plummeted to earth at the controls of his Albatros.

From within the folder, Bodenschatz slowly withdrew a small, yellowed note. He studied the wording for a few moments. It was written in the Baron's hand. It read: "In the event that I do not return, First Lieutenant [Wilhelm] Reinhard [Jasta 6] shall take command of the squadron. [Signed] Frh. von Richthofen, Rittmeister."

These few words were the Baron's entire will and testament. They applied only and alone to J.G. 1. Bodenschatz said that he considered the will a truly soldierly act. Nothing within it related to Richthofen's personal life, nothing to his family. Clearly his life belonged, without exception, without conditions, without retrospect to the Fatherland and to his squadron. Free and without care, firm in the conviction that he was fulfilling his responsibilities to the Fatherland and emperor as preordained by his lineage and character, he had risen daily to do battle in the sky. More conscious at the end than ever, that he was not immortal, he had in his typically Prussian manner provided that the command of the squadron was put into the best available hands.

The Baron, of course, never stated the reasons why he had decided upon Reinhard as his successor. But they were not difficult to fathom. At twenty-six years of age, Reinhard, who had joined the Jagdgeschwader on June 17, 1917, was a mature and serious officer. While he lacked the elan of other J.G. 1 pilots, he more than made up for it by his abundance of courage and stable temperament. Respected by his fellow pilots, Reinhard, Richthofen apparently felt, would best serve to lead the squadron to greater accomplishments and glory.

(A native of Dusseldorf, Reinhard was a lieutenant with the 14th Artillery Regiment when war erupted. In the very early days of the fighting, he was badly wounded in the leg. Surgeons twice considered amputation. Eventually, however, the shattered leg healed and he returned to duty. He was accepted for flying duty in June 1915. By the end of the year, he was placed on active duty as a flying officer. Again wounded, he saw aerial service during the battle of Verdun in 1916, flying G-type aircraft with Fl. Abt. (A) 205. As a first lieutenant, he was transferred to the Balkan front where he was soon hospitalized with typhus.

He applied in early 1917 for service as a fighter pilot. He was accepted and completed his required training at Warsaw. He then was posted to J.G. 1. Taking command of this elite unit on April 23, 1918, he had scored twenty official victories before crashing to his death on July 3, 1918. Reinhard had taken a prototype fighter aircraft, Dornier's Zepp (lindau) D. 1, up to some three thousand feet above Aldershof when the top wing tore off. He never had a chance. The machine dove to earth, killing him on impact. He was succeeded in command of J.G. 1 by 1st Lt. Hermann Goering. The future leader of the Luftwaffe in World War II led the squadron until the Armistice, at which time he had chalked up twenty-two confirmed air victories.)

German Headquarters, meantime, was best wondering how to tell the embattled populace that its Teutonic hero was missing, and, perhaps, even dead. As yet there was still no word on his fate from the enemy. Headquarters could wait no longer; the people must not learn from the enemy that their idol was captured or dead. A brief and official press release was put out: "Rittmeister von Richthofen failed to return from a flying raid over the Somme, April 21." This and nothing more. The people, like the staff at Headquarters, had to wait for further information.

On April 22 this enemy message was intercepted: ". . . famous German fighter pilot Richthofen was shot down over Corbie and after landing near Australian troops . . ." There the message was interrupted, according to Bodenschatz. For him and the waiting German nation it only added to the mystery. Richthofen had landed. But what had happened to him then? Why did the enemy remain silent? Why did they not tell the world, as they always had in similar cases when a great victory was theirs?

Daylong on April 22 all British prisoners were interrogated about any knowledge they might have regarding Richthofen's ultimate fate. English pilots taken at the time could only relate that to their best knowledge Richthofen was dead. The Germans refused to believe it. Other English prisoners reported that a badly wounded German pilot, whose name was a carefully guarded secret, had been removed to a hospital near Amiens. At least this report gave the Germans some hope.

But even this hope was dashed forever on the evening of the day the Australians buried the Rittmeister with full military honors at Bertangles. General Headquarters of the British Expeditionary Force finally released the news of Richthofen's death. The information was handed to Reuters which relayed it to neutral sources. From those sources, it was forwarded on April 23 to the German press. The British communique read: "After a long spell of stormy weather, which greatly hampered aerial activity, the 21st inst. brought a change and our airplanes were to be seen in the air from dusk to dawn . . . The pilot of one of the hostile machines which was brought down in combat was the well-known German airman and fighter, Rittmeister Freiherr von Richthofen, who claimed to have brought down eighty Allied machines. His body has today (April 22) been buried with full military honors."

On that day, too, a German soldier found the message dropped on the evening of April 22. That was the RAF message which informed his comrades that: "Rittmeister von Richthofen was fatally wounded in aerial combat and was buried with full military honors."

The dreadful loss of the Red Baron to the German nation could no longer be denied. The glorious hunter was dead. The nation had to be told the blunt truth. General von Hoeppner, chief of the German Imperial Air Service, released this official communique: "Reittmeister Freiherr von Richthofen has not returned from a pursuit of the enemy. He has fallen. The German Army has lost its greatly admired pilot and the fighting airmen their beloved leader. He remains the hero of the German peoples for whom he fought and died. His death is a deep wound for his Geschwader and for the entire Air Service. The will by which he conquered, and led, that he had handed down, will heal that wound."

With the Baron officially listed as dead, Reinhard, the new J.G. 1 commander, sent out numerous messages of condolences. The initial one was forwarded to Major Albrecht von Richthofen at Kortryk. By return telegraph, the Major wired: "To Jagdgeschwader Nr. 1. My son still lives as your model. Father Richthofen."

The official news of Richthofen's death reverberated around the world. Richthofen's fame, or notoriety, depending upon which cause fealty was pledged, had long been widely publicized. *The New York Times* front-paged his death on April 24. In Germany and elsewhere among the Central Powers, the newspapers carried lengthy obituaries about the Flying Uhlan. Dr. Max Osborn urged the readers of the *B.Z. am Mittag* to revere forever the memory of the deceased ace. In the *Tagliche Rundschau,* Johann Scheuermann, its crack war correspondent, wrote thousands of words about the Baron's last dogfight.

Not all the German newspapers were magnanimous in their treatment of the role played by the British in the death of the national hero. Despite the British accounts of Richthofen's death and burial, with the accompanying photographs, many German editors bitterly assailed the enemy.

In the *Deutsche Tageszeitung,* Count von Reventlow wrote: "This homage is nothing but the latest manifestation of the British self-advertisement of sportsmanlike knightliness. For our part we cannot look upon the ceremony shown as sincere. The Allied Press is full of this cant and is beating the big drum of absurd British magnanimity in the accustomed fashion. But they say nothing about how many and how large money prizes were for the one who succeeded in killing von Richthofen. In truth, the monies must have amounted to an enormous sum. This explains why such bitter controversy raged around the body of the fallen pilot, for there was money waiting for the one who inflicted the mortal wound. The very flying officers who bore our hero were all fortunate money-makers."

Throughout Britain the death of Richthofen was broadly reported and prominently displayed in the daily press exchanges. Despite the bitterness engendered by four years of war and the fearful toll it had exacted from the British populace, the accounts were mostly free of any triumphant acclaim. The noted *Times of London* for example commented: "While probably not as brilliant as Captain [Albert] Ball, all our airmen concede that Richthofen was a great pilot and a fine fighting man."

The *Aeroplane,* a renowned British aviation publication, stated: "Richthofen is dead. All airmen will be pleased to hear that he has been put out of action, but there will be no one amongst them who will not regret the death of such a courageous nobleman. . . ."

One British ace was most generous in his observations. This unidentified flyer, toasting the memory of the Red Baron in the mess of No. 56 Squadron, RAF, said, "Richthofen, our most worthy enemy."

The body of the Baron remained in the desecrated grave at Bertangles until 1925 when it was removed to the much larger cemetery at Fricourt, France. That same year Bolko von Richthofen, the surviving male member of the family, went to Fricourt to recover the body of his famous brother and return it to Germany. The Baroness wanted her son to be laid to rest at Schweidnitz next to his father, Albrecht, who had died peacefully after the war, and his brother, Lothar, who had died in that commercial plane crash in 1922.

However, the Baroness' wishes were not to be. The idol of the Fatherland still belonged to the people. The Baron's remains were claimed for the nation and plans were made to inter the Baron in his new zinc-lined coffin in Berlin's Invaliden Cemetery. There the Rittmeister could rest among illustrious peers.

From Fricourt the Baron's body was taken, inside a small truck, across France. However, once the German border was reached, his return became a national event. The coffin was placed aboard a special train and, much in the same manner as the body of Senator Robert Kennedy was taken from New York to Washington, the trip to Berlin was begun. All along the way, church bells tolled, flags hung draped in black bunting at half-mast, and officials paid their respect at every stop.

The train ended its sorrowful passage on November 18. A guard of honor removed the coffin from the train and bore it through the hushed streets of Berlin to the Gnadenkirche. There it was laid in state. Upon the casket were placed Richthofen's numerous decorations, including the Blue Max and an Uhlan officer's helmet and sword. The wooden cross taken from the military grave at Fricourt rested against the flower-banked casket. An escort of officers, all holders of the Pour le Merite, mounted watch around the clock.

On November 20, 1925, the casket, following religious

services, was carried by eight holders of the Blue Max out of the church and placed on a horsedrawn gun-carriage of the 4th Machine-gun Company, 9th Prussian Infantry Regiment. This unit represented the then nonexistent German Air Service which had been temporarily disbanded under the terms of the Versailles Treaty. Walking right behind the military escort were Baroness Kunigunde von Richthofen, the dead ace's mother, and Bolko. In their rear followed Field Marshal Paul von Hindenberg and state officials. Next came former members of J.G. 1 and the 3rd Squadron of No. 1 Uhlan Regiment.

Upon reaching the Invaliden Cemetery, the casket was borne past a guard of honor comprised of members of the Reischwehr. After a few simple prayers at graveside, the coffin was lowered into the grave. Von Hindenberg tossed the first handful of dirt into the grave. In October of the following year, a large, flat tombstone was placed over the gravesite. With Hitler's rise to power, a huge memorial was erected at the tomb in 1938. Hermann Goering, the grand field marshal of the Luftwaffe and the last commander of J.G. 1, unveiled the memorial. A red triplane, Dr.-1152/17, once flown by the Red Baron, was displayed at the cemetery during the unveiling. This triplane and a red Albatros, also piloted by the dead ace and kept on display in the Air Museum, were destroyed during the Allied bombing of Berlin in 1944.

Goering always evinced a great interest in the details concerning the death of the Rittmeister. He constantly had various representatives or groups tracking down the answer to the mystery surrounding the death of the Red Baron. In the years after the new German Luftwaffe was created on March 1, 1935, Goering sought to imbue the new German Air Force with pride and enthusiasm by reestablishing the traditions of the World War I Squadrons. On March 14, 1935, the Luftwaffe's first staffel was christened Jagdgeschwader Richthofen.

Goering, as commander-in-chief of the Luftwaffe, found it impossible to admit that Richthofen could ever have been vanquished in midair combat. So it was not too surprising that Nazi Germany officially announced in 1942, at the height of World War II, that the Rittmeister "fell undefeated in his element, in which he so often staked his life for his earthbound comrades." In a word, the German version was that their great hero had been downed by ground fire.

✝ ✝ ✝

Chapter 8

THE FINAL ANSWER

"The manner in which Richthofen met his death may be historically unimportant, but what is important is that no doubt should be cast on the accuracy of the official history. If by any chance the official history says that an RAF pilot shot the great German aviator down, the tendency will be to doubt the accuracy of other narratives of events, at least in the minds of the hundreds—possibly thousands of eyewitnesses—who could see with their own eyes, that Richthofen was not shot down by one of our fighters."

MAJ. GEN. L. E. BEAVIS
OFFICER COMMANDING THE 53RD
BATTERY, 5TH DIVISION, AIF

✠ ON April 24, 1918, *The New York Times* printed this version of the Red Baron's last flight:

"The Captain with his Flying Circus of more than twenty followers, came toward the British lines near Sailly-le-Sec, on the Somme, about noon on Sunday. . . . As they neared the fighting front they encountered two British airplanes. Captain von Richthofen . . . separated himself from his followers and started on a furious pursuit of one of these machines.

"Meanwhile a score of British planes came swirling up and engaged the Germans. The Captain kept after his man and tried to outmaneuver him. The British plane which was accompanying the one under attack got above the German. The three machines raced towards the British lines. . . . Meanwhile the other German machines were fighting the British squadron more than three miles away.

"Machine guns and rifles on the ground came into action against Captain von Richthofen, who was also being fired at by at least one of his adversaries in the air. Suddenly the machine turned its nose downward and crashed to the earth.

Lt. Wilfred May, No. 209 Squadron, RAF.

"Examination later showed that the German pilot had a bullet through his heart. It was difficult to say whether the bullet came from the ground or from a British machine. . . ."

This is one of the earliest printed accounts of the controversy that has raged to this day. And like most of the other accounts, the *Times'* story is replete with errors and misinformation, easily understandable when one recalls the conditions under which the Allied brass forced war correspondents to work. About the only point of value in the account is the final sentence: "It was difficult to say whether the bullet came from the ground or from a British machine. . . ."

This controversy, of course, could have been quickly put to rest at the time if Ted McCarty, who prepared Richthofen's body for burial, had come forward with the bullet he found in the Flying Uhlan's clothing. A check with the Federal Bureau of Investigation by Carisella confirmed the fact that there were armament specialists of sufficient skill in 1918 to determine the death weapon from the ballistic markings on the retrieved slug. Their study of the markings could have pinpointed from which weapon the fatal bullet was fired: one of the R.E. 8's; Brown's Camel; the Vickers machine gun manned by Popkin and Weston; the Lewis guns manned by Franklyn, Buie, and Evans; or the weapon of any other claimants.

This observation received the support of Raymond Collishaw, the Canadian ace who tallied sixty confirmed kills during World War I. Writing to Carisella in September 1966, Collishaw noted: "In respect to the bullet retained by the Australian medical orderly of No. 3 Squadron. If this is so, it would be an easy thing to determine whether it was fired from the ground or from the air, because the RAF ammunition used in aircraft was quite different to that used by ground AA machine guns. Also the air machine guns had a different rifling, so that the barrel markings on the bullet itself would be quite different."

Alas, McCarty did not come forward with the bullet. But if he had, aviation historians and buffs alike would have been deprived of one of the great controversies of aviation history. Without the mystery surrounding his death, Baron von Richthofen would never have attracted the attention paid him during the last half century. As the war's greatest ace,

Capt. A. R. Brown, No. 209 Squadron, RAF.

deservedly he would have received his share of notice and acclaim and there would have been the usual biographies—but undoubtedly little more. The fascination with the Red Baron's life paradoxically stems from the manner in which he exited it.

As for the controversy itself, that is, whether Richthofen was shot at from the air or from the ground, and who did the actual shooting, it must be obvious to any reader that the authors have ruled out any possibility that Richthofen's death resulted from an air-to-air shot. With all the information now available, one cannot defend, with any credibility, the position that the Red Baron was killed by a British airman. A review of the facts will irrefutably substantiate the impossibility of any Allied flier's having conquered the Rittmeister in air combat.

The claim of Lt. E. C. (Edmond Clifford) Banks, the observer-gunner aboard one of the two R.E. 8's attacked by the Red Baron west of Hamel on April 21, 1918, can be quickly dismissed. Again, Carisella reveres Banks as a personal friend and cherishes their long correspondence but cannot support the old air fighter's claim that machine-gun fire from the R.E. 8's of No. 3 Squadron, Australian Flying Corps, killed the German ace.

Briefly, the site of Richthofen's fight with the R.E. 8's was more than two and a half miles from where the Red Baron finally crashed beside the Bray-Corbie Road—and remember that's as the crow flies. Richthofen flew many more miles when you consider the dogfight with the Camels and his chase of May along the Somme Valley.

Richthofen could never have flown that distance with the mortal wound he suffered on April 21, 1918. The wound was fatal, even if he had received immediate medical attention. Contemporary medical experts say the effects of the wound must have been violent and noticeable immediately. The machine-gun bullet, entering on the right side, below the armpit at the ninth rib, and passing through his chest cavity, must have—at the very least—punctured both lungs before exiting some two inches below and lateral to the left nipple. Even if the big slug missed the heart or the aorta, it caused massive internal bleeding.

Dr. Frank L. Geiger Jr., medical adviser at the U. S. government's Northeastern Radiological Health Laboratory in Winchester, Mass., told the authors that Richthofen's lungs must have become flooded with blood that rose through his trachia to his mouth, inevitably drowning him in his own blood. Other pronounced reactions, he said, would have included: gasping for air, uncontrollable choking, and rapid and sharp clenching of his arms. Dr. Geiger said that the machine-gun bullet wound in the chest cavity resulted in an immediate response to the nervous system. No matter how intent Richthofen was on flying and trying to shoot down an Allied aircraft, his concentration would have been instantly interrupted, Dr. Geiger added.

With such a hit in the chest cavity and the accompanying severe trauma of the body's nervous system, the Red Baron would have had to crash even before his fight with Brown's Camels of No. 209 (Naval) Squadron!

Banks' position has received little backing from Australians who might tend to be prejudiced in his favor. F. M. Cutlack, in his highly regarded history of the *Australian Flying Corps,* briefly mentions the gallant fight put up by the two R.E. 8's but also makes it quite clear that he does not credit them with Richthofen's death.

Lt. H. N. Wrigley, a onetime commanding officer of No. 3 Squadron, AFC, wrote in his admirable squadron history, *The Battle Below,* that two R.E. 8's of No. 3 Squadron tangled with the Flying Circus about the time the Red Baron was shot down. However, Wrigley added ". . . they were not concerned in the actual shooting down of their celebrated enemy."

The authors also contend that the view that Capt. Arthur Royal Brown shot down Richthofen is indefensible. Brown himself never at any time claimed that the red tripe he fired at was Richthofen's. Note, we said "fired at!" In his combat report written on his return to Bertangles, Brown made no mention of Richthofen by name and said that the "pure red triplane" he "got a long burst into" was observed to crash by Lieutenants Mellersh and May. Brown did not see it crash. And could you imagine two more unreliable witnesses than Mellersh and May? We will return to them shortly.

Brown received a bar to his Distinguished Service Cross for his role in the Baron's last air battle. Note, though, that the RAF, while anxious to gain the credit for Richthofen's fall, still was sensitive enough to criticism not to specifically men-

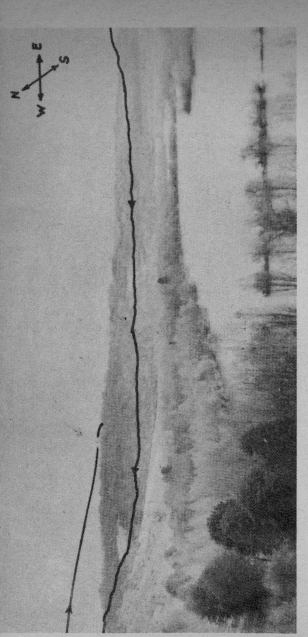

Richthofen chased May along the slope shown above. When both planes cleared the rise at left, Richthofen turned right, gained altitude, turned sharp right again towards the east, and was killed. He crashed 150 yards beyond the chimney stack (arrow), beside the Bray-Corbie road.

tion the Red Baron by name in the citation accompanying Brown's bar to his D.S.C. Surely, if the RAF was that certain Brown got the Rittmeister, its brass would not have hesitated to say so publicly.

Brown's citation read: "For conspicuous gallantry and devotion to duty. On the 21st, April, 1918, while leading a patrol of six scouts he attacked a formation of twenty hostile scouts. He personally engaged two Fokker triplanes, which he drove off; then, seeing that one of our machines was being attacked and apparently hard pressed, he dived on the hostile scout, firing the while. This scout, a Fokker triplane, nosedived and crashed to the ground . . ."

Brown might have shot down a Fokker tripe on April 21, 1918, but it was not that of Baron von Richthofen. All his life Brown never once publicly stated that he was the conqueror of the Red Baron, despite several spurious articles to the contrary by hack writers. Remember that Brown was painfully ill at the time he fought the Flying Circus on April 21, 1918, and that he told several airmen at Poulainville aerodrome the next day that he had to break off the fight with the tripe because he was in agony from dysentery. At that time, he also was quoted as saying that the RAF higher-ups already were pressuring him to state unequivocally that the tripe he fired at, and which was observed to have crashed by Mellersh and May, was that of Richthofen.

Raymond Collishaw, one of Canada's top aces of the war, told earlier in this work how he flew by to see Brown on April 20, and found him "definitely in a bad way, both mentally and physically. . . ." In another letter to Carisella, Collishaw said that Brown on April 20 "was shaking like an aspen. I just cannot imagine him tackling the redoubtable von R and trying to beard him."

Again Collishaw wrote: ". . . I did not see Brown for quite some time afterwards when he explained to me that the von R business had largely been foisted upon him by the press correspondents. . . . Brown himself never claimed that he shot down von R. In his conversation with me, he said that he had fired at a red aeroplane (triplane) in the high altitude battle beforehand. However, I am aware that Brown's combat report presents a different story."

Brown, in the February 1930 issue of *Reveille,* an Australian veterans' magazine, is quoted as saying that he was at

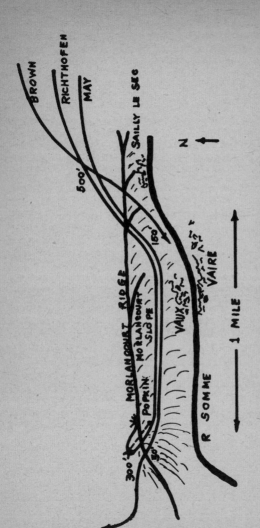

Diagram of flight paths of May, Richthofen, and Brown.
Note Popkin's gun position at left.

lunch after returning from the fight with Richthofen's Circus when Wing Commander W. J. Cairns of No. 209 Squadron walked into the mess. "We got to our feet," Brown reportedly told *Reveille*. "He [Cairns] came toward me. His face was grave. In his manner there was no hint of congratulations. His tone gave me a chill. 'Well, Brown, so you claim to have killed Richthofen?' 'No, sir, I claimed to have shot down an all-red Fokker triplane. I don't know who the pilot was.' Said Cairns: 'It was Richthofen. But the point is this: Australian machine gunners say they got him from the ground. There is also a report that he was downed by one of the R.E. 8's. Then there is your report. It looks like a mess.' "I said nothing," Brown is quoted to have said.

From his home at 97 Garfield Avenue, Toronto, Brown wrote the following note for the November 1930 issue of *Reveille* magazine: "As far as I am concerned, I know in my own mind what happened, and the war being over, the job being done, there is nothing to be gained by arguing back and forth as to who did this and who did that. The main point is that, from the standpoint of the troops in the war, we gained our objectives."

Inevitably, in regard to those who support the view that Brown killed Richthofen, we have to return to the combat reports of Brown himself, May, and Mellersh. But as stated earlier in this work, Richthofen could not have crashed near Vaux-sur-Somme as contended by Brown, May, and Mellersh in their reports. He did not crash there, quite obviously, because his all-red tripe was seen by hundreds of Australian troops chasing May's Camel along the Somme Valley for almost two more miles before coming up over Corbie Hill and crashing alongside the Bray-Corbie Road.

May stated in his combat report that: "while the triplane was on my tail, Capt. A. R. Brown attacked, and shot it down. I observed it crash [*sic*] onto the ground near Vaux-sur-Somme."

It is past belief that May, in his state of near panic could have seen anyone, including Capt. Brown, coming to his rescue from the rear. No novice pilot, in his frame of mind and at the controls of a tricky Camel, could possibly observe what was going on behind him. With Richthofen hot on his heels and death imminent, May would scarcely maneuver his Camel so that he could see behind himself as to what Richt-

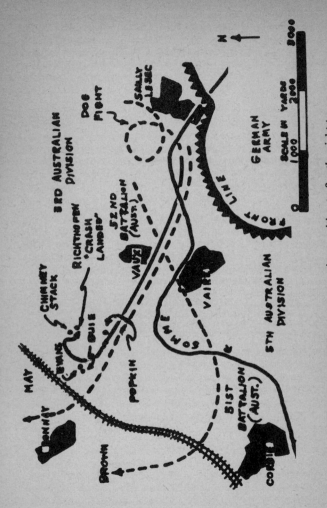

Note that Buie and Evans were not in a position to fire the right-to-left shot that killed Richthofen, while Popkin and Weston were in a good position to fire such a shot at two times.

hofen was doing and as to whether any friendly machine was coming to save him.

Canadian ace Collishaw already has observed in this work that "a Camel pilot, flying at full speed very close to the ground cannot see anything to his rear, without altering his course forty-five degrees to both flanks."

May certainly was zigzagging to escape the Baron's fire; but we cannot believe that May would have repeatedly changed his course forty-five degrees to his flanks, thus losing headway just to find out what his pursuer was up to. May already knew what Richthofen had in mind—May's life! And May was doing everything possible to save it! One of the best ways he could do it was to keep a sharp eye to his front—since he was flying very close to the ground and at times just skimming the treetops.

The same argument applies to Mellersh who stated in his report that "a bright red triplane crashed quite close to me as I looked up I saw Capt. Brown's machine." Mellersh, too, was fleeing for his life when he claimed that he saw the triplane crash. With Joachim Wolff and the one-armed Walther Karjus fastened onto his tail, Mellersh dove to within fifty feet of the earth in a desperate attempt to save himself. He then hedgehopped for home. Given his state of mind, Mellersh can hardly be considered a reliable witness. Even if he did take the time to look up from his very low altitude and see Capt. Brown's machine, that is no reason to believe Brown was responsible for the downing of the "bright red triplane."

Mellersh is quoted later (not in his official combat report) as saying that he saw the bright red aircraft glide to a rude landing about a mile and half west of Sailly-le-Sec. Maybe so, but the Fokker couldn't possibly have been Richthofen's. About a mile and a half west of Sailly-le-Sec and you would be smack in the center of Vaux. The Red Baron's tripe crashed some distance from that spot.

Mellersh, in this later account, has shaken off Wolff and Karjus. On seeing the red Fokker go down, he states that he flew over to have a close look. Mellersh then reports that he observed Capt. Brown circling the site and wobbling the wings of his red-nosed Camel.

"It was more than a recognition signal. By its exuberance, I could tell it was a victory sign. Although I knew, of course, that Richthofen flew a pure red tripe, it just never occurred

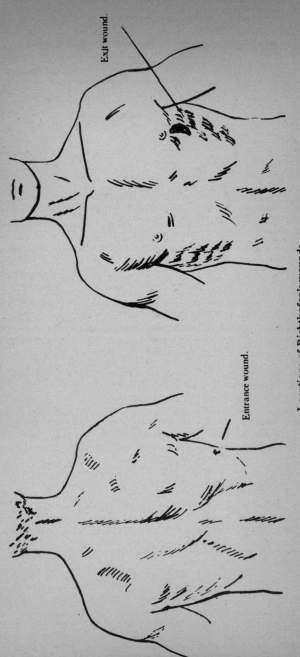

Locations of Richthofen's wounds.

to me at the time that I was witnessing the Baron's final exit."

This entire account appears to be based more on imagination than fact. The tripe didn't go down where Mellersh said. Brown dashed for home after firing a burst at Richthofen's tripe. He certainly didn't circle about. Mellersh himself was in no mood to hang about that area of embattled sky.

In any case, the triplane Mellersh and Captain Le Boutillier, also of No. 209 Squadron, believed they saw crash west of Sailly-le-Sec as the big dogfight broke up could not, under any possible stretch of the imagination, have been that of the Red Baron. The Flying Uhlan's plane, again, went down well over two miles from that point. Its final fall was watched by hundreds of Aussie ground troops.

And again, as in Banks' case, the wound suffered by the Baron was of such a mortal nature that it could not have been sustained at that point—some half mile east of Vaux— where Brown said he fired his burst. With such a devastating injury to his body, Richthofen would never have been able to continue flying his tripe for another sixty-five to seventy seconds before diving to earth atop Corbie Hill.

Richthofen not only continued to fly his tripe from the point where Brown said he shot down the "pure red tripe," but the German ace remained fixed on May's tail, outmaneuvered the Canadian flier at every turn, fired his Spandaus, was observed moving his head, and tossed off his goggles only seconds before the crash.

Dr. Geiger, our medical expert, said that Richthofen's immediate concern upon being hit in the chest would have been to make an immediate landing. This would occur, the physician said, because Richthofen's tendency to choke, become unconscious, and drown in his own blood, would have been rapid. The Baron might have returned his plane to its rightful attitude through the utmost and determined concentration after being wounded, but only momentarily. Dr. Geiger said this would be so because the Baron's wound would have caused his entire body to jerk convulsively. These movements would have been relayed to the stick by which he flew the tripe.

The direction, too, that the bullet took through the Red Baron's body also made it impossible for Brown to have fired it. Brown attacked from the right rear and from above,

Position of body when fatal slug entered it.

swooping down and across the Baron's flight path. Richthofen would have had to twist his torso some ninety degrees to the right in his tight cockpit to permit one of Brown's bullets to inflict the wound. Remember that the bullet not only pierced the Baron's body from right to left but also went through it in a distinctly upward course. Brown was firing from behind and from above!

The claim that the Baron contorted his body in such way to make such a wound possible because he was checking on the effects of Australian ground fire upon his machine must be ruled out. There were no reports of any such fire being directed at Richthofen at the time Brown approached him. Allied gunners would not be apt to fire at a German plane with one friendly aircraft just to its front and another approaching from the rear.

Brown definitely has to be ruled out henceforth in any serious study of the death of Baron Manfred von Richthofen. He might very well have dived onto Richthofen's tail and fired a burst at him, and honestly believed in his own mind that he got the Red Baron, but the evidence does not support the view that he killed the Rittmeister. Remember, too, that from Vaux onward, the hundreds of ground witnesses observed only May's Camel with Richthofen's tripe in hot pursuit. Where was the second Camel? Where was Brown's Camel? There was no such third aircraft anywhere near when the Baron broke off his fight with May and turned for home.

The authors, in dismissing Brown as the victor over Richthofen, do not seek in any way to belittle his outstanding contributions to the Allied war effort. Throughout his life, he was a brave and honorable gentleman. The ill health that plagued him throughout his service days gave him no letup after April 21, 1918. He reported sick the day after the Baron's funeral, then flew the next day. But he was ill again the following day. He left No. 209 Squadron on April 30 for the hospital. His illness was diagnosed as battle fatigue and critical gastritis. Invalided back to England, he was attached to the staff of the Second School of Fighting. However, his bad health gave him no release. In July he fainted while flying and was severely injured in the resulting crash. His doctors despaired of saving him.

However, he grimly clung to life and was still on the

Gunr. Cedric Bassett Popkin.

invalid list at the Armistice. On April 9, 1919, Brown was placed on the retired list of the RAF. His old squadron, No. 209, still convinced that Brown killed Richthofen, has for its unit insignia: "A red eagle—falling."

After the war Brown married Edith Monypenny and the couple had two daughters and a son. He was engaged mostly in commercial aircraft ventures during the 1920's and the 1930's. In 1939 he tried unsuccessfully to enter the RCAF. Forced to retire from business by ill health, he found temporary employment in 1943 as an executive editor for a Canadian aviation magazine. He loved the work, but time was running out for Roy Brown. He was only fifty years old when he died at Stouffville, Ontario, on March 9, 1944.

With the elimination of any flier as the person who killed the Red Baron, we must now focus our attention on the cast of ground gunners who claimed credit for his end.

The claim of Sgt. Alfred G. Franklyn, formerly of the 110th Section, F Battery A.A.; Royal Horse Artillery, need not be dwelt on. The wartime records of the Fourth Antiaircraft Defenses, to which his unit was attached, state that a member of F Battery did, indeed, shoot down a German plane. However, the record clearly notes that the incident occurred on April 22, 1918, and not on April 21, 1918.

Franklyn might well have been the gunner who dropped the enemy aircraft on April 22. In his mind, hearing later of the death of Richthofen on April 21 and seeing the word "yesterday" in the report, he might well have thought that "yesterday" referred to April 21. Franklyn, in any case, could not have shot Richthofen down. The sergeant's Lewis gun was not sited as having inflicted the wound suffered by the Baron.

So it comes down, after all those years since April 21, 1918, to the claims of Sergeant Popkin and Gunners Buie and Evans, all of whom, unfortunately, are deceased at this writing. Fortunately, Popkin and Buie have left us their reports of that day, not only in official records but in their voluminous correspondence with P. J. Carisella.

It is an indisputable fact, if we reread their reports and the supporting evidence of their adherents, that this trio of Aussie warriors had ample opportunity to fire at Richthofen as he zipped his tripe up over Corbie Hill and turned, when his Spandaus guns malfunctioned, for home. But we are still left

Gunr. Rupert F. Weston.

Pvt. George Ridgeway.

with the question: Which of the three Aussies killed the Red Baron? The answer would have been readily determined if Ted McCarty had come forth with the bullet he found. But he did not and the bullet is lost forever. However, the authors of this work have a final answer of their own based on the evidence available.

We adamantly oppose any view that the Red Baron was shot down from the air. The arguments to refute this position have been, we feel, convincingly put forward. Likewise, Sergeant Franklyn did not shoot down the Rittmeister. So again we return to Sergeant Popkin and Gunners Buie and Evans.

In conclusion, we believe that Sergeant Popkin, with the assistance of Private Rupert F. Weston,[1] shot down Baron Manfred von Richthofen.

Why? Because Popkin, firing a mounted Vickers machine gun, had the first opportunity to score a telling blow on the Baron's tripe. The authors believe that Popkin's initial burst did some damage. Pieces of the machine were seen to fall off.

Private George Sowerbutts[2] of the 44th Battalion, AIF, also fired on the Baron as he passed overhead. He was in an excellent position to observe the fire of Popkin's weapon. He testified later that he thought that Popkin had hit the Baron as the tripe had swerved to the right before straightening out and flying over Corbie Hill in the direction of Buie and Evans.

If Popkin's fire was not fatal at that point, although Richthofen was to crash shortly, the Aussie was presented with a near perfect target when the Baron turned away from the guns of Buie and Evans. Swerving sharply and desperately fighting for altitude, the Baron was fatally fixed in Popkin's gunsight. Richthofen had climbed quickly for another several hundred feet and was involved in an extremely vertical banking turn to the right when Popkin's second burst struck. It was at that time, the authors feel, that Popkin inflicted the fatal wound that killed the Red Baron.

Buie and Evans, on the other hand, fired their Lewis guns practically head on at the tripe. Evans died in the early 1920's and never made his views known. But Buie, who died

[1] Still alive, December, 1968.
[2] Died in 1939.

Gunner Popkin behind Vickers machine gun.

in 1964, made his account readily available. In it he stated that "his tripe was flying frontal and just a bit to the right of me." The tripe at the same time must have been flying frontal and even more to the right of Evans because his Lewis gun was sited ten yards forward and some fifty yards to the left of Buie.

Richthofen's tripe, hit by the burst from Popkin's Vickers, passed some fifty feet over the guns manned by Buie and Evans. It then turned sharply to its right (north), rose several hundred feet, became somewhat erratic (Popkin once more blazed away at the tripe), and turned even more to the right (northeast) before leveling off and gliding to a crash landing beside the Bray-Corbie Road.

Since Richthofen's wound was right to left through the chest, Buie and Evans could not have inflicted it with their Lewis guns as Richthofen roared towards them, still in pursuit of May. Nothing has ever been reported about their firing on the tripe once it passed overhead and turned northward and then northeast. Even if they had fired then, they would have been too close to have inflicted the wound suffered by the Baron. While the bullet passed through him from right to left and on a slightly upward course, Buie and Evans were so close that a bullet from their guns would have cleaved his body at a more upward angle. Additionally, because of the close range, any bullets from their guns undoubtedly would have passed through the Baron's body and wallet, thus not having been found by Medical Orderly Ted McCarty.

Not so for the second burst fired by Sergeant Popkin and Gunner Weston. They had a clear right to left shot as the Baron turned to escape the fire from the Lewis guns of Buie and Evans. Popkin and Weston were at such a location that their gun easily would have inflicted the wound suffered by Richthofen as he made a sharp bank to the right, its wings at one time almost vertical to the ground. Popkin and Weston also were far enough away so that the fatal slug had enough velocity to penetrate the Baron's body, but not enough force to pierce the wallet located in his left breast pocket.

This view coincides with that of Dr. Geiger. It is his opinion from reading the half-century-old medical testimony and that of the other witnesses that Richthofen was fatally shot almost immediately before his descent to earth. His wound, Dr. Geiger stated, caused the Baron to descend rapidly into a state of unconsciousness or semi-consciousness. Control of his triplane was then impossible, Dr. Geiger added. The wound could not have occurred earlier!

The authors position that Richthofen was wounded as he turned for home is further supported by the fact that the Baron flung off his goggles at that point. On one other occasion when he was wounded he had flung off his goggles. This was an action he performed instinctively in a desperate attempt to gain the best possible visibility. He undoubtedly knew that his wound was mortal, or at the very least extremely critical. The blood was rising in his mouth, choking him. As the plane lurched and rose up several hundred feet, he fought for control, gained it momentarily, flung off the goggles, and sagged into unconsciousness. The tripe straightened out, once his hand stopped its jerking, and glided to earth. Richthofen, more than likely, was dead before the tripe nosed into the mangel heap.

In conclusion, it is to Sgt. Cedric Bassett Popkin[3] and Gnr. Rupert F. Weston of the 24th Machine-gun Company, 4th Division, that the credit goes for the downing of Baron Manfred von Richthofen. In our estimation, with the evidence now available, the distinction for the Baron's fall must go to those two Aussies, Sergeant Popkin and Gunner Weston, who stood to their gun and faced the Red Baron eyeball to eyeball. May men of their heroic breed always be with us.

[3]Popkin died 1968.

✠ ✠ ✠

Chapter 9

EPILOGUE

✠ FOR the second consecutive year I decided to accept the invitation of the Old Grey Eagles to attend the anniversary ceremonies marking the death of Manfred von Richthofen. The 1969 invitation to the observances which were held in Newburg-on-the-Danube, was personally extended by Hans a.D.v.d. Osten, the secretary of the organization and a close friend of the late Baron. Although the ceremonies were impressive, an event of far more importance to those interested in the Rittmeister's life and death occurred in France en route home.

I had planned my trip in 1969 so that I could spend at least a day in the Corbie-Bertangles area. I was eager to revisit that area for two reasons: (1) to rephotograph Corbie Hill, the site where Richthofen crashed; and (2) to recover the identification plaque from the empty coffin lid at Richthofen's gravesite in the Bertangles Cemetery. The plaque, as previously mentioned, had been made by No. 3 Squadron Air Mechanic Harold Edwards and was attached to Richthofen's coffin on the day he was buried. When his body was removed in 1925, the lid with the plaque was replaced in the grave and covered again. It was my feeling that the plaque is of historical interest, too valuable to be rusting away in the earth; and I was determined to obtain permission to remove it.

Arriving at Amiens on Friday, April 25, 1969, I traveled by bus the seven mile ride to Bertangles. There I immediately contacted Marcel Cavillon, the farmer whom I had met the year before on my visit to Bertangles. At that time he had told me how he had personally witnessed the exhumation of the Baron's body in 1925. His testimony had been somewhat puzzling, for he had claimed in our 1968 conversation that the two Germans who had exhumed the gravesite removed only the skull, placing it in a small box. I had questioned him on this, believing he must be wrong. Surely the Germans would have taken all the Baron's remains, but he had stubbornly adhered to his story. He had also referred to his having seen the plaque attached to the lid, saying that the Germans did not take the coffin out of the ground but only took the lid, removed the skull, and tossed the lid, with the plaque attached, back into the grave which was then refilled.

I had paid little attention to his testimony about the skull, confident that he was in error—especially when I knew the effort the Germans had made to obtain the remains and later the impressive state funeral held for the Baron in Berlin. My thoughts after our conversation and until my return visit in 1969 constantly returned to the plaque. If it was still in the grave, I must go back to the cemetery and recover it.

Mr. Cavillon remembered me immediately when I arrived at his home. I told him of my mission and, with his daughter acting as interpreter, he said I would need permission of the mayor to open the original grave and search for the plaque. From his home I walked a short distance to the Bertangles Chateau, the home of Mayor Francoise de Clermont Tonnerre—a member of a distinguished family of minor nobility that had long lived in the region. The mayor himself responded to my knock and, fortunately, spoke excellent English. I introduced himself, as I had not met him the year before, and told him my reason for returning to Bertangles.

Mayor Clermont-Tonnerre was most gracious and interested in my request. He assured me at once that no one else

GEDENKSTÄTTE DES
MANFRED FREIHERR VON RICHTHOFEN
GEBOREN AM 2. MAI 1892   GEFALLEN AM 21. APRIL 1918

DEM
ERFOLGREICHEN
KAMPFFLIEGER
DES
WELTKRIEGES

DEM
UNERREICHT GEBLIEBENEN
SIEGER
IN
79 LUFTKÄMPFEN

ERBAUT 1938 ERRICHTET
AUS SPENDEN DER DANKBAREN HEIMAT

Richthofen's present grave in East Berlin.

had ever been buried in Richthofen's gravesite and that if a plaque had been put back into the grave in 1925 by the Germans, it was still there. He pointed out that when one digs down about a foot and a half in that region he reaches chalk which acts as a fairly good preservative. Agreeing to give me permission to open the grave, he wrote the orders in French for the local public works official, Mr. Etienne Legagneur. He seemed very willing to cooperate with my research endeavors.

As it was late in the day, the mayor asked his son to drive me back to Amiens for the evening. The next morning I again went by bus to Bertangles and directly to the home of Mr. Cavillon. It was Saturday, April 26, 1969, a wet, dismal day, which suited my mood as I felt rather reluctant and uncertain about reopening the Baron's grave. Together he and I drove to the cemetery. On arriving there, we saw not the public works official, but one of his workers, a young man named Michele Destomles. Incidentally, I had agreed that I would pay Mr. Legagneur thirty francs for the digging. When he was through, I also gave Mr. Destomles a five-franc tip.

I immediately saw that the young man was digging in the wrong place, as I know the right location from the photos and films of the burial which I have studied for years and also from visiting the site in 1968. Asking him to stop his work for a moment, I pushed aside one of the two vats and suggested that he dig closer to the little path. This he did.

Two hours passed in the rain while Mr. Destomles dug with a pick and shovel through the hard chalk soil. To pass the time, I took photos of the scene which became rather sloppy as the tossed chalk quickly turned to a muddy, plaster-like substance, making the walking beside the grave extremely hazardous.

Finally the young man reached the outline of a coffin. He had gone straight down and landed right on target, for the coffin was just where I had been confident it would be without an inch to spare on either side of it. I was positive it was the coffin of the Rittmeister, as it was made of wood painted black but the lid was missing.

Mr. Destomles searched but could not find any trace of the plaque. I asked him to dig the dirt out of the coffin, thinking t had fallen into the empty box. With a hoe that Mr. Cavillon had returned home to fetch, he began scraping away

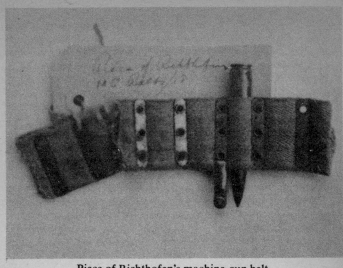

Piece of Richthofen's machine-gun belt.

Sight from one of Richthofen's Spandau machine guns.

at the chalk that seemed to fill the coffin. At the time he was standing on a chalk mound that was in the center of the coffin and about a foot higher than the rest of the area. Next he took a pick and felt for the plaque. Still nothing.

Finally he reached for his shovel and dug into the earth at the foot of the coffin. Up came a spadeful of wet chalk and with it—an anklebone! Mr. Cavillon grabbed for it and yelled that it was Richthofen. I was stunned! My God, it couldn't be. Wasn't the Red Baron's body completely removed forty-four years earlier? Mr. Cavillon brushed off the chalk and handed the bone to me. I reluctantly took it. Could it actually be from the Flying Uhlan's remains? If I had for a moment thought that I would find any trace of the dead German ace still in the old grave, I would never for a moment have touched it.

Mr. Destomles continued his shoveling. As more spadefuls of earth came up, so did other parts of the skeleton, including leg bones, the spine, and the hands. As Mr. Cavillon kept handing them to me, I took them to one of the vats, which was filled with rain water, and gently washed them clean. Then I set them down on a small manhole cover nearby.

Then it became too much for me. The bones had to be from the Baron's remains, for the mayor had assured me the site had not been touched since the Germans came in 1925. I recalled then what Mr. Cavillon had told me the year before that, as a boy in 1925, he had seen the Germans take only the skull from the grave. He must have been right after all!

My mind became filled with a whirlwind of conflicting thoughts. I had never expected such a find and became deeply concerned with what was occurring. It was all too much for me. I told Mr. Destomles to stop any further digging immediately. "But what about the plaque?" he apparently asked me in French. I motioned for him to forget it, although I believe the plaque is still there in the vicinity.

We placed the bones and a section of the coffin, the right-hand side and the footboard, into the rear of Mr. Cavillon's station wagon. The coffin was still in pretty good condition, even the old-fashioned nails had not rusted very much.

After thanking Mr. Destomles and leaving him to refill the

Left—Helmet in which Richthofen received head wound.

Goggles, handkerchief, scarf, and belt found on Richthofen's body, April 21, 1918.

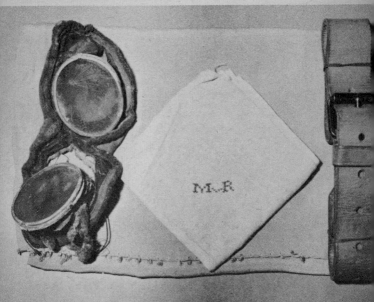

grave, Mr. Cavillon and I drove back to his home. I was rather shaken by what we had found and eagerly took the glass of wine he offered me. His married daughter was there and she interpreted while Mr. Cavillon and I discussed the situation. I told him no one would ever believe that I found the remains of Richthofen in the old gravesite in Bertangles Cemetery. It was all too fantastic. I asked him to write out in French what he had witnessed while I did the same in English. He agreed to do so and then he and Mr. Destomles, who entered the house a few moments earlier, signed the statements. I have both these statements in my possession.

We then took a box from the garage and placed the bones in it. With a French newspaper, we wrapped the box and tied it tightly with string. I also wrapped some of the newspaper about the section of coffin. I thanked both men for their help and, with my two awesome packages, went down the road to see the mayor.

In most cordial tones he asked how the search went. I said, "Well, Mr. Mayor, I don't know how to tell you. It's incredible! I went to find the plaque and found Richthofen's remains still in the coffin."

He didn't seem too surprised and his only comment was, "Very good."

I said, "I'm not too sure that it is very good. The fact is I have Richthofen's remains in this box and I don't know what to do with them."

He only smiled and replied that he had given me permission to open the gravesite, so the remains were mine. "We thought the grave was empty and that you were digging only for the plaque. So the remains are yours." And that was the end of it.

By that time the sun had appeared for a brief period. We went outside, and his sister, a Resistance leader in that region during World War II, snapped several photographs of us together. I have both his letter of permission and the photographs of us. We shook hands, I thanked him for his cooperation, and walked off to the bus stop for my ride back to Amiens.

The following Monday, after two rather sleepless nights in the Amiens hotel, I took the train to Paris. After registering at a hotel I washed up, put on a clean suit, and with my two

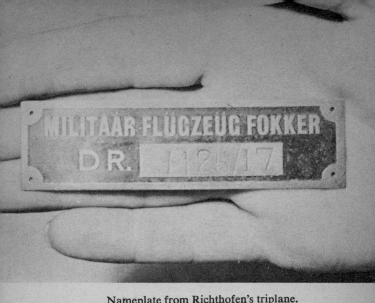

Nameplate from Richthofen's triplane.

Lady's dressing-table set — buttonhook, cuticle pusher, and nail cleaner—made from bits of Richthofen's triplane.

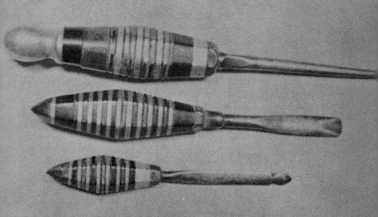

packages walked some twelve blocks to the office of the German Consulate at 34 Avenue d' Gena. It was Monday, April 28, 1969. Reaching the Consulate I walked in and told the man inside the door that I wanted to talk to whoever was in charge. Just then another gentleman walked by and inquired in perfect English whether he could help me. I told him as succinctly as possible that I had in my possession something I was certain was of great importance to Germany. "In these two packages," I said, "are the remains of Baron Manfred von Richthofen and a section of his coffin."

He seemed to be taken aback because he repeated, "Oh you have in that box the remains of Baron von Richthofen?"

I said, "Yes."

He then asked me to sit down and gave me the distinct impression that he thought I was insane. Another official then came in and asked me, "What's this now about you having the remains of Manfred von Richthofen?"

I told him that's just what I had.

"You got them in Germany?" he asked.

I said, "No, in France. In Bertangles, France." He then asked me how I had come into possession of them. I told him the story. By that time another official had joined us and I went through the entire interrogation again.

This last official decided that the matter was not of concern to the Consulate as it was "a military matter" and out of its jurisdiction. He said that there was nothing he could do for me and that I should take the matter up with the military attaché at the German Embassy in Paris. Being a little disturbed by this time, I informed him that I was not leaving with the remains. If Germany wanted them, then Germany better claim them right then and there.

The official obviously sensed my determination and asked me to wait for a moment. He then called the Embassy, and they sent around a chauffered automobile for me. I rode then to the Embassy at 13/15 Avenue Franklin D. Roosevelt. There I was met by two Embassy officials who put me through another round of stiff questioning about the remains and how I had come to possess them. Apparently satisfied that there was something to my claims, they scheduled an appointment for me with the Military Air Attaché at 4:30

Four-bladed propeller used as cross on grave at Bertangles.

Plaque attached to the Baron's coffin, made by Harold Edwards, No. 3 Squadron, AFC.

P.M. the same day. I then left, leaving my two packages behind.

After killing a few hours' time on various errands, I returned at the appointed time, only to undergo further interrogation. At last I was told to take the elevator to the fifth floor where the Military Air Attaché was awaiting me. This I did. He was a Luftwaffe colonel; and as I entered his office, I noticed a large framed photograph of Manfred von Richthofen fastened to the wall along with a wall plaque of an R emblem of the contemporary Richthofen Geschwader.

The colonel was very cordial and asked me whether I would take a refreshment. Since it was a hot day and I had been walking about, I requested a cold beer, which was immediately served. With both of us sitting I told him that the two packages, which I had picked up downstairs, contained the remains of Manfred von Richthofen and a section of his original coffin. He asked me how I could be sure. With that I recounted at length my interest in the Baron since the age of ten and told him of the many years I had spent researching the Baron's life, with special emphasis on the incidents of April 21 and 22, 1918. I told him about this book and how it was soon to be published. Additionally, I recounted my visits to Corbie and Bertangles in 1968 and again in 1969; how the chalk would act as a preservative; and why I was so certain that the spot we had dug was in fact the Baron's 1918 gravesite.

"Believe me," I repeated, "those are the remains of Baron von Richthofen. I don't expect you to believe me fully, but check with the mayor of Bertangles and you'll find I'm right." I also showed him a letter from Congressman Torbert H. Macdonald of Massachusetts, who is a very close friend of mine and who has always been of valuable assistance in helping me gain further knowledge about the Baron. The letter of Macdonald's asked "whomever it may concern" to give me every possible assistance, as I was, indeed, a serious researcher in regard to the Baron.

The colonel then assured me that he would look into the matter and let me know his findings. He kept the two packages and the congressman's letter. In conclusion I made two requests of him: (1) that if the plaque was found, it be forwarded to me, and (2) that the remains be sent to Baron Bolko von Richthofen, a personal friend whom I had last seen only the week before at the anniversary observances in Neuburg, Germany. We then shook hands and I left.

P. J. Carisella

May 7, 1969

✠ ✠ ✠

APPENDIXES

FACTS AND MYTHS
OF THE RICHTHOFEN LEGEND

✠ DURING Carisella's 1968 trip to Bertangles, France, he learned that many Germans had made pilgrimages to the Baron's former gravesite. During World War II many German occupation troops had their pictures taken at the old gravesite to send home.

When Richthofen's body was being prepared for photographing at the Poulainville aerodrome, it was noticed by photographer John Alexander that the Baron's face was dirty and dark. Alexander ordered one of his men to locate some facial powder to put on the Baron's face. When none could be found, Alexander used baking soda. If you look closely at the photograph of the dead Baron you will see that some of the baking soda fell on his flying jacket.

The French farmer showed Carisella the exact spot where the stripped remnants of Richthofen's tripe were dumped. He informed Carisella that for many days after the Baron was buried French civilians and soldiers picked at the tripe until nothing was left of it.

Today two metal vats used for rubbish, are located over the exact location of the Baron's grave in Bertangles. The cemetery has changed very little since April 22, 1918. The hemlock trees that were ten feet tall in 1918 are now fifty feet.

The old 1918 Poulainville and Bertangles aerodromes are now one large farm.

Many writers in describing the death of Manfred von Richthofen, give the impression that he came under the fire of Captain Brown and the ground troops at the same time. This was not so. Captain Brown fired at the Rittmeister at the eastern end of Morlancourt Ridge, while the Australian diggers opened fire at the western end of the Ridge, one and one half miles away.

Of the men that participated in the April 21, 1918, air battle, only Sir Robert Foster and Oliver Le Boutillier are alive today (1969). Both flew in No. 209 Squadron RAF.

While inspecting the Corbie Hill area, Carisella learned that the present chimney stack is located some forty yards north of the 1918 stack. Richthofen crashed a little over one hundred yards east of the old stack along the Bray-Corbie Road. The present stack is still used to manufacture bricks.

Very few mementoes of Richthofen are to be found today at the Richthofen Museum in Wittmund, Germany. One showcase houses a helmet, goggles, flying gloves and a blue scarf left behind the day the Baron flew off on his last flight. Other items to be found at the museum are a scrapbook, photo album, a copy of Richthofen's request to Ernest Udet to join the Circus, and a small piece of red fabric from the 425/17 triplane.

Karl Bodenschatz, Richthofen's adjutant in J.G. 1 and a longtime friend and correspondent of Carisella, said that there never was anything to the rumors about a romance between Richthofen and some mystery woman. Bodenschatz described such talk as a "fairy tale." He said the rumors apparently began when newsmen saw the Baron strolling with Sister (nurse) Katie Otersdorf while he was convalescing from his severe head wound at St. Nicholas Hospital in Courtrai during the summer of 1917.

The color scheme of Richthofen's 425/17 tripe has always been a mystery to aviation historians and buffs. Some have said that the 425/17 was painted a dull red and others said it was a bright red. Through the years Carisella has collected some twenty different pieces of fabric from this historical aircraft. Several of these pieces have been painted a color that fitted either of the above descriptions. (Under the red was a layer of sky blue paint.) When Carisella attended the Richthofen reunion in West Germany in 1968, he asked several surviving members of J.G. 1. about the exact color of the 425/17 and they described it to the best of their memory as being painted a bright red. When shown a piece of the dull red fabric they said that it had undoubtedly turned that color due to exposure. Carisella believes that Richthofen's 425/17 was painted a vermillion red. The tripe was in the process of being repainted when the Baron was shot down.

The rudder of Richthofen's 425/17 was painted white. The rest of the aircraft was painted a vermillion red. Even the cowling and wheels were painted a bright red.

Similarly, Carisella, through his extensive research, located the soldier who had Richthofen's coveralls, machine-gun belt, and the step-up of his tripe. He was former Air Mechanic Frank Rawlinson of No. 3 Squadron. In 1963 Rawlinson donated all of his Richthofen memorabilia to the Australian Imperial War Museum.

When the advancing Russian troops entered Richthofen's hometown of Schweidnitz in 1944, they went first to the town hall to seize the records. Next, according to report, they rushed to the Richthofen estate and removed all the World War I relics from the Baron's museum. These relics of his victories were carefully boxed and forwarded to a warehouse museum near Moscow. Here, the relics, which include the famous 60 victory cups, have remained in their boxes to this day. Attempts by the West German government to have them returned have been rebuffed.

The propeller from the tripe was removed before the aircraft was hauled off Corbie Hill. It was sawed into some forty pieces and distributed to Aussie diggers.

In 1962 Carisella received a section of one of the German crosses from Lt. Malcolm Sheehan, a member of No. 3 Squadron, AFC. Lt. Sheehan also was a pallbearer at Richthofen's burial. The cross obviously was of the straight Latin type framed by an unbroken white border. The many artists' impressions of the Baron's crashed aircraft inaccurately show it bearing the Cross Patee.

The magneto from the tripe's Oberursel engine is to be found today on a dusty shelf in the Australian outback region. The present owner received it many years ago from his brother, who served in France.

The Aussie who removed the instrument bar from the tripe later sold it for junk. One elderly Aussie digger still uses a walking stick he made out of a section of one strut from Richthofen's tripe.

The twin Spandau machine guns from Richthofen's tripe were last seen during the night of April 22, 1918, lying alongside the remnants of the aircraft at the Poulainville aerodrome. They were found to be missing the next morning.

Carisella says that parts of the Spandaus (#695 and #1795) are in Australia and Canada. He possesses one of the locks from the #1795 weapon. Its firing pin is broken.

Richthofen's machine gun belts were cut up and distributed to various Australian diggers at the crash site atop Corbie Hill. The lacerated remnants of the belt were taken by Air Mechanic Frank Rawlinson of No. 3 Squadron, AFC, at Poulainville.

The whereabouts of the Baron's diamond ring, wristwatch, and identification disk is still unknown. The ring was or

Richthofen's finger when the body arrived at Poulainville, but
t disappeared that night along with other personal effects.
The wristwatch disappeared while being taken from the crash
ite to Army headquarters. The ID disk was last seen at the
rash location.

Adjutant Bodenschatz and Baron Karl Bolko von Richthofen both informed Carisella at their 1968 meeting that no
personal effects of Richthofen were ever returned to his
amily at any time.

For years the Australian Imperial War Museum displayed
one of Richthofen's flying boots. In 1965 Carisella discovered that the other boot was in the possession of Mrs. W.
Herbert in Australia. Her late husband had been a member
of No. 3 Squadron, AFC, and was given the boot by one of
the air mechanics who had "removed" it during the night of
April 21. When Mrs. Herbert was informed by Carisella of
the importance of the boot, she donated it before her own
death to the museum.

Several of the souvenirs removed from the tripe were lost
or destroyed during the disastrous floods that ravaged Aus-
ralia in 1954.

Captain Brown years ago supplied Carisella with the
following pertinent information:

". . . it is difficult for me to recall now exactly the marking
hat I used on my Camel in 1918, but if I remember
correctly they were as following—

"(1) The engine cowling and back as far as the metal
vent on the fuselage was red, about the shade of Merrimack
Chemical Co.'s Stearman Vermillion. The disks on the wheels
were also red, and the top plane had a red V outlined in
white, also a red V on the top, bending over the side on the
fuselage, which if I remember rightly, started from the rear
of the pilot's cockpit . . .

"(2) Vickers guns were fed from disintegrating belts made
up by aluminum alloy clips.

"(3) The aircraft was powered with a Bentley Rotary
engine.

"(4) No Very pistols were carried.

"(5) The red of Richthofen's biplane [*sic*] was a shade something between Merrimac Chemical Co.'s International Orange and Stearman Vermillion.

"I have no photographs of any aircraft I ever flew."

Richthofen's assignment on the day of his death was to patrol along a line extending from Marceaux to Uchvillers. Adjutant Bodenschatz said that the Baron's primary objective was to prohibit Allied reconnaissance fliers from scrutinizing the countryside north of Hamel, where preparations were underway for a local offensive.

A German mark, carried by the Baron on the day he died, now is in the Carisella collection. It was removed from the Rittmeister's body while it lay on the ground and given then to "Snowy" Evans.

Richthofen's body was never at any time placed within a church, despite several reports to the contrary. The pallbearers at the funeral were not all captains. They were lieutenants, from No. 3 Squadron, AFC.

The identification plate on the cross over Richthofen's grave disappeared within hours of his burial. Carisella believes that the plate was removed by either revanchist French civilians or souveniring Aussies. He sought information in vain in regard to the plate during his 1968 visit to Bertangles. None of the contemporary villagers had ever heard anything about the plate.

Another fascinating item in the Carisella collection is the scarf worn by the Red Baron the day he was killed. It still shows visible evidence of the wound he suffered.

The whereabouts of Richthofen's flying gloves has never been solved. They were last seen at the crash scene. They never reached Poulainville.

There is a Mount Richthofen located just west of Rocky Mountain National Park. It is named after Ferdinand von Richthofen, a cousin of the Red Baron.

Carisella's research disclosed that the fabric used on the Baron's death plane was of a better quality than that placed on other German aircraft.

At least two Australian diggers were wounded by Richthofen's machine-gun fire as he chased Lt. May along the Somme Valley. Several other Aussies were hit by the German artillery barrage laid down around the tripe.

The stripped remnants of Richthofen's tripe were carried off the aerodrome at Poulainville on April 23, 1918, and discarded on top of a junkpile of wrecked aircraft. The location of this dump was off the side of the dirt road leading to the town of Bertangles. Even the airmen and soldiers kept souveniring the aircraft until only the framework remained.

The many artists' impressions one sees of the Baron's death, of an aircraft with the Cross Patee, are inaccurate, being probably drawn from the plane parked in the background of the photograph taken just before his final flight. This aircraft was not the 425/17. Most of the tripes assigned to Richthofen's Circus had adopted the straight Latin Cross in January, 1918.

The three highest scoring German units during World War I were Jastas 2, 5, and 11.

Jasta 2 destroyed three hundred and thirty-six Allied aircraft while losing only thirty-six men in aerial combat. Jasta 5 scored more than three hundred confirmed kills against the loss of only seventeen of its men.

Jasta 11, which was Richthofen's own squadron, destroyed three hundred and fifty Allied planes while losing only fifteen men to enemy air action.

LIST OF RICHTHOFEN'S VICTORIES

DATE	AREA	AIRCRAFT
1 - Sept. 17, 1916,	Villers-Plouich,	F.E. 2b
2 - Sept. 23, 1916,	Beugny,	Martinsyde
3 - Sept. 30, 1916,	Freicourt,	F.E. 2b
4 - Oct. 7, 1916,	Ypres,	B.E. 12
5 - Oct. 10, 1916,	Ypres,	B.E. 12
6 - Oct. 16, 1916,	Ypres,	B.E. 12
7 - Nov. 3, 1916,	Loupart Wood,	F.E. 2b
8 - Nov. 9, 1916,	Beugny,	B.E. 2c
9 - Nov. 20, 1916,	Guedecourt,	B.E. 12
10 - Nov. 20, 1916,	Guedecourt,	F.E. 2b
11 - Nov. 23, 1916,	Bapaume,	D.H. 2
12 - Dec. 11, 1916,	Mercatel,	D.H. 2
13 - Dec. 20, 1916,	Monchy-le-Preux,	D.H. 2
14 - Dec. 20, 1916,	Noreuil,	F.E. 2b
15 - Dec. 27, 1916,	Ficheux,	F.E. 2b
16 - Jan. 4, 1917,	Metz-en-Coutrure,	Sopwith Pup
17 - Jan. 23, 1917,	Lens,	F.E. 8
18 - Jan. 24, 1917,	Vitry,	F.E. 2b

19 - Feb. 1, 1917,	Thelus,	B.E. 2e
20 - Feb. 14, 1917,	Loos,	B.E. 2b
21 - Feb. 14, 1917,	Maxingarbe,	B.E. 2d
22 - Mar. 4, 1917,	Acheceville,	Sopwith 1½ Strut
23 - Mar. 4, 1917,	Loos,	B.E. 2d
24 - Mar. 3, 1917,	Souchez,	B.E. 2c
25 - Mar. 9, 1917,	Bailleul,	D.H. 2
26 - Mar. 11, 1917,	Vimy,	B.E. 2d
27 - Mar. 17, 1917,	Oppy,	F.E. 2b
28 - Mar. 17, 1917,	Vimy,	B.E. 2c
29 - Mar. 21, 1917,	La Neuville,	B.E. 2c
30 - Mar. 24, 1917,	Givenchy,	Spad 7
31 - Mar. 25, 1917,	Tilloy,	Nieuport
32 - Apr. 2, 1917,	Farbus,	B.E. 2b
33 - Apr. 2, 1917,	Givency,	Sopwith 1½ Strut
34 - Apr. 3, 1917,	Lens,	F.E. 2d
35 - Apr. 5, 1917,	Lembras,	Bristol F2A
36 - Apr. 5, 1917,	Quincy,	Bristol F2A
37 - Apr. 7, 1917,	Mercatel,	Nieuport
38 - Apr. 8, 1917,	Farbus,	Sopwith 1½ Strut
39 - Apr. 8, 1917,	Vimy,	B.E. 2e
40 - Apr. 11, 1917,	Willerval,	B.E. 2c
41 - Apr. 13, 1917,	Vitry,	R.E. 8
42 - Apr. 13, 1917,	Monchy,	F.E. 2b
43 - Apr. 13, 1917,	Henin,	F.E. 2b
44 - Apr. 14, 1917,	Bois Bernard,	Nieuport
45 - Apr. 16, 1917,	Bailleul,	B.E. 2c
46 - Apr. 22, 1917,	Lagnicourt,	F.E. 2b
47 - Apr. 23, 1917,	Mericourt,	B.E. 2c
48 - Apr. 28, 1917,	Pelves,	B.E. 2e
49 - Apr. 29, 1917,	Lecuse,	Spad
50 - Apr. 29, 1917,	Inchy,	F.E. 2b
51 - Apr. 29, 1917,	Roeux,	B.E. 2d
52 - Apr. 29, 1917,	Billy-Montigny,	Nieuport
53 - June 18, 1917,	Strugive,	R.E. 8
54 - June 24, 1917,	Ypres,	Spad
55 - June 26, 1917,	Keilbergmelen,	R.E. 8
56 - June 25, 1917,	Le Bizet,	R.E. 8
57 - July 2, 1917,	Deulemont,	R.E. 8
58 - Aug. 16, 1917,	Houthulster Wald,	Nieuport
59 - Aug. 26, 1917,	Poelcapelle,	Spad
60 - Sept. 2, 1917,	Zonnebeke,	R.E. 8

61 - Sept. 3, 1917,	Bousbecque,	Sopwith Pup
62 - Nov. 23, 1917,	Bourlon Wood,	D.H. 5
63 - Nov. 30, 1917,	Moevres,	S.E. 5A
64 - Mar. 12, 1918,	Nauroy,	Bristol F2B
65 - Mar. 13, 1918,	Gonnelieu,	Sopwith Camel
66 - Mar. 18, 1918,	Audigny,	Sopwith Camel
67 - Mar. 24, 1918,	Combles,	S.E. 5A
68 - Mar. 25, 1918,	Contalmaison,	Sopwith Camel
69 - Mar. 26, 1918,	Contalmaison,	Sopwith Camel
70 - Mar. 26, 1918,	Albert,	R.E. 8
71 - Mar. 27, 1918,	Aveluy,	Sopwith Camel
72 - Mar. 27, 1918,	Foucaucourt,	Bristol F2B
73 - Mar. 27, 1918,	Chuignolles,	Bristol F2B
74 - Mar. 28, 1918,	Mericourt,	A.W.F. K.
75 - Apr. 2, 1918,	Moreuil,	R.E. 8
76 - Apr. 6, 1918,	Villers-Bretonneux,	Spad
77 - Apr. 2, 1918,	Moreuil,	R.E. 8
78 - Apr. 7, 1918,	Villers-Bretonneux,	Spad
79 - Apr. 20, 1918,	Bois-de-Hamel,	Sopwith Camel
80 - Apr. 20, 1918,	Villers-Bretonneux,	Sopwith Camel

On April 21, 1918, Manfred von Richthofen was
shot down and killed.

PERSONNEL OF RICHTHOFEN'S J. G. 1 PILOTS

**COMMANDERS: MANFRED von RICHTHOFEN -
W. REINHARD - H. GOERING**

**JASTA 11 - FLIGHT LEADERS: W. VOSS, K. WOLFF, (K),
L. von RICHTHOFEN, (W), E. UDET, H. WEISS, (W)**

PILOTS:
ALLMENRODER, LT. K. (K)
BAHR, LT. (K)
BOCKELMANN, LT. (K)
CONTA, von, LT.
DORRIEN, von, LT. (W)
EISERBECK, UFFZ. (K)
ESSER, LT.
FESTLER, LT. (K)
FÖRSTER, LT.
GABRIEL, VFW.
GERSTENBERG, LT. (W)
GROOS, LT.
GUSSMANN, LT.
HOFFMAN, LT. (K)
HOHENAU, von (W)
JAGLA, LT.
JUST, LT.
KARJUS, LT.
KÖCKERITZ, von LT.
KREFFT, LT.
LAUTENSCHLAGER, LT. (K)
LINSINGEN, von (W)
LÜBBERT, LT. (W)
NOLTENIUS, LT.
MARTENS, UFFZ.

MEYER, LT.
MOHNICKE, LT. (W)
MÜLLER, OBLT.
NIEDERHOFF, LT. (K)
NIEMZ, VFW.
OSTEN, von (W)
PASTOR, LT. (K)
RACZEK, von
REINHARD, OBLT. (K)
RICHTHOFEN, von LOTHAR (W)
RICHTHOFEN, von W.
SCHAEFER, LT. K. (K)
SCHEFFER, VFW
SCHOENEBECK, von LT.
SCHOLZ, VFW. (K)
SCHULTE-FROHLINDE, LT.
SCHWEINITZ, von LT.
SIMON, LT.
STAPENHÖRST, LT. (POW)
STEINHAÜSER, LT. (W)
WEDEL, von LT.
WEISS, LT. (K)
WENZ, LT.
WENZL, LT.
WOLFF, K. LT. (K)

JASTA 10 - FLIGHT LEADERS: A. DOSSENBACK (K), W. VOSS (K), E. LÖWENHARDT (K), A. LAUMANN, H. KLEIN (W)

PILOTS:
 ADOMEIT, LT.
 ALTRUS, von LT.
 AUE, Offz. (W)
 BARTH, Vfw. (K)
 BELLEN, LT.
 BENDER, LT.
 BIEWERS, Uffz.
 BOHREN, LT. (K)
 BOHLEIN, LT. (K)
 BRETTEL, Uffz. (W)
 BURGGALLER, Vfw.
 DELANG, Vfw.
 DEMANDT, LT. (K)
 DERFLINGER, Uffz.
 FEIGE, LT. (K)
 FRIEDRICHS, LT. (K)
 GILLES, LT.
 GRASSMANN, LT.
 HARDEL, Uffz. (W)
 HECHT, Vfw. (K)
 HELDMAN, LT.
 HENNIG, Uffz.
 HENSCHLER, Fefr.
 KESELING, LT. (K)
 KIRST, LT. (K)
 KLAMT, Uffz.
 KOEPSCH, LT.
 KOHLBACH, LT.

KRAYER, LT.
KUHN, LT.
LAUTENSCHLAGER, Vfw.
LEHMANN, LT. (POW)
MALETSKY, LT.
MEISE, LT.
MOLLER, Gefr.
NITSCHE, Fl.
OHLRAU, LT.
OTTO, LT. (W)
ROEMER, LT. (K)
RADEMACHER, LT. (K)
RIENSBERG, LT.
RUDENBERG, Vfw. (W)
SCHAEFER, Oblt.
SCHAFFEN, Vfw.
SCHIBILSKY, LT. (POW)
SCHRÖDER, LT.
SCHUMACHER, Vfw. (W)
SIENZ, LT.
STOY, LT. (W)
STRECKER, Uffz.
STUMPF, Vfw.
WAWZIN, Vfw.
WEIGAND, Oblt. (W)
WERKMEISTER, Uffz. (K)
WOLFF, LT. H. J. (W)

JASTA 4 - FLIGHT LEADERS: E. von ALTHAUS - K. WURSTHOFF - E. UDET

PILOTS:
 ALVENSLEBEN, LT.
 ANDERS, LT.
 BAHLMANN, LT.
 BOENIGK, von LT.
 BOUILLON, LT.
 CLAUSNITZER, Vfw. (POW)
 DOERING, von LT.
 DRECKMANN, LT. (K)
 FISCHER, LT.

FLASSBECK, Fl.
GEPPERT, LT.
GLUCZEWSKI, von LT.
GRAUL, LT.
GROSCH, Oblt. (W)
HARTMANN, Oblt.
HELD, LT.
HERTZ, LT.
HILDBRANDT, LT.
HIRSCHFELD, LT.

HÜBNER, LT. (K)
HÜBNER, LT. A. (K)
JESSEN, LT.
JOSCHKOWITZ, LT.
KLEIN, LT.
KOEPSCH, LT.
KRAUT, LT.
KRÜGER, LT. (1)(K)
KRÜGER, LT. (2)
MARQUARDT, Vfw.
MATTHIES, LT.
MAUSHAKE, LT. (W)
PATERMANN, Vfw. (K)

PUTTKAMER, LT.
RAUTTER, LT. (K)
REINHARDT, Oblt. (W) (KIA)
RHODE, Fl.
ROUSSELLE, LT. (W)
SCHMUTZLER, Sgt. (K)
SCULZE, Vfw. (K)
SIEMELKAMP, LT.
SKAURADZUN, LT. (W)
SUCK, LT.
WILDE, LT.
WINTERFELD, von LT.
WÜRSTHOFF, Vfw. (POW)

JASTA 6 - FLIGHT LEADERS: E. von DOSTLER, (K), - H. KIRSCHSTEIN, W. REINHARD - J. NECKEL

PILOTS:
ADAM, LT. H. (K)
BACHMANN, Vfw. (K)
BLOCK, LT.
BLUMENER, LT. (K)
BREITEN-LANDENBERG,
  LT. von (W)
BROCKE, LT.
CZERMAK, LT.
DEGEN, Vfw. (K)
DEILMANN, LT.
DOSTLER, Oblt. (K)
FISCHER, LT. U. (K)
GALETSCHKY, LT.
HARTMANN, LT.
HEIDENREICH, LT. (K)
HEMER, Vfw. (W)
JANZEN, LT. (POW)
KIRSCHSTEIN, LT. (K)
KOCH, LT.

KREBS, Vfw. (K)
KULLMER, Vfw.
KUPPERS, LT.
SCHIEMANN, LT.
SCHLIEWEN, LT.
SCHMIDT, LT.
SCHUBERT, Fw. LT.
SKOWRONSKI, LT.
STOCK, LT. K.
STOCK, LT. W.
STUMPF, Vfw. (W)
TUXEN, LT.
WENSE, LT. (K)
WENZL, LT. P. (W)
WOLFF, LT. (III) (POW)

J.G. 1 VICTORIES
644

J.G. 1 CASUALTIES
KILLED 56
WOUNDED 32
POW 6
TOTAL   94

LEADING AIR ACES OF
WORLD WAR I

BRITISH AND BRITISH EMPIRE ACES	VICTORIES
Maj. E. Mannock	73
Lt. Col. William A. Bishop	72
Maj. Raymond Collishaw	60
Capt. James McCudden	58
Capt. Donald McLaren	54
Capt. A. Beauchamp-Proctor	54
Maj. William G. Barker	52
Capt. George E. H. McElroy	48
Capt. Frank G. Quigley	34
Maj. G. Murlis-Green	32
Maj. J. L. M. White	31
Capt. M. B. Frew	30
Capt. S. M. Kinkead	30
Capt. J. E. Gurden	29
Capt. T. R. C. Hoidge	27
Maj. G. J. C. Maxwell	27
Capt. John Leacraft	25
Capt. W. E. Shields	24
Capt. John Andrews	24

FRANCE	VICTORIES
Capt. Rene Fonck	75
Capt. George Guynemer	53
Lt. Charles Nungesser	43
Lt. George Madon	41
Lt. Maurice Boyau	35
Lt. Michel Coiffard	34
Lt. Jean Pierre Leon Bourjade	28
Capt. Armand Pinsard	27
Sous-Lieutenant Rene Dorme	23
Lt. Gabriel Geurin	23
Sous-Lieutenant Claude Marcel Haegelen	23
Sous-Lieutenant Pierre Marinovitch	22
Capt. Alfred Heurtaux	21
Capt. Albert Deullin	20
Capt. Henri J. H. de Slade	19
Lt. Jacques L. Ehrlich	19
Lt. Bernard de Romanet	18
Lt. Jean Chaput	16
Capt. Armand O. de Turenne	15
Capt. Paul V. d'Argueeff	15
Lt. Gilbert Sardier	15

ITALIAN

VICTORIES

Maj. Francisco Baracca	34
Lt. Silvio Scaroni	26
Lt. Col. Pier Ruggiero Piccio	24
Lt. Flavio Torello Baracchini	21
Capt. Fulco Ruffo di Calabria	20
Sgt. Marziale Cerutti	17
Lt. Ferruccio Ranza	17
Lt. Luigi Olivari	12
Lt. Giovanni Ancillotto	11
Sgt. Antonio Reali	11

RUSSIAN

VICTORIES

Capt. Alexander A. Kazakov	17
Capt. P. V. d'Argueeff	15
Liet.-Com. A. P. Seversky	13
Lt. I. W. Smirnoff	12
Lt. M. Safonov	11
Capt. B. Sergievsky	11
Ensign E. M. Tomson	11
Capt. E. N. Kruten	7
Ensign G. E. Suk	7

AUSTRO-HUNGARIAN

VICTORIES

Hauptmann Godwin Brumowski	40
Offzierstellvertreter Julius Argi	32
Oberleutnant Frank Linke-Crawford	30
Oberleutnant Benno Fiala, Ritter von Fernbrugg	29
Leutnant Josef Kiss	19
Leutnant Franz Graser	16
Stabsfeldwebel Stefan Fejes	15
Feldwebel Eugen Bonsch	15

AMERICAN

VICTORIES

Capt. Edward V. Rickenbacker 26
Lt. Frank Luke 18
Maj. Gervais Raoul Lufbery 17
1st. Lt. George Vaughn 13
Capt. Field E. Kindley 12
1st. Lt. David E. Putnam 12
Capt. Elliot W. Springs 12
Maj. Reed G. Landis 10
Capt. Jacques M. Swaab 10
1st. Lt. L. A. Hamilton 9
Capt. Frank O'Driscoll Hunter 9
1st. Lt. Chester E. Wright 9

AND OTHERS

BELGIAN

VICTORIES

Capt. Willie Coppens 37
Adj. A. de Meulemeester 11
Lt. E. Thieffry 10
Capt. F. Jacquet 7
Lt. J. Olieslagers 6